FILTON COLLEGE

A0051688

Learning Resource Centre
WISE
New Road
Stoke Gifford
Bristol. BS34 8LP
Tel: 0117 9192647 or 9192648

Return on or before the last date stamped below.

Critical acclaim for Ashes Victory:

document to be preserved about an oft ... agonising drama, the outcome of which remained uncertain until about an hour before that light-meter whimpered the end'

P. J. Kavanagh, *The Spectator*

'The skill is in the retelling of the action through so many different voices'   *Independent on Sunday*

'In *Ashes Victory* Hayter has taken on the toughest test of his versatility yet, the entire England team. He has managed to convert what must have been hundreds of snatched interviews and phone calls into a seamless narrative that captures the intensity of the series and roars along . . . Sharp, vivid and can be read in a session'

Christopher Douglas, *Wisden Cricketer magazine*

D1348133

ASHES VICTORY

*The official story of the
greatest ever Test series
in the team's own words*

The England Cricket Team

with Peter Hayter

WISE LRC
FILTON COLLEGE
NEW ROAD
STOKE GIFFORD
BRISTOL
BS34 8LP

An Orion paperback

First published in Great Britain in 2005
by Orion
This paperback edition published in 2006
by Orion Books Ltd,
Orion House, 5 Upper St Martin's Lane,
London WC2H 9EA

1 3 5 7 9 10 8 6 4 2

Copyright © The England Cricket Team 2005

The right of The England Cricket Team to be identified as the authors
of this work has been asserted by them in accordance with the
Copyright, Designs and Patents Act 1988.

All rights reserved. No part of this publication may be
reproduced, stored in a retrieval system, or transmitted, in
any form or by any means, electronic, mechanical,
photocopying, recording or otherwise, without the prior
permission of the copyright owner.

Every effort has been made to fulfil the requirements with
regard to reproducing copyright material. The authors
and publisher will be glad to rectify any omissions
at the earliest opportunity.

A CIP catalogue record for this book is available
from the British Library.

ISBN-13 978-0-7528-8075-4
ISBN-10 0-7528-8075-6

Printed and bound in Great Britain by
Clays Ltd, St Ives plc

The Orion Publishing Group's policy is to use papers that
are natural, renewable and recyclable products and
made from wood grown in sustainable forests. The logging
and manufacturing processes are expected to conform to
the environmental regulations of the country of origin.

www.orionbooks.co.uk

CONTENTS

PREFACE

The Greatest Summer Ever

In 2004 England had won ten out of eleven Tests. Could it get any better?

Absolutely it could! And it wasn't just the regaining of the Ashes; it was the amazing spirit in which the series was played, the utter professionalism of the England team and the nail-biting spectacle of it all as new heroes were made and old heroes honoured. I feel a fortunate man to have witnessed it.

This year the cricket arena has grown bigger, more intense, more public, and the boys have more than risen to the occasion. Team England deserves every plaudit for the best Test series ever, but they'd be the first to tell you that Ashes series and team performances like this do not materialise magically. There are years of hard graft, unsung heroism and dedication behind these great and enduring moments. Tiger Woods once said, 'No matter how tough you think you are, you cannot do it on your own.' So congratulations are due to the ECB, the England management, the county coaches and administrators for getting our great game to where it is today.

Thanks are also due to all the loyal sponsors and supporters of English cricket. In particular, Vodafone, npower and NatWest have been immense, while Channel Four and Sky have provided the best coverage in the world. Brit Insurance and Accenture also deserve special mentions for outstanding and innovative support.

Finally, we look to the future of our game, and there is excitement as we seek to build on the success of this epic summer. The players are keen to play their part both on and off the pitch.

Thank you all for supporting us.

Richard Bevan, PCA chief executive

FOREWORD

Building a successful team is not just about the eleven players that take to the field at any one time. Ability gets you part of the way, hard work and preparation are fundamental, but it is the creation of a winning environment that really makes the difference. There are many people the team would like to thank, who have contributed to making this the most amazing summer possible, putting everything in place, allowing us to do our stuff.

Top of this list are Duncan Fletcher and his management team. Duncan is a special coach and a special person who has carefully put together perhaps the world's best support team. His knowledge of the game and his ability to challenge convention are an inspiration. Kirk Russell, our unflappable Kiwi physio, works tirelessly to keep us on the park. Nigel Stockill, physiologist, has been instrumental in changing the mindset of our team from a group of cricketers to a team of athletes. We are simply the fittest we've ever been. Tim Boon, our assistant coach and analyst, is one of the unsung heroes, glued as he is for hours to his laptop, while the introduction of Matthew Maynard has brought a new dimension to our preparation and some welcome Welsh influence. Troy Cooley has worked wonders with the bowlers, developing the best and most varied attack in world cricket. We'll forgive him for being an Australian. No team could survive the pressures of modern international cricket without an excellent team manager and media relations manager. In Phil Neale (he used to play for Lincoln City, you know), we surely have the most efficient and fastidious manager in world cricket. Where would we be without his throw-downs or text messages! Andrew

Walpole, our media manager, is officially a legend. Appearances can be deceiving but he does really know his stuff, and he isn't bad in goal either.

Further thanks must go to Steve Bull, for getting all of us thinking correctly, Doc Peter Gregory for his appropriate diagnosis, and masseurs Paul Roberts and more recently Mark Saxby, a valued addition to the party.

Throughout a summer there are many people, round the country, who work so hard on our behalf, so we can turn up and enjoy playing the game we love. Thanks must go to them, too numerous to list individually, but I'll have a go: the dressing-room attendants who do our washing, clean up our mess and keep the toasted sandwiches coming; the security guards who keep back some of the slightly over-zealous autograph hunters as well as often helping with our bags; Medha Laud at the ECB who quite simply sorts out everything – the darling of the team; Emma Barnes at the PCA who has been instrumental in developing our family programme around the country; all the groundsmen and ground-staff for creating great wickets, the best in the world; the dinner ladies, especially at Lord's, quite magnificent; the substitute fielders – good job, 'nuff said; the net bowlers – a life-threatening job when bowling to Fred and KP; all the hotel staff at the Marriott Regent's Park, the Landmark, the Birmingham Marriott, Harts in Nottingham, the Worsley Park Marriott and the Grange City in London. Special thanks to the sushi chef at the Grange City – you are a legend. Merlin, the spin wizard, thanks for enduring the continued maintenance and the gallons of WD40 – a massive contribution.

Thanks also to the thousands of cricket fans, both old and new, that have parted with your hard-earned to watch us this summer. You are an inspiration and we are proud to play for you. To Paul Burnham and the Barmy Army, you are simply the best fans, in any sport from any country. To Trumpet Man, awesome. To Jimmy Savile, another cricket legend and an honour to have you on stage in Trafalgar Square – see you in Pakistan. And, of course, to Pink Panther and Sylvester – we know who you are!

To all the staff at both the ECB and the PCA, your continued hard work and professionalism are outstanding and we appreciate all that is done for us. To Richard Bevan, so instrumental in the development of central contracts and the creation of representational and commercial stability through the Team England Player Partnership, all current and future England players owe you a huge debt of gratitude. To Jim Souter, for your support and professionalism over the past six years and for making this book a reality. To Vodafone, our team sponsor, a massive thanks for all your support over the years; here's to another four. And to npower, our series sponsor, for bringing a refreshing face to Test cricket.

To our happy gang of cricket media, we know you love our game as much as we do; we hope you enjoyed the summer. To Channel Four, Sunset + Vine, Gary Franses and the team – 'super effort that'.

To Peter 'Reggie' Hayter, whom I've known personally for many years, thanks for all your hard work, sleepless nights and endless interviews.

Also thanks to Robert Kirby and to Malcolm Edwards, and to everyone else who has worked so hard to produce this book so quickly, including Ian Marshall, Ian Preece, Ian Smith, Philip Parr, Helen Ewing, Fiona McIntosh, Jon Fordham, Lorraine Baxter, Sarah Jackson, Nick May and Rabab Adams.

And finally, to the wives, girlfriends, family and friends, without your support on the bad days, the good days would simply not happen. Thanks.

Marcus Trescothick – England vice-captain

INTRODUCTION

England's coach Duncan Fletcher has little doubt that 21 September 2004 was the date when England's Ashes victory on 12 September 2005 became more than a distant dream. From the outside, laudable though England's victory over Australia in the ICC Trophy semi-final at Edgbaston was, it hardly seemed to offer conclusive proof that Michael Vaughan's side were ready to take on and beat the world champions at Test cricket. But Fletcher saw in the six-wicket victory a demonstration that this England side had no psychological scars after years of being under the Australian whip. They chased down Australia's 259 for 9 in a steady, methodical fashion, and won with 3.3 overs to spare. The victory needed no heroics, no one-man show, just solid teamwork, with Flintoff's continuing maturity giving Vaughan the edge he required.

Fletcher explains: 'From my point of view that result and the way we played there put down a marker for us and for them. Up to that point, you always thought that for us to win a game against Australia they had to have a real débâcle and play terribly for all one hundred overs, either batting or bowling. This was different: Australia didn't play badly; England just played better. We went in to bat and there was a cool calmness about the side which I liked. There was this mental strength, off the field, and you got this feeling that there was a belief that this was our time.

'Australia got 259, definitely a score they would have felt confident of defending, but Trescothick, Vaughan and Strauss clinically cut down that total and we went on to win comfortably. It was done in a manner that showed there was no fluke about it; there was no luck. One side was just better on the day, and that side was England. It showed me there was potential there.

'I held that up as an example to the players and as a target. And we referred to it over and over again just to re-emphasise our belief. We could beat Australia because we did it there and then. We said, "No man stands alone." We could win the Ashes.'

England went on to lose the final to the West Indies at The Oval, when a ninth-wicket stand of 71 between Courtney Browne and Ian Bradshaw frustrated the home side's hopes. But that was a rare setback in a summer of success that included seven straight Test wins over New Zealand and the Windies, as well as that seminal semi-final.

The next big target for Fletcher was to win the forthcoming Test series in South Africa. England had not done that for forty years, although for half of that time South Africa had been in sporting isolation in reaction to its apartheid policy. Since the Proteas had returned to international cricket in 1992, only one team had travelled to South Africa and won. That team was Australia, and they'd done it twice.

The last England tour had been Fletcher's first as coach and Vaughan's first in Test cricket. Batting at number four and prior to facing a ball, Vaughan had looked at a scoreboard that read 2 for 4 on the first morning of the series. England lost that Test and the New Year game in Cape Town, but the Fletcher–Hussain partnership gained its first victory in dramatic (and later controversial) fashion at Centurion Park.

When Vaughan returned in 2004 he did so as England captain with a young side that had won ten out of eleven Tests in the year. That form continued at Port Elizabeth where Strauss showed he was a natural for Test cricket abroad as well as at home with 126 and 94 not out. England's fast-bowling quartet of Harmison, Flintoff, Hoggard and Simon Jones, supported by spinner Ashley Giles, continued the trend of taking twenty opposition wickets well inside the time allowed. The tourists won by seven wickets.

The winning streak came to an end in Durban, but there were still plenty of positives to take from that match. England recovered brilliantly after being bowled out for 139 in their first innings and starting their second 193 runs behind. Centuries from Trescothick, Strauss and Thorpe would have given England victory but for bad light. The team ended the Test year with eleven wins, two draws and no defeats – a great achievement.

Unfortunately, though, Vaughan's men started 2005 in disastrous fashion as once again the Cape Town jinx saw England defeated, this time by an embarrassing 196 runs. That made it three heavy defeats at Newlands since England had started visiting again in the nineties.

Fletcher knew the setback would test his side's resolve and resilience, especially with the final two games being played in Johannesburg and Pretoria. They proved up to the task. Strauss and Trescothick provided the runs and Hoggard the wickets (an aggregate of 12 for 205) that put England back ahead in the series with a 77-run victory at the Wanderers. It was a gutsy performance, especially on the final day after Trescothick had given his team the quick runs they needed to have a chance of bowling out the South Africans.

The final match at Centurion Park was a rather scrappy affair, although Thorpe showed his class, as he and Flintoff put on 141 for the fifth wicket. There was a slight wobble on the final afternoon, but Vaughan was still there at the death and England had their fourth series win in a row when the game was drawn.

Harmison had had a quiet series, even though he still finished it with a record number of Test wickets in a year for England (67), beating Ian Botham's former mark. However, his wickets in the South Africa series cost 73.22 each. Vaughan, too, was not at his best.

'People said that England could not win unless I was

taking wickets and Vaughany was scoring runs,' reflected Harmison afterwards. 'Well, we showed in South Africa that we can. The one man we cannot do without is Andrew Flintoff. England need his runs and wickets. Still, it was a great team effort, with everyone chipping in when needed. This is not a fair-weather England team. In fact, we play better cricket when our backs are to the wall and we are under pressure. That's the sign of a good side.'

Another part of the Ashes jigsaw puzzle fell into place as Kevin Pietersen then returned to the land of his birth and, despite bucketfuls of abuse from the home support, carried all before him with the bat. England lost their way towards the end of that one-day series, but Fletcher just put that down to tiredness. The main objective of the winter, Test victory, had been achieved. The early winter problem of visiting Zimbabwe was now history. The team was united, the Ashes were only a few months away, and Flintoff, recuperating back home after the operation to cure a persistent ankle injury, was well on the road back to full fitness.

It would not have been Team England's preferred option to prepare for the best team in the world by taking on the worst, Bangladesh. To most observers the two-Test series was an utter waste of time, with Richie Benaud voicing most people's opinion that the ICC should withdraw Test status from both Bangladesh and Zimbabwe. As usual, he seemed to be talking a lot of sense when the Lord's Test ended on the Saturday with England winning by a monumental innings and 261 runs. Trescothick and Vaughan scored centuries and the four-man pace attack skittled out the visitors for 108 and 159. The Durham Test struggled into Sunday as England used the occasion for batting practice. Both Trescothick and Bell passed 150, with the latter's Test average now a 'healthy' 297! This time Bangladesh were bowled out for 104 (local boy Harmison collecting 5 for 38) and 316. In spite of that respectable second-innings knock, the winning margin was still an innings and 21 runs. It was Thorpe's 100th Test match and he sauntered through with an unbeaten 66. Some had argued that Pietersen should have played in these Tests, but the selectors saw no reason to disrupt a settled and successful side. That was their line for the time being, anyway. England had lost only six wickets in the two matches, with Strauss's 8 at the Riverside the only single-figure score.

The arguments over whether Pietersen should be risked in the Ashes series grew heated during the two one-day series that followed. The contests against Australia got off to a cracking start, for England anyway, when the tourists were bowled out for 79 at a packed Rose Bowl when chasing 180 to win the first Twenty20 international in England. Pietersen hit 36 and took three catches, with Darren Gough and Jonathan Lewis running through the Aussies, who had been 31 for 7 at one stage, a score which had sent the fans delirious.

Later the same week Australia were defeated by Bangladesh in Cardiff. Skipper Ricky Ponting labelled his team's performance 'humiliating', while Andrew Symonds was hauled over the coals for turning up on the morning of the match clearly the worse for wear. (He'd been sampling the delights of the Welsh capital the night before.) The comparison with England couldn't be starker: they started the NatWest series with two wins. Pietersen hit an undefeated 91 in Bristol to sentence Ponting's side to back-to-back defeats over the weekend.

Paul Collingwood grabbed the limelight with an excellent display against Bangladesh at Trent Bridge. After an undefeated 112 in England's massive 391 for 4 (Strauss hit 152), the all-rounder took 6 for 31, the best one-day figures by an England bowler. Sir Vivian Richards is the only other cricketer to have managed a ton and a five-wicket haul in a one-day international.

Australia got some revenge at Durham with a 57-run victory after the home side had collapsed to 6 for 3. The papers had been full of stories of Aussies being kept awake by the ghost of Lumley Castle, their Northumbrian hotel. It was too good an opportunity for Gough to miss, and he sneaked up behind Shane Watson and gave him his best 'Boo!' during the match.

Bangladesh duly lost both matches over the second weekend of the series to set up an England–Australia final. The last group match between the two had been rained off, and Lord's was packed for this first truly significant battle of the summer. England won the toss and bowled Australia out for 196, with Mike Hussey top scoring. But Australian fears that they were way short of what was needed faded as England collapsed to 33 for 5. The big five – Trescothick, Strauss, Vaughan, Pietersen and Flintoff – had all gone.

Collingwood and Geraint Jones led the fightback. They got England close before being dismissed, but Gough and Giles still needed 19 off the last 2 overs to win. Eleven balls later, with 3 runs required off McGrath's last delivery for an unlikely victory, Giles scrambled 2 and the match was tied. The NatWest Challenge Trophy and the series were shared.

England had a wicket to spare and felt they could have won, but yet again the team had proved it would fight to the very end. 'At 33 for 5 I thought we were out of it,' insisted Vaughan. 'I would certainly have settled for a tie then. Australia bowled well at the start and we had some poor shot selection. But Geraint and Colly batted beautifully. I always thought if we managed to reduce the target to about 60 off the last 10 overs with tail-enders to come, we would be in with a chance. It was an enthralling finish and I have never played in a tie before.'

Both sides were ready for the main event, but the Lord's Test was still nineteen days away. First there was the NatWest Challenge – three more one-day matches against Australia. (Bangladesh were presumably by now deemed surplus to requirements.) This was the series of the supersub, the latest innovation from the ICC.

At Headingley England inflicted their heaviest ever one-day defeat on Australia – winning by nine wickets – with

Trescothick's century leading the way after Collingwood had run through the Aussie top order. But Vaughan's team faltered over the next two matches and handed the trophy to Australia at The Oval after a batting display that was 150 runs short of a decent score, despite Pietersen's belligerent 73. Simon Jones was dumped for supersub Vikram Solanki without ever stepping on to the field, Adam Gilchrist hit an undefeated 121 and the tourists won with more than 15 overs to spare.

Had England peaked too soon? Was delaying the Test series to late July a mistake? Should England have tried to catch Australia cold? Gilchrist certainly thought so: 'We've had a slow start and copped it on and off the field. We've had stories made up about us, pictures of us carrying handbags in the papers and people laughing at us and all sorts of things. So the last two results have shown great character from the team. We realised that all that stuff is irrelevant as long as we focus on our cricket, and that's what we've done. Now the most important thing is to get our minds in order for next week because the Ashes is the big challenge of the summer.' Gilchrist did not need to add that the Australian squad was about to be joined by the greatest bowler in the history of the game, Shane Warne.

England, though, were far from feeling that they had missed the boat. The past year had told them they had the capacity to beat Ponting's team. Now it was simply a case of putting it into practice.

David Graveney, who celebrated 100 Tests as England's chairman of selectors during the summer, was the one member of the England set-up who had personal experience of the bad old days. Now he predicted a 2–1 win to England. Like Duncan Fletcher, he was convinced that the ICC semi-final victory was a clear sign that Vaughan's team had a chance. 'That day was the turning point, and was all the more important because this was a competition Australia had missed out on during its great run. Ponting's team were desperate to win in order to make their trophy cabinet complete. No one will admit it now, I suppose, but there must have been one dressing room thinking that they were invincible, especially against England, and the other thinking, Are we ever going to beat this lot? Our last victory in a "live" one-day day game had been way back in 1999, and our World Cup defeat four years later in Port Elizabeth was one of several setbacks. But on 21 September last year not only did England win, but the manner was emphatic. I accept it was only one victory, and in a one-day game, but after many years England's building blocks were in place.

'After our heavy defeat in Australia on Hussain's tour, when our Ashes challenge lasted three Tests and eleven days, most pundits believed that our earliest chance for success would be in 2007. That assumption mainly rested on the fact that most of the Australian team would be too old to put on their boots by then, although don't rule out the thirty-seven-year-old Warne and McGrath just yet! I did not share that view for several reasons. First, under Michael and Duncan, the team was quickly developing into a really tight unit, ironically displaying many of the qualities that have made Australia such a force in recent times. Second, we had learned to win "ugly". We were not at our best in South Africa last winter; two of our main match-winners, Vaughan and Harmison, were below their best. Yet the team prevailed because of its team unity and every one of the squad made a contribution.

'Our early-season performances began to show that we could stand toe to toe against a formidable opposition, whoever they were. Victory at the Rose Bowl showed that we, too, could be aggressive. I also found it revealing that partisan crowds could genuinely rattle the Australian fielders. But, as interesting as these one-day games were, they were becoming more and more like the hors d'oeuvre before the main course, which seemed to be taking ages to come around. As the months became weeks, and the weeks became days in July, the media hype increased to frenetic proportions. I found Glenn

McGrath's comments predicting a 5–0 win for his team, an interesting sideshow. By then, I am sure both sides were yearning for 21 July to arrive, for the talking to stop and for battle to commence.

'As far as the selectors were concerned, the playing of a five-man attack was crucial to our cause. It was imperative that we reduced the workload on Freddie. We also knew that Simon Jones could cause the Aussies serious problems as he was already showing the rewards of the work put in by Troy Cooley.

'It was no secret that our early-season selection meetings were dominated by the name "Kevin Pietersen" after his dazzling batting in South Africa. I have to reveal that it was not until his final one-day England knock of the summer, against the Aussies at The Oval, that we were convinced he was ready for Test cricket. This conclusion meant leaving out Graham Thorpe. I have never found those phone calls easy, particularly when the player concerned has been such an outstanding performer. But, for me, the bottom line was that we couldn't take the risk with his fitness.

'I never felt the match venues would be such a contentious issue as many were suggesting. That said, I knew that if we could get past Lord's without too much damage, then our home crowds would have a huge part to play. What can beat the atmosphere at Birmingham on a Saturday?'

All that remained was for Fletcher and Vaughan to gather together their troops and re-emphasise the message that they had been preaching all summer. According to Fletcher: 'We use the term, "Get in their space."'

And how they did.

FIRST TEST
LORD'S

PREVIEW

By the time the cricketers of England and Australia arrived at Lord's on Monday 18 July to begin their final preparations for the first Test of the 2005 Ashes series, the only residents of the two nations without an opinion as to the outcome were those who had recently arrived from another planet. From Freddie Flintoff to Glenn McGrath, from Mike Gatting to Allan Border, from the Queen's corgis to Skippy the bush kangaroo, it seemed everyone had had their say. According to McGrath, the pace spearhead of the world-champion team, who needed just one more wicket for 500 in Tests, there could be only one result: 5–0 to Australia. In an extensive *Mail on Sunday* interview, he explained his thinking: 'You see, I'm between a rock and a hard place here because I go into cricket doing everything I can to make sure, and fully expecting, to win every game I play and I never expect to lose. And if that is the case I can only give one prediction. Five–nil. I'd be letting myself and my team-mates down if I said anything less.'

Ah yes, but surely even the massive confidence on which McGrath and his team-mates base their success must have been dented when this tour started with defeats by England in the inaugural Ashes Twenty20, by Somerset and, incredibly, by Bangladesh. Then there were two more one-day international losses and that amazing tie in the final of the NatWest series at Lord's. The Aussies were finally rocking, weren't they, Glenn?

'Not really,' he said with a grin. 'No, not at all. To be fair, our intensity was not high enough against Bangladesh, [but] the result was a kick up the backside and our team discussion afterwards was very honest. A few things needed to be sorted out. Ricky Ponting said we had been embarrassed and humiliated and he wasn't far wrong. Andrew Symonds, who had let himself down, apologised to us, we all refocused and since then we have played well.

'But despite what was being written and the stick we were getting, we never thought our early form was anything serious. We are the victims of our own success. When you are the champions people are always looking for signs that you might not be the champions much longer, so they latch on to things which might not be relevant in the long run. Our attitude is that whether we win or lose is totally up to us. Above all else, the reason we have been so successful is that we don't fear defeat. If you take the fear out of your game, it is amazing what you can achieve.'

Whatever he might have thought about the rest of McGrath's comments, England captain Michael Vaughan seemed to concur with that final sentiment. The captain used his pre-Test briefing for Sunday newspaper journalists to insist that his players' relative inexperience in terms of Ashes cricket meant they would not carry the psychological baggage that had weighed down England teams after perennial losses to Australia since 1989. He was making this point just two days after it had been announced that England would be going into a Test match without Graham Thorpe for the first time since the Surrey man's emotional comeback to international cricket in 2003 against South Africa at The Oval. While Thorpe was out, Ian Bell (three caps) and Kevin Pietersen (none) were in.

Thorpe had been a major player in England's brilliant, record-breaking run over the previous two years, contributing fully to the sequence of results that had shot them up the world rankings to number two. The left-hander had helped England beat Bangladesh, the West Indies (twice), New Zealand and South Africa in that time. When he won his 100th cap against Bangladesh at Chester-le-Street at the start of June, it was widely assumed that he was a shoo-in to play in the first Ashes Test, provided his long-term back complaint continued to be successfully managed. Having undergone a series of injections to ease the problem – five cortisone and one epidural – the thirty-six-year-old had pronounced himself fit and ready to play. However, on the eve of the Test squad being announced to the world, David Graveney, the chairman of selectors, rang Thorpe to tell him: 'Graham, I'm afraid I'm the bearer of bad news ...'

'... we do not fear playing them and we are actually looking forward to what is a massive challenge. The players are not thinking, Oo-er, it's Australia at Lord's.'
MICHAEL VAUGHAN

Thorpe soon expressed his disappointment to the press and informed them that he was thinking seriously about his future.

According to Vaughan: 'No disrespect to Graham or the teams of the past eighteen years, but they were full of experienced players. Our attempts to win the Ashes have largely been based on experience and we haven't competed. Only time will tell how successful we are this summer, but why not go for young and potentially exciting new players and back them to rise to the challenge?

'We would be kidding ourselves if we think Australia are not going to have great sessions and great days against us. But we do not fear playing them and we are actually looking forward to what is a massive challenge. The players are not thinking, Oo-er, it's Australia at Lord's. They are thinking, What a great opportunity to go out and express ourselves, for batsmen to score hundreds, for bowlers to take five-wicket hauls and for the team to do well. The fact that we don't have that much experience in the side could work in our favour. There are not many cobwebs in the England dressing room, and not many bad tastes of what can go wrong.'

Of all the views offered by those on the periphery, perhaps those that most closely mirrored the mood of expectancy abroad in the land came from Brian Lara, the greatest batsman of his generation, and Mike Gatting, the last England captain to experience the thrill of beating Australia at cricket.

Lara said: 'England can beat Australia by playing continuously aggressive cricket. Against Australia you have to be prepared to play fifteen aggressive sessions per match. You cannot play a patience game with them. They like to take command, and if you let them, they will. You've got to match them stride for stride and do it over a long period of time.'

At a pit-stop during his 1,000-mile walk for charity, Gatting boomed: 'With Steve Harmison, Freddie Flintoff and Simon Jones, if fully fit, we have three guys all bowling at 85 m.p.h.-plus; one bouncing it, one seaming it and one swinging it. That sort of attack and the back-up of Matthew Hoggard and Ashley Giles mean we definitely have the best chance of winning the Ashes since my time. Whereas in the past we might have had one outstanding bowler, or two at a pinch, the fact that we have four or five bowlers capable of dominating on their day gives England the means to put and maintain pressure on opposing batsmen heavier and longer than we have been able to for years. Let's see how their batsmen react to our bowlers coming at them in waves.

'And look at their attack in comparison. I hope I'm not tempting fate, but they do not seem to possess the all-round threat that they used to. Is Shane Warne as dangerous as he was? Is he the shock he was when he bowled me that ball on his Ashes debut at Old Trafford? Is Glenn McGrath as penetrative as he has been? Is Jason Gillespie? And if they rely on a four-man attack, what do they do if anything goes wrong?

'I remember sitting down in the dressing room at the end of the Ashes-winning series in 1986–87 and feeling tired but elated. At that moment you simply could not have imagined that no England captain would feel the same way for so long, but I really believe Vaughan could this summer. I bloody hope he does. It's been a privilege to be called the last England captain to win the Ashes, but I'd rather not be the last one ever!'

As for England's new boys, Pietersen, not renowned for keeping a low profile, said: 'I was playing grade cricket in Sydney when England were last in Australia and, jeez, they copped it. They copped it all day, every day, on chat shows, on adverts, on everything. The English got absolutely crucified by Australia and I think the English press and media should do the same to them.'

Aussie coach John Buchanan contented himself with the following assessment of Pietersen, gleaned from his side's experience of him in the recent NatWest one-day internationals: 'A very poor starter.'

'They like putting themselves in the spotlight and bigging themselves up, but we're second in the world now and very capable of beating them.'

MATTHEW HOGGARD

The War of Words was becoming more than a minor skirmish. Even Matthew Hoggard, whose acerbic views were normally reserved solely for the England dressing room, reacted to McGrath's 5–0 forecast. 'They are always trying to put us down,' said the Yorkshire swinger, 'but the last Test match we played against them we beat them, and, as they're getting on a bit and we've got some back-to-back matches, it will be interesting to see if they can put in consistent performances for twenty-five days. They like putting themselves in the spotlight and bigging themselves up, but we're second in the world now and very capable of beating them. I think they know that. They're scared and they're trying to be bullies.

'It's going to be interesting to see if Warne can reproduce some of his best form, because he's getting on a bit as well. He's not the force he was: he's having to come round the wicket instead of over, which I think is a defensive ploy. It's going to be interesting to see if they've got the firepower to bowl us out twice.'

Shane Warne offered the hope that 'the last Test at The Oval has something riding on it'. No doubt someone immediately warned him to be careful what he wished for.

Interestingly, the world champions chose as their final warm-up opponents a team from the *Sun* newspaper. In a match for the paper's photographers and Aussie sponsors, Travelex, the greatest leg-spinner the world has seen bowled in flip-flops. Later, their fab four fast bowlers obligingly posed for a beautifully judged photo: McGrath, Brett Lee, Jason Gillespie (in bare feet) and Michael Kasprowicz re-enacting the famous zebra-crossing cover shot from *Abbey Road* on the very crossing itself, which is half a mile from Lord's.

When, at long last, the hype subsided just enough to allow the 2005 Ashes series to begin in earnest, every seat at Lord's was occupied, and every square foot of standing room in the Marylebone Cricket Club Members' Pavilion was jostled over, albeit with unremitting politeness.

Australian captain Ricky Ponting won the toss and opted to bat first under cloudy skies. As the England players left the dressing room to make their way on to the field, they encountered something none of them had ever experienced before or is likely to again. Geraint Jones remembers: 'Outside the door of our dressing room, a guard of honour had formed that stretched all the way down the stairs. As we passed through it the noise was unbelievable. It built up and up so that when we entered the Long Room the place erupted. Normally at Lord's you might get a few quiet "good lucks" from the MCC members. This was something else. They were cheering and clapping and shouting. It was like being in a movie.'

Pietersen, in his first Test, agrees: 'That was the most incredible feeling I have ever had in cricket: walking through the Long Room to the loudest roar I had ever heard. It was just amazing. And we felt the support was just so strong. They thought we had a real chance and they wanted to let us know that.'

Marcus Trescothick said: 'You just could not have got any more people in there. It was like a boxing match. They were giving it: "Yeah, come on, lads. You can do it!"'

Such an assault on their senses could have knocked England's young and largely inexperienced side badly off course. Clearly, as they stepped on to the immaculate Lord's turf, they were pumped to bursting point, fighting to control their emotions and their energy. Sensing this, Michael Vaughan brought them together on the outfield to give them a moment to collect themselves and concentrate. He recalls: 'The atmosphere that day at Lord's, the build-up and the response we got in the pavilion and from the supporters, was so intense that it was difficult to handle, because we'd never been in that situation before. We'd spoken about how we were going to act on that first morning, how we were going to go out and try to be as positive as possible. But I could see everyone was nervous, so it was a case of reminding them what we wanted to focus on. It was so important that we came out and hit Australia hard right from the start because in previous series that is what they had done to us.'

Now they were ready, and when Steve Harmison ran in to

bowl the first delivery of a series between the two best sides in international cricket for the biggest (albeit smallest) and oldest prize of all, every pair of eyes in the packed house and watching live on Channel Four was fixed upon the centre of the stage. From that moment on, they never looked away all day, or all series.

Rarely can a cricket match or a series have had so much to live up to. Over the course of the next fifty-five days, how it delivered ...

DAY ONE: AUSTRALIA 190;
ENGLAND 92 FOR 7

Peering at the partial cloud cover overhead, Michael Vaughan was not too unhappy that Ricky Ponting had decided to bat after winning the first toss of the 2005 Ashes, for it enabled him to unleash his fast bowlers at the Australian batsmen right from the beginning. Vaughan and Duncan Fletcher had decided very early that the key to the series would be a positive refusal to be intimidated by Australia, by their record against England, by their status as world champions, or by the aura that surrounded great players such as Warne, McGrath, Hayden, Ponting and Gilchrist. Respect them, by all means. But any sign of fear and England were doomed.

Fletcher explains: 'We spoke a lot about our approach to playing against Australia and said, whatever else we do, we must get in their space. We identified that, in previous series, England had just been bullied by Australia. We were determined that was not going to happen to this team. We said that normally the best way to fight a bully is to hit him harder than he hits you. We were seen as the small guy and we were just going to go in there and fight back. And none of the players was going to be left to stand alone.'

According to Vaughan: 'Deep down it was all about showing Australia an "anger" and an attitude which they hadn't seen in an England team for a long while. As at the Twenty20 game the previous month, it was very important on that first day to get across to them that we weren't going to be intimidated by them and the way they are. We just had to show an intent from the minute they arrived. We'd been to Australia and knew that if you get hammered in the early games, that can be it for the rest of the tour. We wanted to make sure that we showed them a new England body language: of going out and wanting to enjoy playing cricket and having a real go and not being intimidated by the opposition. The message was just try to control everything you can, by preparation, hard work and having your plan. If the opposition then comes out and plays better than you, you have to hold your hands up. But don't allow all that psychology and bravado they radiate to affect the way that you are going to play.

'I think Steve Harmison's first over really set the tone for the whole series. That was as good a first over as you could ever wish for: the manner in which he bowled, with pace, right at them.'

A huge amount was expected of Harmison. While most pundits gave England little chance of getting their hands on the Ashes urn for the first time in sixteen years, those who at least foresaw a 'competitive series' generally agreed that the Durham man was crucial to England's cause. He had disappointed in South Africa the previous winter, but if he could rediscover the form with which he had blitzed the West Indies and New Zealand twelve months before, it was thought the home side could at least sneak one Test.

With the second delivery of the match, Harmison produced a monster of a ball that smashed into Justin Langer's right arm just above the elbow. The Australian opener seemed to realise at that point that this was unlike any England side he'd ever faced. Harmison recalls: 'We were determined to go out and play with high intensity and get them rattled. We wanted to get a few blows in, show aggression, hostility and make the experience as uncomfortable for them as we could. One way to do that was to get them out; another was to scare them; and a third was to hit them. It was not a case of trying physically to hurt people but to put them on the back foot technically and psychologically. The way it turned out, it was like Wild West cricket out there. There were bodies everywhere.'

Indeed there were. In five overs from the man dubbed by the *Sun* 'Grievous Bodily Harmison' Australia's top three had all been hit, and hit hard. When the television cameras zoomed in on Langer's bruise, the nation could see a lump the size of a golf ball. Matthew Hayden then had his senses scrambled by a bouncer that crashed into his helmet, unsettling him enough for Matthew Hoggard to bowl him for the first wicket of the series: 35 for 1.

Then the Australian captain Ricky Ponting, rising to the challenge, attempted to hook Harmison, missed and felt blood dripping down his cheek after the metal grille of his helmet cut into his face. Play was delayed for five minutes while Ponting received treatment. England's captain and fielders looked on from a distance, another signal that they were going to play this Ashes series tough. Ponting later criticised England's lack of one of the game's common courtesies and claimed it motivated him.

Simon Jones remembers: 'No one wants to see a player hurt but they weren't going to get any sympathy from us. We were there to do a job. It was about controlled aggression, not going over the top.'

Andrew Strauss admits to feeling conflicting emotions. Langer, after all, was a friend and colleague from their time together at Middlesex. 'We wanted to let Australia know that they wouldn't be able to bully us. We wanted to hit the ground running and really show them that we meant business and that our quick bowlers were going to cause them problems. Looking back on it now, though, I think we probably got a bit carried away with that. You know, if a guy

*'I remember when Ponting got hit and we were just
leaving him to it, Langer said to me: "This really is a
war out here, isn't it? You're not even going up and
seeing if he's all right." And no one said a word.'*

gets hit, regardless of the situation, you should probably go
up and see if he's all right. But I think that first session,
walking out there that morning and the sort of roar that went
up in the Long Room as we walked through and realising the
enormity of what lay ahead put us on edge a little bit more
than we'd normally be.

'It's a tricky one. Langer's a good mate of mine and I get
on very well with him on and off the pitch, but that first
morning, the first hour, it was all about setting the tone for
the rest of the series. We were very keen to get under their
skin and maybe that thing about being mates went out of the
window for a session or so. I remember when Ponting got hit
and we were just leaving him to it, Langer said to me: "This
really is a war out here, isn't it? You're not even going up and
seeing if he's all right." And no one said a word.'

Whatever the protocol, Ponting was dismissed soon after,
with Kevin Pietersen's drop in the gully counting for nothing
as the Aussie skipper edged Harmison to Strauss at third slip.
'I really enjoyed that wicket,' says Harmison, 'probably more
than the others because I rate Ricky so highly. When I'm
bowling well and getting the ball to stand up off a length I
know how difficult it is for batsmen to get on top of it. Ricky
does it better than almost anyone I've bowled against. He is
the best batsman I've bowled to, but what pleased me most
was that I felt I set him up. When I hit him on the helmet that

sent him back into his crease and I'd got him right in the area I wanted him to be. Then the plan is to put the ball just outside off stump for him to nick it. All I had to do was execute it, and it came out perfect. It was also probably the most hostile spell I've ever bowled.'

The normally reserved Lord's crowd were lapping it up. This was what they'd come to see: a proper England pace attack sticking it to the world champions. Suddenly all the hype seemed like understatement.

Despite his heavily bruised arm, Langer had looked the most at ease until he mistimed a hook off Flintoff's fourth ball in Ashes cricket to Harmison. Australia were 66 for 3, and three of the England pace quartet had already registered in the scorebook.

Then, with his first ball of the match, the fourth, Simon Jones, had Damien Martyn caught behind with a beauty. It was the first delivery Jones had bowled at an Australian batsman in Test cricket since he had suffered a horrendous and career-threatening injury to his right knee in the Gabba's outfield in 2002. His reaction was entirely in keeping with the moment. He explains: 'I was so desperate to make an impact, not just because of trying to win the Ashes but because of what happened to me that day in Brisbane. I was lying on the ground, my right knee twisted and busted, in so much pain that I was ready to punch anyone who tried to touch it. And when I looked up I saw one guy shouting at me at the top of his voice. Because of the state of shock I was in, I couldn't really hear what he was saying at first. Then I realised he was shouting: "Get up, you weak Pommie bastard." It had been a fine day; I had done well to get back in the side after the rib injury I suffered in my debut against India that summer. I felt I bowled half-decent, at quite good pace, and, having taken the wicket of Justin Langer in my first spell, I was ready for another blast. But then, out of a clear blue sky, a bloody freakish accident happens and I'm sitting there asking myself, "Is that it? Is that my career?" To say that I wasn't ready for the abuse would be putting it mildly. Obviously we all understand the Aussie mentality: they want to win at all costs and that attitude is passed on to the crowd, who tend to express it in hostility – especially towards the Poms. I've no grouse with the Australian players. Jason Gillespie helped Steve Harmison carry me off on the stretcher, all of their players came into the dressing room to see me afterwards. And, to be fair to the guy who abused me, there is no way he could have known the extent of the damage. But at the same time he could see I was in serious pain, so he could just have bitten his lip. As for the bloke who threw the can, what do you need to say? Harmison told me he was so upset he was on the point of jumping the fence and doing a Cantona.

'I'm not saying I was on a mission or out for revenge, but things like that stay with you. I was extremely nervous before the start of that day and hardly slept at all, but I was also very determined. When I nicked Martyn off first ball it was an emotional moment but it also helped me relax.'

When the Glamorgan man struck again to remove Michael Clarke LBW, the noise inside Headquarters reached the top of the dial. Looking out from the roof terrace of the recently refurbished Marylebone Cricket Club Pavilion, one member was heard to remark: 'We might be about to see the first ever MCC wave!'

At lunch, the world's top-ranked team were 97 for 5. Game on.

On the resumption of play, several of the players noticed a pronounced dip in the atmosphere among the crowd. Most of them put it down to spectators allowing themselves an extra glass or two in celebration of what they had witnessed before returning to their seats. It was not until half an hour into the afternoon session that the awful truth was passed on to them: for the second time in a month London had fallen under the shadow of terrorism. Thankfully, the incidents turned out to be nowhere near as catastrophic as on the previous occasion, 7 July. But Strauss conceded that the news still affected him and his colleagues, at least initially.

'No one really had a clear idea of what was happening, and before we knew it we were out on the field playing again. Of course, your first reaction is to think, Oh, no, not again; and there was a lot of uncertainty. The noise levels fell quite dramatically. It was eerie. But as more information gradually filtered through to us and it became clear that the situation was under control, the mood lifted. I don't think we played any differently, but maybe a bit of the wind had been taken out of everyone's sails. For a few overs maybe the aggression we had been showing seemed a little inappropriate.'

Australia took advantage while they could, with Katich, Gilchrist and Warne combining to stage a brief recovery, dragging their side to 175 for 6 in typically defiant style. The dismissal by Flintoff of Adam Gilchrist, everyone's idea of the principal Aussie danger man, helped concentrate England's minds again, especially as it proved that their homework was paying dividends. Flintoff, charging in round the wicket, sought to cramp the great stroke-maker for space to play his big, booming shots. Gilchrist's nick was gratefully pouched by Geraint Jones, and the ferocity of the all-rounder's celebration showed just how vital they considered the wicket to be.

Then Harmison removed the Australian tail in a manner that was clinical and hostile. The last four wickets were all his: Warne was bowled, Katich was caught behind, as was Lee (already dropped by Pietersen, his second fumble of the day), and the job was finished when Gillespie was trapped LBW. The packed Lord's crowd could not quite believe what they had seen. England's bowlers had put Australia to the sword in less than two sessions. Harmison led the players in after taking his sixth five-wicket haul in Tests, and earning his place on the Lord's honours board.

'I was relieved, to be honest,' he says. 'I felt a lot of pressure going into the match because so much was expected of me. People were saying, "Oh well, we've only got a chance if Harmison bowls them out," which I thought was not only unfair on me but just mad. Sure, you back yourself and you believe you can do what you need to. You wouldn't go on the field if you didn't think that. But to take those wickets against the best team in the world gives you facts with which to back up the hope. You don't say to yourself, "I think I can do it against these blokes." In that moment of coming off the field you say to yourself, "I *have* done it against these blokes."'

The feeling of euphoria among England's supporters was boosted by the news that temporary disruption to London's transport system was the worst outcome of the terrorists' efforts. Now all concerned, and particularly the England cricket team, could focus on the next part of the task. The few pundits who had believed this was England's time started to say, 'Told you so.' Even those who thought such optimism was a waste of words began to wonder.

But what happened next suggested that the old order would still be in place for some time yet. It was simply one of the best bowling spells ever seen at Lord's and it came from the hand of Glenn McGrath. In less than an hour the man who had predicted a whitewash ran through England's top order, taking 5 wickets for 2 runs in 32 balls. The first victim, Marcus Trescothick, brought McGrath his 500th Test wicket with the first ball of the final session. No sooner had Langer taken the catch at third slip as the left-hander attempted to whip the ball through midwicket than the bowler was slipping into something more comfortable: a special pair of boots inscribed with '500' in gold. In his 110th Test, McGrath had just become the fourth bowler (the second fast bowler and the one with the lowest average) to reach the milestone, following Courtney Walsh, Muttiah Muralitharan and Shane Warne. 'My sponsors made these boots for the occasion,' he said. 'I was going to sneak off at the end of the over, but Michael Kasprowicz [twelfth man] ran out with them, so I had to put them on. I'm not normally much of a show pony, but I thought today I probably deserved it.'

Strauss, a first-slip catch by Warne, went later in the same over. Then Vaughan was squared up and looked to have been beaten by one that shot along the ground. But first impressions were deceptive: the ball hit nearer the top than the bottom of off stump. McGrath also rattled Bell's castle (dragging one on) and Flintoff's (beaten by a delivery that cut back sharply). Having waited seven years and forty-eight Tests since his international debut to play an Ashes innings – easily an England record – this fourth-ball duck was a huge disappointment to the Lancastrian and his fans. England's reply was in ruins at 21 for 5. McGrath held the ball aloft to signify his eighth five-wicket haul against England and his third at Lord's.

> '[McGrath was] bowling like God ... I was thinking,
> How on earth am I going to score a run here? Every ball, constantly asking the question.'
>
> MARCUS TRESCOTHICK

Whereas Harmison's spell had been hostile and physically testing for his opponents, McGrath gave their technique a thorough examination with probing deliveries that left no margin for error, especially as the Lord's slope is ideally suited to his angle of attack outside off stump with the ball cutting back at right-handers from the Pavilion End. Trescothick describes the paceman as 'bowling like God. How well did he bowl? Let's just say I was thinking, How on earth am I going to score a run here? Every ball, constantly asking the question.'

Strauss agrees: 'I don't think any of the batsmen were necessarily at fault against McGrath. I must admit the thought did cross my mind that maybe he was just too good for us. Playing against him, then watching everyone else get out to him, the overriding feeling was shock.'

Bell's introduction to Ashes cricket was anything but

welcoming. 'I was struck by how fast everything was happening. I'd played a little push through the covers for four off Brett Lee and was just starting to feel as though I might be able to settle down and play, when – *bang* – McGrath bowled me all ends up. Thanks for coming.'

Even the normally irrepressible Flintoff was, well, repressed: 'As with all new experiences it probably took me a little time to find my feet. Going into the first Test at Lord's there was so much hype and expectation and I probably built it all up a bit too much in my own mind and put too much pressure on myself. I play my best cricket when I'm relaxed, and at Lord's I probably wasn't in that state of mind.'

Amid the carnage, though, Kevin Pietersen, on debut, not just against the Australians but also in Test cricket, stood firm. It was clear that playing forward was likely to extend a batsman's time at the crease, and that suited Pietersen, who had walked out boldly with the score on 18 for 3. Geraint Jones fancied his chances in that situation, too. The pair prevented a total collapse and began to give spectators hope of finishing the day with no more catastrophes as they amassed the highest stand of the innings, 58. But then Lee got the ball to lift sharply, it came off the splice of Jones's bat and flew to wicket-keeper Gilchrist. The disappointment was doubled when Giles went to the last ball of the day. Originally, the scorecard registered another 'c Gilchrist b Lee', but as England's spinner trod on his stumps at the same time, it was later changed to 'hit wicket'.

If 17 wickets had fallen for 282 runs in 77.2 overs on the first day of a county match, the pitch inspectors would probably have been summoned. Here the fans had seen two exceptional fast-bowling performances – one rough and tough; the other smooth and sublime – but many of the players still felt that there had been too much in the wicket on day one of a showpiece Test match. Langer's top score of the day (a mere 40) bore witness to that.

DAY TWO: ENGLAND 155 ALL OUT;
AUSTRALIA 279 FOR 7

Prior to the start of the series, almost all of the speculation over the make-up of the England side had concerned Kevin Pietersen. His dramatic exploits in the one-day series in South Africa, including three centuries, had clearly marked him out as a Test batsman of the future. But what of now? And what of that ever-changing hairstyle, which drew the following comment from his mum: 'No matter what happens, a mother will always love her son.'

'At the start of the summer I wasn't interested in looking too far ahead,' Pietersen insists. 'I wanted to cement my place in the one-day team, but I didn't think I was going to be in the early Ashes Tests because I thought the team that played against Bangladesh was going to be the team that played against Australia. I hoped to get a go somewhere along the line, though.

'So it was a massive confidence boost and a massive thrill when they picked me for the first Test at Lord's. People talked a lot about my innings in the one-day match against Australia in Bristol, but I felt the one in which I maybe showed I was ready for Test cricket was the one later against them at The Oval because I had to come in with the side in trouble, build a platform and play a Test match-like innings. The Australians were giving me the biggest amount of banter. They were saying: "The Test match is around the corner. Can you hack it? This is Test match bowling, you know. Can you hack it? What can you do?" And I really enjoyed that and got myself

'No matter what happens, a mother will always love her son.'
KEVIN PIETERSEN'S MUM ON HER SON'S HAIRSTYLE

into a zone. I knew that to play through that innings would stand me in good stead. I think that knock got me in the side. It showed the character and the strength and the discipline to go on and be successful against the Aussies in the Test match, and after that I thought I'd have a go at it.

'I got the call from David Graveney on the eve of the announcement of the squad, and I'd actually fallen asleep on the sofa at the time. He just said, "I'm the bearer of good news. We have picked you for the first Test." I wondered at first if I had woken up or if I was still dreaming.'

But then, inevitably, came the questions. In plumping for Pietersen over the great left-handed stalwart Graham Thorpe England had thrown their faith behind youth; and, on the surface, bold, brash, even impetuous youth at that. Pietersen was slightly taken aback, but not for long: 'Sure, when you step up to international level everyone starts to scrutinise your technique and everything else about you. Everyone thinks they know everything about your game. And a lot of people were saying, "Well, the way he plays across the line all the time, that might be OK for one-day stuff, but not Test cricket, against the best bowlers in the world." I was under fire from the doubters before I'd even played!

'I don't mind constructive criticism. In fact, I enjoy it, because you go away and you think about it and I'm a very quick learner. I mean, I can change things around very quickly. So the technical side was something that I went away and thought about, and I changed different things. I'd already had a meeting with Duncan Fletcher early in the season. He told me the best thing to do is to limit yourself by trying to stand as still as possible. I do still favour the leg side, but so did Mark Waugh, and that bloke made thousands of runs. It's all about playing to your strengths, and that's a strength of mine.

'As for temperament, I think I proved myself in that regard at Lord's on day one, where I scored 29 off 70 or 80 balls in really testing circumstances. That proved a lot of people wrong. It showed that the temperament's there, the mental strength's there and the discipline's there.

'Generally speaking, I don't bother too much with what I read. I know what I need to do to succeed, and a newspaper article's not going to fire me up and get me angry. I need to prepare myself in the nets or prepare myself in the gym. I need to prepare myself mentally. A newspaper article, or someone saying, "Pietersen's a muppet" or "He can't do this or that" is not going to hurt me. As for what John Buchanan said about me being a poor starter, we all know the psychological games they try to play. I knew Buchanan said stuff about people, and McGrath said stuff about me. Warney was the only bloke who was complimentary about me. He was the only bloke who said England should select me: "You'd better pick him if you want to compete." I was grateful for that. But you do have those little snide remarks from the Aussies, and in the end it was up to me to stand up and show what I could do. And at the end of that first innings I thought, If this is Test match cricket, I want it every single day.'

On day two, England's tail managed to wag as much as could be hoped, even though Hoggard was out cheaply, to a juggling catch by Hayden at slip off Warne. That left the home team at 101 for 8, but the precarious position did not seem to bother the debutant, who now had licence to challenge the Australian bowlers. First he hit McGrath into the middle tier of the Pavilion Stand, then stroked the next delivery gracefully through the covers. The battle between Pietersen and Warne had been eagerly anticipated because the pair had spent spring and early summer together at Hampshire, becoming bosom buddies. In county games, when Warne was bowling and Pietersen was standing at slip, the two men had studied each other for clues, weaknesses and ideas for the contest ahead. Warne had cheekily nicknamed Pietersen '600', as he reckoned his new mate's wicket would be the one to take him past that milestone at some stage in the series.

'I just tried to relax and enjoy it,' says Pietersen. 'I certainly enjoyed hitting McGrath back over his head for six! As for my tussle with Warney, it helped that we were mates. It relaxed me out there and helped me be positive against him. I knew I needed to be quick on my feet and I knew he'd be trying his hardest to get me out, and, yeah, I really, really enjoyed facing him.'

Just after Pietersen had completed his maiden Test fifty in his debut innings he hoisted Warne into the second tier of the grandstand. The leg-spinner, still clearly the master of his art, then offered him the opportunity to do the same again. This time Pietersen did not get as much leverage and he was brilliantly caught by Damien Martyn diving at full stretch just inside the ropes on the midwicket boundary.

'I winked at Shane Warne when I hit him for six, but then he just patted me on the bum and said, "Well batted." Then he got me out next ball! You're always learning.'
KEVIN PIETERSEN'S FIRST TEST INNINGS COMES TO A CLOSE

'I was a bit disappointed to get out having reached 57. Yes, it's fantastic to get a fifty on your debut and first time in, but it was disappointing to get out when I know that I could have got a few more and got us a little closer. I do set myself really high standards. I don't want to settle for doing OK. Before I played, people were questioning what I would do if I came in at 50 for 3. Well, we were 21 for 5 at one stage and I coped with it. I winked at Shane Warne when I hit him for six, but he just patted me on the bum and said, "Well batted." Then he got me out next ball! You're always learning.'

Geraint Jones, who had earlier made 30 in his partnership with Pietersen, said: 'I wasn't surprised by how quickly he made himself at home at Test level because of what I'd seen him do in South Africa. What did surprise me was how he scored his runs. He is an amazing front-foot player, but in that innings he played the short stuff so well, too. I could see he was really up for it. At one stage, when Brett Lee was flying in at him, we came together in mid-pitch for a chat at the end of the over and he just said: "Sorry, China. Can't talk now. Too pumped."'

During the day, the man who had been left out to make way for Pietersen, Graham Thorpe, announced his retirement from Test cricket. He had played exactly 100 Tests in a career that began against Australia at Trent Bridge in 1993 with a century.

England were still 68 runs behind when Pietersen went, to a standing ovation, not only in tribute to what he had achieved in that innings but in recognition of the possibility that, with his brave approach and toe-to-toe aggression, he might have shown his colleagues the way forward for the rest of the series. Certainly his example appeared to inspire the last pair, Steve Harmison and Simon Jones, who reduced the deficit to just 35 after a whirlwind tenth-wicket stand of 33 from 29 balls.

'He played the short stuff so well and I could see he was really up for it. At one stage when Brett Lee was coming flying in at him, we came together in mid-pitch for a chat at the end of the over and he just said: "Sorry, China. Can't talk now. Too pumped."'

GERAINT JONES ON PIETERSEN'S MAIDEN TEST FIFTY

Vaughan believed England's position was retrievable, provided his bowlers got stuck in again and every half chance was taken.

By lunch, Australia were 82 runs ahead for the loss of Langer, brilliantly run out by Pietersen's direct hit from point.

After the resumption Flintoff accounted for Hayden, and Ponting, who had just become the seventh Australian to reach 7,000 Test runs. The captain was caught by a substitute fielder (James Hildreth), which seemed fairly irrelevant at the time, but was to gain considerable pertinence later in the series. Australia were 100 for 3, and England felt one more push could bring the breakthrough that would keep alive their slim chance of victory.

The chance came when Michael Clarke, on 21, drove the ball firmly, knee-high, to Pietersen at extra cover off Simon Jones. For the third time in the match the debutant could not hold on. For a man considered one of the best outfielders in the country, this was the easiest of the three catches – and the most costly drop. Clarke went on to score another 70 runs in a partnership of 155 with Martyn that took Australia far out of England's reach.

'That was a catch I should have taken ten times out of ten,' admits Pietersen. 'There are no reasons why I dropped so many; no excuses. If the ball touches my hands, I should catch it. That's the standard I set myself. But I'm not going to sit there and hum and haw over it. Once it's happened, that one split second, there's nothing I can do about it.'

Amazingly, twenty-four hours after Ponting's team had looked in deep trouble, they were firm favourites to continue England's disastrous Ashes record at Lord's, much to the pleasure of watching Australian Prime Minister John Howard. There's no doubt that Clarke will be one of Australia's batting heroes over the next decade, as his fine array of shots proved, but the word was he was playing for his place after a run of low scores. (His last six Tests had brought just 121 runs.) This performance, especially the manner in which he played the spin of Giles, whose leg-stump attack went at 5 an over, guaranteed him his place for the summer, as well as putting Australia in total control. Instead of being 139 for 4 (as the score would have been if Pietersen had held on to the catch), Australia reached 255 for 3.

Pietersen missed another opportunity when he failed to run out Clarke (on 53). As Flintoff's delivery was also a no-ball, and Pietersen's throw raced to the boundary for overthrows, 6 runs were added to Australia's total.

The final hour gave England some respite and rekindled a little optimism. A Lord's century and a place on the honours board were there for Clarke if he was patient, but he threw away both by playing on after a wild drive at Hoggard. Martyn, who had just passed 4,000 Test runs, went LBW next ball when Harmison got one to nip back. Flintoff scored a Gilchrist double by coming around the wicket again and bowling the Aussie wicket-keeper with one that cut back. He then mimicked the head-bobbing celebration with which Courtney Walsh used to greet his wickets.

Harmison closed the day with a brute of a ball to Warne that lifted from a length, and Giles took the catch in the gully. The loss of 4 wickets for 24 runs in the final 31 deliveries had halted Australia's charge and shown that England were prepared to keep fighting, even when on the back foot. But with Ponting's side now 314 ahead with three second-innings wickets standing, and McGrath and Warne waiting to pounce, few Englishmen held out much hope.

DAY THREE: AUSTRALIA 384 ALL OUT; ENGLAND 156 FOR 5

If they were to have the slightest chance, England needed early wickets on the third morning. But to most observers it looked as though the stuffing had already been knocked out of them. There was no doubting their effort or commitment, but the aggression that had been so evident on the first morning was nowhere to be seen, and the belief appeared to have drained out of them as well.

The apparent loss of confidence manifested itself in their fielding, as three clear-cut opportunities came and went begging. England did manage to remove Lee, run out by Giles from point, and Gillespie, clean bowled by Simon Jones, but the tourists really should have been all out by lunch. Instead, Katich (10 not out overnight) had moved on to 66 and still had a partner to keep him company. McGrath was given two lives: Flintoff dropped a regulation chance at second slip; and Geraint Jones, who had already missed a tough chance off Gillespie, failed to gather a much easier opportunity when diving forward. Simon Jones was the unlucky bowler on all three occasions. This was the one session of the summer that left England fans worrying that, when it came to Ashes cricket, nothing had changed. Questions were being raised at Headquarters about whether Vaughan's side were up for the fight.

Geraint Jones finds little comfort in the fact that his mistakes came at a time when the match was already out of reach. 'There just is no hiding-place for a wicket-keeper,' he says. 'Obviously, at the start of the season I knew my position would be under scrutiny because I didn't have a particularly great series in South Africa. It was a tough tour and I felt I contributed along the way, but I was definitely under a bit of pressure and I needed to have a good season, especially bearing in mind the opponents we were coming up against. It was going to be the biggest test of my character and my ability.

'I felt really good with the gloves the whole way through the series against Bangladesh and throughout the one-dayers, so I had a lot of confidence going into the Test with the way I'd been playing. But the one thing that came across fairly quickly was the difference between keeping to the white ball and keeping to the red. That immediately threw me. I don't know if it was my eyes or Lord's difficult background, but straight away, because it was harder to see, all that rhythm I had had was harder to achieve. I remember thinking, What's happened here? I've been seeing everything so well but now the red ball feels a bit foreign.

'I had also felt confident with my batting in the first innings, even though wickets had tumbled. I love those situations because you go out there and you show your character. That's what I love doing in both aspects of the game. But then I dropped those two catches and the demons were back. I knew everything I had tried to quash about my wicket-keeping would resurface. It didn't make me feel any better that they probably didn't have a bearing on how the match turned out.

'The first one, off Gillespie, I went for one-handed. It was off Simon Jones, and the wicket would have brought him level with his dad, Jeff, for Test scalps. So it was disappointing personally for me to drop it, but also I knew what it meant for him. I remember everything felt so good going for it: the positioning, everything. I felt in total control the whole way. I really couldn't have done anything better … except hold on! For a keeper, that is frustrating, because you can take some catches when you're not perfect and think, How did that stay in? And then something that you feel so good going for just pops out. If anything, it was a two-handed catch, but I felt in such control going for it one-handed that instinct took over.

'The second one looped up off McGrath and initially I thought I was never going to reach it. I saw it go up and thought, I'm going to have to give it everything to get to it. I was at full speed and straining. Then I suddenly realised I'd misjudged it and I almost went past the ball. And, of course, you feel dreadful. It's not like there is a blackboard and you can just rub off your mistake and the board is clear when the next ball comes down. Your brain doesn't work that way; you've got a memory. But you have to push all of your focus on the next ball, and concentrate even harder after you drop a catch. We're all human, though, and your mind is still in overdrive thinking about what you should have done. I can honestly say that I can describe in great detail every error I have made in my Test career. And what is doubly hard is that when it happens again it brings all the others to mind.

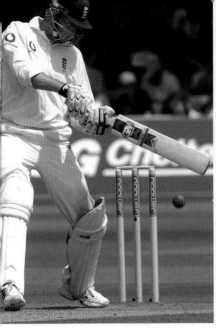

ABOVE, LEFT: The summer got off to a flying start for Marcus Trescothick, whose 194 helped England to a score of 528 for 3 declared against Bangladesh. (*Getty Images*)
RIGHT: Graham Thorpe on his way to making 66 not out in his 100th and final Test for England in the second Test. Before the Ashes series, the big question was which two of Thorpe, Ian Bell and Kevin Pietersen would start. (*Getty Images*)

Matthew Hoggard celebrates taking his 150th Test wicket – Javed Omar was his victim. (*Getty Images*)

Glenn McGrath has his middle stump knocked flying by Steve Harmison at the end of the first-ever Twenty20 international, at the Rose Bowl, where England won by 100 runs. It was a great start for the summer ahead. (*Getty Images*)

ABOVE, LEFT: Steve Harmison celebrates as Adam Gilchrist is caught behind in the NatWest Series game at Bristol. He finished with 5 for 33, and had already made his mark. (*Getty Images*) RIGHT: Kevin Pietersen's 65-ball 91 in the same match won over any who still doubted that he could deliver at the highest level. (*Getty Images*)

TOP: Matthew Hayden squares up to Simon Jones, after the England paceman had thrown the ball at him when preventing a run. This England side was not going to back down. (*Getty Images*)

ABOVE: Paul Collingwood and Geraint Jones during their 116 partnership in the NatWest Series final at Lord's, which helped tie the match after England had been reduced to 33 for 5. (*Getty Images*)

RIGHT: Vikram Solanki during his innings of 53 not out in the NatWest Challenge match at The Oval, where he became England's first ever full substitute. (*Getty Images*)

Michael Vaughan and Ricky Ponting pose for the cameras ahead of the most eagerly anticipated Ashes series in years. Even they could not have dreamt what was to happen in the coming weeks.
(*Getty Images*)

Duncan Fletcher addresses the England squad the day before the first Test at Lord's. He had done everything possible to prepare the team so they could regain the Ashes.
(*Getty Images*)

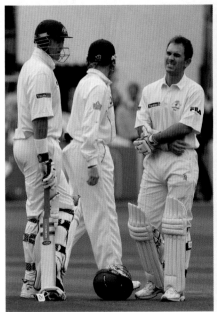 

ABOVE, LEFT: The Ashes series was less than an over old when Steve Harmison hit Justin Langer a painful blow on the arm: England meant business. (*Getty Images*) RIGHT: Later that morning, and it was Ricky Ponting on the receiving end. (*Empics*)

Kevin Pietersen and Michael Vaughan join Andrew Flintoff as he celebrates having Adam Gilchrist caught behind. Australia were skittled out for 190 in just 40.2 incredible overs. (*AP Photo/ Alastair Grant*)

Harmison the destroyer: first Ricky Ponting then Shane Warne tumbled to the irresistible pace of Steve Harmison, who took 5 for 43. (*Getty Images, Sean Dempsey/PA*)

ABOVE, LEFT & RIGHT: Glenn's revenge: McGrath bowls Michael Vaughan then Andrew Flintoff to seize the initiative, and by the end of the first day England were reduced to 92 for 7. (*Chris Young/PA, Getty Images*) BELOW: Kevin Pietersen is brilliantly caught on the boundary by Damien Martyn to bring an end to his defiant knock of 57. (*Empics*)

Shane Warne celebrates after trapping Ian Bell LBW in the second innings. Only his Hampshire friend and team-mate Kevin Pietersen seemed to have any answer to him, making an aggressive 64 not out. But it was not enough to save England from a 239-run defeat. (*Getty Images*)

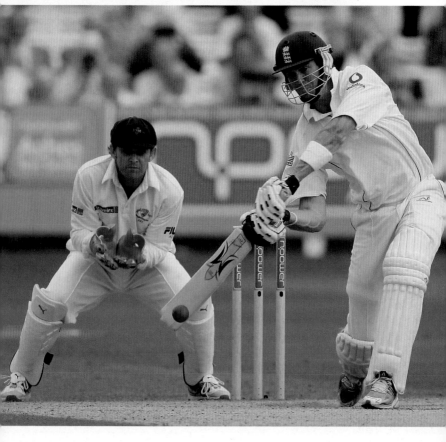

'They say all keepers are mad. I think I'm well on the way!'

Harmison finally finished the job when Simon Jones provided the safe pair of hands that had been missing when he'd been bowling and took a sharp catch at third man to end Katich's resistance.

England's victory target was an unlikely 420, even though Vaughan's team had plenty of time to reach it: two full days and 58 overs. History was not in their favour. England's highest total to win a Lord's Test was the 282 they had amassed in 2004 against New Zealand. Their Ashes best was 332 for 7 at the Melbourne Cricket Ground on the 1928–29 tour. The highest by any team at Lord's was 344 (admittedly for only one wicket lost!) by the West Indies in 1984; while the most in Ashes history was the 404 for 3 at Leeds by Don Bradman's 1948 Invincibles. The highest fourth-innings total of all time was the West Indies' 418 for 7 against Australia in 2003. Few at Lord's gave this England team any chance of surpassing all of those records in one fell swoop against a side containing two of the best bowlers in cricket history.

That said, there was some wishful thinking at tea after Trescothick and Strauss had reduced the target to a seemingly more manageable 355. They must have taken some heart from the manner in which they batted positively against McGrath second time round. However, as sides around the world had been discovering for a decade against Australia, if the pitch is not assisting one of their stars, it will be offering plenty to the other. Even before tea, England's opening pair had seemed baffled by the wiles of Warne. One factor may have been the technical problem that had effectively taken Merlin (Loughborough's bowling machine which was designed to help them deal with everything the leg-spinner could send their way) out of the game.

Duncan Fletcher explains: 'I'd been told about this machine by Troy Cooley, our bowling coach. He had said, "It's not only a leg-break machine; it's a bowling machine. It bowls all balls and it's programmable. It can even bowl balls close to what Glenn McGrath does. You programme in: 'I want the ball to come out this way, this speed, this length.' It's fantastic." But you're always a bit sceptical about this kind of thing, so I said to Michael Vaughan, "You don't live too far away, go and try it out." There was some spare time between the one-day series and the Test match and Michael wanted to do some work on his batting anyway. So he went down to Loughborough, tried it out and said it was very, very useful.

'As soon as that happened I said, "Right, bring it down to Lord's." But it didn't get off to a good start. Until that point the guys had been using it indoors, and the way it works is that a series of lights come on, like at the start of a Formula One race, so the batsman can get ready for the ball to be bowled: four lights, three lights, two, one, bowl. But when they brought the machine outdoors so that we could practise batting in patches of rough that we had kicked up, you couldn't see the lights because of the glare. It confused the guys, they didn't see it very well and the timing was wrong.

'After that we fixed the machine and it has since played a tremendous part. You cannot replace the human element, but in terms of replicating the angles of delivery, once we got over the teething troubles, it really helped the batsmen.'

Which may explain why both openers attempted to defend against Warne almost exclusively with their pads first and bats second.

Strauss recalls: 'After I played for Middlesex against Hampshire, Warne made a few comments about how I was going to be his next rabbit. I took them all with a pinch of salt. Certainly something that we discussed as a team prior to the series was the fact that the Australians were going to use the press as a medium to try to get under our skin, but we decided just to remain classy and not get lured into having a slanging match through the papers. We had to remain smart enough to realise what they were trying to do rather than biting at anything they said. It's tough, though, when they're talking about you.

'I had the feeling that Warne genuinely thought he had something over me, anyway. So that, combined with the way he was acting on the field, did get on my nerves a little. But also you know the only way to answer him is by scoring runs. It's as simple as that. You can't come back and say, "That's not true, I'm not your rabbit," if the guy is continually getting you out. So trying to prove someone wrong can act as a motivation as well, and certainly that was the way I tried to look at it when I read it in the papers.'

Strauss evaded the spinner's clutches this time, and he and Trescothick managed to reduce the target to 340. But then Lee started a collapse with an acrobatic catch off his own bowling to get rid of the Middlesex man, who had tried to leave the ball.

Then it was Warne's turn. In an inspired spell from the Nursery End he took 3 wickets in 32 balls. To all intents and purposes, after an hour or so of carnage, England were dead in the water. First Trescothick was caught by Hayden at slip. Then, after Lee had again exposed Vaughan's footwork for a second-innings 4 to add to his first-innings 3 and raise genuine concerns about his form, Bell padded up, expecting turn. The ball went straight on and Aleem Dar's finger went straight up. Most observers were convinced Bell had been undone by Warne's infamous slider, the ball he had used to dismiss him in the county match between Hampshire and Warwickshire. Bell,

> '*I had a few comments ... Obviously they were meant to make me feel uncomfortable. "Is that how you're going to play Shane Warne?" Stuff like that ... he very much plays a mental game with you, slowing things down, waiting at the end of his mark, then rushing you. It was an education.*'
>
> IAN BELL

though, was not convinced, arguing that the ball was actually a 'leg-spinner' that Warne simply didn't spin. There was much less doubt about what the Australians thought of his batting. 'I had a few comments,' he recalls. 'Obviously they were meant to make me feel uncomfortable. "Is that how you're going to play Shane Warne?" Stuff like that. And he very much plays a mental game with you, slowing things down, waiting at the end of his mark, then rushing you. It was an education.'

The masterclass was completed when Flintoff, attempting to cut, was caught by Gilchrist. England had plunged from 80 for 0 to 119 for 5 in 13 overs. It could have been even worse: Aleem Dar turned down several impassioned pleas from Warne before giving one in the affirmative.

Pietersen and Jones added 37 runs before bad light ended play for the day at 5.36. England still trailed by 264 runs, and it was now a question of when, not if, Australia would go one up in the series. Once again there was Australian talk of a whitewash. Lee declared that night: 'We've come over here to try to win five–nil. There's no point trying for a three–two result. This first Test is important because it sets up the series. When you try to write off Shane Warne and Glenn McGrath, they come back bigger and stronger. Warne is the world's best. His persona and presence out there are fabulous. I definitely believe he is the best he has ever been: he gets better with age.'

DAY FOUR: ENGLAND 180 ALL OUT; AUSTRALIA WON BY 239 RUNS

England lasted late into Sunday, but only because of the weather. At one stage it looked likely that there would be no cricket at all, but the Lord's outfield had been recently relaid to improve the drainage, and play started less than an hour after the rain had stopped. There were 42 overs remaining in the day, but in the event only 10.1 were needed as England tamely folded.

Pietersen was left undefeated on 64, having become the eighth England player to hit two half-centuries on his Test debut. He added 22 on the Sunday while the other five England batsmen totalled ... well, absolutely nothing. Geraint Jones was out for his overnight score of 6 when he pulled McGrath to mid-on. Then Giles (out second ball in the gully), Hoggard (collecting a pair when he was LBW to McGrath), Harmison (another LBW, first ball) and Simon Jones (edge to Warne at first slip off McGrath) all made ducks. His catch to dismiss Jones ended what was almost certainly Warne's last chance of getting his name on the Lord's honours board. His absence from the roll-call of visiting Test bowlers who have taken five wickets in an innings or ten in a match will remain one of the great anomalies of sport.

McGrath's spell this time was 4 for 3 in 23 balls, as England seemed to have no answer to these two thirty-five-year-old masters of their craft. McGrath's match figures of 9 for 82 gave him a total of 26 Test wickets at Lord's for 299 runs, an average of just 11.50. The winning margin was an embarrassing 239 runs and the fans were less than happy with England's capitulation. Play had started at 3.45 and ended at 4.46 (and there had been another 12-minute rain break in the middle of that). There were no refunds for the 28,000 capacity crowd, even though they had seen only 49 minutes of play and 61 deliveries. The ECB policy is to refund half the ticket price when fewer than twenty overs are bowled *because of bad weather*. But this does not apply if the day is shortened because of a result: there is no indemnity against poor batting.

Vaughan sympathised with the fans but insisted: 'There's nothing I can do. There will be England supporters who will be disappointed we are one–nil down to Australia, but there are still four games to play and we have to up our performance levels. I think there's a real opportunity to play some good cricket against them. For the first two days they knew they were in a contest.

'Dropping catches has happened before and it's happened again. They are good fielders dropping them, so it's difficult to explain. A lot of us need to go away and work on our games and make sure we are ready for the second Test. But you don't become a bad team because you've lost one game. These are young players; give them a chance, they've lost one game. We have a bowling unit who can bowl Australia out twice, as we have proved. Australia have a knack of taking the game away from you if you give them opportunities – and that's what we did.'

England were promptly pushed to 9/1 outsiders to win the Ashes; Ponting's side were cut to 1/8 on. The Australian skipper reckoned the bookies had got their odds spot on. 'The gap between the sides in this game has been quite vast,' he said. 'We've got a very good chance of winning five–nil. This Test match has lots of similarities to the first Tests of other Ashes series, because they made lots of big mistakes at crucial times.'

Only three Ashes series since the Second World War had been won by the side losing the first Test: England in 1954–55 and 1981; and Australia in 1997. When Australia next come in 2009, it will be 75 years since England have last won a Lord's Ashes Test, and that 1934 victory will be the only success there in 111 years. Maybe Nelson will come to England's rescue.

The loss brought England's record run of ten successive Test wins to an end. It was only Vaughan's fifth defeat in twenty-eight Tests as captain.

Duncan Fletcher did not like what he saw: 'I think, for some reason, after that first morning, we just relaxed too much. When we went in after bowling the world champions out for such a low total, I think we suffered from some sort of delayed shock. It was as though we couldn't believe what we had just done, and from then on the players' minds weren't focused on the job. And if McGrath and Warne are bowling at you and you are not focused, you're history.'

Matthew Hoggard recalls: 'Obviously, when you've been pretty well hammered by the best team in the world, you have a tendency to think, Oh my God! It was vital we got off to a good start. We knew that if we didn't, they would be full of confidence and full of talk,

> *'It was vital we got off to a good start. We knew that if we didn't, they would be full of confidence and full of talk, saying that we couldn't pull a pint.'*
>
> MATTHEW HOGGARD ON THE OPENING TWO DAYS OF THE FIRST TEST

saying that we couldn't pull a pint. So, after the first game, they start up the band and sing the old songs. It was: "You've played everybody else and you've won because everybody else is not very good. Now you've played the best team in the world, us, and you're lacking."'

First Test, Lord's, London

Result Australia won by 239 runs   **Toss** Australia

Umpires Aleem Dar (Pak) and R.E.Koertzen (SA) **Match Referee** R.S.Madugalle (SL)
Man of the Match G.D.McGrath

Australia First Innings		R	M	B	4s	6s
J.L.Langer	c Harmison b Flintoff	40	77	44	5	0
M.L.Hayden	b Hoggard	12	38	25	2	0
*R.T.Ponting	c Strauss b Harmison	9	38	18	1	0
D.R.Martyn	c G.O.Jones b S.P.Jones	2	13	4	0	0
M.J.Clarke	lbw b S.P.Jones	11	35	22	2	0
S.M.Katich	c G.O.Jones b Harmison	27	107	67	5	0
+A.C.Gilchrist	c G.O.Jones b Flintoff	26	30	19	6	0
S.K.Warne	b Harmison	28	40	29	5	0
B.Lee	c G.O.Jones b Harmison	3	13	8	0	0
J.N.Gillespie	lbw b Harmison	1	19	11	0	0
G.D.McGrath	not out	10	9	6	2	0
Extras	b 5, lb 4, w 1, nb 11	21				
Total	all out, 40.2 overs, 209 mins	190				

FoW   1–35 Hayden (8th ov), 2–55 Ponting (13th ov), 3–66 Langer (15th ov), 4–66 Martyn (16th ov),
5–87 Clarke (22nd ov), 6–126 Gilchrist (29th ov), 7–175 Warne (37th ov), 8–178 Katich (37th ov),
9–178 Lee (39th ov), 10–190 Gillespie (41st ov)

Bowling	O	M	R	W
Harmison	11.2	0	43	5
Hoggard	8	0	40	1
Flintoff	11	2	50	2
S.P.Jones	10	0	48	2

England First Innings		R	M	B	4s	6s
M.E.Trescothick	c Langer b McGrath	4	24	17	1	0
A.J.Strauss	c Warne b McGrath	2	28	21	0	0
*M.P.Vaughan	b McGrath	3	29	20	0	0
I.R.Bell	b McGrath	6	34	25	1	0
K.P.Pietersen	c Martyn b Warne	57	148	89	8	2
A.Flintoff	b McGrath	0	8	4	0	0
+G.O.Jones	c Gilchrist b Lee	30	85	56	6	0
A.F.Giles	c Gilchrist b Lee	11	14	13	2	0
M.J.Hoggard	c Hayden b Warne	0	18	16	0	0
S.J.Harmison	c Martyn b Lee	11	35	19	1	0
S.P.Jones	not out	20	21	14	3	0
Extras	b 1, lb 5, nb 5	11				
Total	all out, 48.1 overs, 227 mins	155				

FoW 1–10 Trescothick (7th ov), 2–11 Strauss (7th ov), 3–18 Vaughan (13th ov), 4–19 Bell (15th ov), 5–21 Flintoff (17th ov), 6–79 G.O.Jones (35th ov), 7–92 Giles (37th ov), 8–101 Hoggard (42nd ov), 9–122 Pietersen (44th ov), 10–155 Harmison (49th ov)

Bowling	O	M	R	W
McGrath	18	5	53	5
Lee	15.1	5	47	3
Gillespie	8	1	30	0
Warne	7	2	19	2

Australia Second Innings		R	M	B	4s	6s
J.L.Langer	run out (Pietersen)	6	24	15	1	0
M.L.Hayden	b Flintoff	34	65	54	5	0
*R.T.Ponting	c sub (J.C.Hildreth) b Hoggard	42	100	65	3	0
D.R.Martyn	lbw b Harmison	65	215	138	8	0
M.J.Clarke	b Hoggard	91	151	106	15	0
S.M.Katich	c S.P.Jones b Harmison	67	177	113	8	0
+A.C.Gilchrist	b Flintoff	10	26	14	1	0
S.K.Warne	c Giles b Harmison	2	13	7	0	0
B.Lee	run out (Giles)	8	16	16	1	0
J.N.Gillespie	b S.P.Jones	13	72	52	3	0
G.D.McGrath	not out	20	44	32	3	0
Extras	b 10, lb 8, nb 8	26				
Total	all out, 100.4 overs, 457 mins	384				

FoW   1–18 Langer (6th ov), 2–54 Hayden (15th ov), 3–100 Ponting (28th ov), 4–255 Clarke (62nd ov), 5–255 Martyn (63rd ov), 6–274 Gilchrist (68th ov), 7–279 Warne (71st ov), 8–289 Lee (75th ov), 9–341 Gillespie (90th ov), 10–384 Katich (101st ov)

Bowling	O	M	R	W
Harmison	27.4	6	54	3
Hoggard	16	1	56	2
Flintoff	27	4	123	2
S.P. Jones	18	1	69	1
Giles	11	1	56	0
Bell	1	0	8	0

England Second Innings

		R	M	B	4s	6s
M.E.Trescothick	c Hayden b Warne	44	128	103	8	0
A.J.Strauss	c & b Lee	37	115	67	6	0
*M.P.Vaughan	b Lee	4	47	26	1	0
I.R.Bell	lbw b Warne	8	18	15	0	0
K.P.Pietersen	not out	64	120	79	6	2
A.Flintoff	c Gilchrist b Warne	3	14	11	0	0
+G.O.Jones	c Gillespie b McGrath	6	51	27	1	0
A.F.Giles	c Hayden b McGrath	0	2	2	0	0
M.J.Hoggard	lbw b McGrath	0	18	15	0	0
S.J.Harmison	lbw b Warne	0	3	1	0	0
S.P.Jones	c Warne b McGrath	0	12	6	0	0
Extras	b 6, lb 5, nb 3	14				
Total	all out, 58.1 overs, 268 mins	180				

FoW 1–80 Strauss (27th ov), 2–96 Trescothick (30th ov), 3–104 Bell (34th ov), 4–112 Vaughan (37th ov), 5–119 Flintoff (40th ov), 6–158 G.O.Jones (51st ov), 7–158 Giles (51st ov), 8–164 Hoggard (55th ov), 9–167 Harmison (56th ov), 10–180 S.P.Jones (59th ov)

Bowling	O	M	R	W
McGrath	17.1	2	29	4
Lee	15	3	58	2
Gillespie	6	0	18	0
Warne	20	2	64	4

Close of Play Day 1 Australia 190, England 92–7 (Pietersen 28*)
Day 2 England 155, Australia 279–7 (Katich 10*)
Day 3 Australia 384, England 156–5 (Pietersen 42*, G.O.Jones 6*)

SECOND TEST
EDGBASTON

PREVIEW

After all the months of pre-series hype and hoopla, England's disappointing defeat in the first Test at Lord's had let a large amount of the air out of the balloon of their supporters' hopes. Another poor performance in the second at Edgbaston, starting on Thursday 4 August, and it would either go pop or fly about raspberrying until finally coming to rest on the scrap heap of England's broken Ashes dreams. Australia would be 2–0 up, a world-champion team brushing aside young pretenders while barely able to suppress a chuckle as another collection of Pom supposed heavyweights hit the canvas. Meanwhile, those who specialise in the kind of sporting obituary that created the Ashes in the first place would have enough material to string out the demise of English cricket until the nation once again turned its attention to the question of who would come second to Chelsea in the Premiership.

Within the England camp, Ashley Giles was not alone in thinking the criticism they received after losing at Lord's – which included the extraordinary notion that Ian Bell should be replaced – was unnecessarily harsh, particularly that emanating from former England players. Under the headline 'Traitors', he even suggested some of them seemed to *want*

England to lose. But his strong words masked deeper and darker personal concerns. 'It felt like a lot of ex-players didn't want us to win the Ashes because they hadn't, or because they were the last people to do it, so I said so,' explains the left-arm spinner. 'That might have sounded bitter, but that's the way it felt. Suddenly everyone was on our backs again and it was quite offensive. We felt like we were being thought of as a bad team, that we didn't have the right players, that we had to make changes and we weren't good at this and we weren't good at that. So there was quite a bit of anger and defiance among us. We had to stick together as a team, harness the feelings and say, "I'll show them." Most of what I said was about defending the team.

'But I suppose the reason I reacted so strongly was that some of the most direct criticism was about me. Even before the series began I read an article by Terry Alderman in which he said that if any of their batsmen got out to me they should hang themselves. Now Dave Houghton, the former Zimbabwe captain and someone whose opinions are respected throughout the game, wrote in the paper: "Playing Ashley Giles is like playing ten men against eleven." It was all getting dangerously close to the "What's the point of Ashley Giles?" stuff I had had to contend with the previous year and I was a bit raw. Then, having said what I said, I found myself being attacked from all quarters. It was a tough week for me, especially being away from the team, because I was on my own and all those thoughts are going through your head. Am I good enough? Do they want to get rid of me? I was in a bad place. I was angry and annoyed and found it hard to get my mind back on the game.

'So when we met up prior to the game and I spent some time with our psychologist Steve Bull, he probably had to work harder with me than he had done at any time since our first meetings a couple of years previously. But we sat down with a cup of coffee and he eventually got me thinking about what I do well, about my personal goals, and slowly but surely he brought me round. The support I got from the other players was so important. "We'll get through this" was the message. "Let's get on with the next Test."'

Michael Vaughan, Giles's captain and close friend, 'asked me casually if I was all right and I poured it all out. I told him that it had been a tricky week for me because of all the things that had been written and said. He had absolutely no idea what I was on about because he hadn't read a single newspaper!' Moreover, when Australian coach John Buchanan talked of trying to attack the spinner in an attempt to increase the workload of Steve Harmison and Andrew Flintoff, Giles started to think: 'Hang on, if he's got a plan for me, that must mean he rates me. That made me feel a lot better.'

After the Test was over, Giles reflected: 'Maybe I should have bitten my tongue. Maybe when the reporters approached me I should have said that I needed time for my thoughts to settle. But on the other hand, I didn't say those things to get a reaction or to wind up anyone. That was genuinely how I felt and I was quite pleased to get it all off my chest. The fact was that we had been playing fantastic cricket over the past eighteen months and we had no reason to doubt our strength as a team. But when you read some of the criticism you can be dragged into believing it. Even when someone says, "I wouldn't worry about what so-and-so said or wrote about you," and you haven't even read it, you start to wonder, What has so-and-so said? and run off and try to find out. Nightmare. At least Dave Houghton texted me before the start of the game with the message: "I hope you get the chance to put some egg on my face."'

Giles and his colleagues also received welcome support from their most recent former colleague, Graham Thorpe. In his regular column for the *Mail on Sunday*, Thorpe wrote: 'The first thing England must do as they prepare to try and bounce back this week is to remind themselves of what they have achieved in the past two years. The message from the top down, from the selectors and management, to all the players must be this: we've picked you, we back you, we believe you can do the job. It is the job of coach Duncan Fletcher and captain Michael Vaughan to rebuild the confidence that was a key element in the team's success.'

Thorpe could not have known it, but somewhere in Yorkshire the two men concerned were figuring out exactly how to do what he had suggested.

Marcus Trescothick summed up the mood of the players as they left Lord's: 'It was shock, really, that we had had our arses kicked so badly. I personally thought, Oh no. This is not going to go well, and I was pretty worried. In the first couple of days afterwards I didn't turn on the TV or read any papers because I was dreading every minute what was going to be said. I rang Michael a couple of times and he felt the same.'

But when Vaughan and Fletcher met to review the events at Lord's, their discussion had a massive bearing on how the rest of the summer and the series turned out. According to Fletcher: 'Prior to the series we had spoken so much about how we needed to show positive intent and get in the Australians' space. I think the problem was that we just forgot to do it at Lord's.

'It was crunch time and it was a key meeting. If we waited for the Aussies to come to us after Lord's, we would lose the series. We discussed the attitude of the players and how we could lift them. I didn't think we were intimidated at Lord's but we didn't play well and forgot to be positive. It was a mental thing. I never thought we were in awe of the Aussies. It wasn't a question of telling the players not to be worried about failing in trying to have a go. The key was never to talk about or mention failure, like when you are standing on the golf course and someone

> *'It was shock, really, that we had had our arses kicked so badly. I personally thought, Oh no. This is not going to go well, and I was pretty worried.'*
> MARCUS TRESCOTHICK

says to you "Don't hit the ball in the water." The word "fail" was never used. We had to be positive. What Michael and I did was offer a clear direction.'

Michael Vaughan recalls: 'On the day we arrived at Edgbaston I got the team together and told them we had to erase from our thoughts what happened at Lord's. I reminded them there were still four games to go and we were still in the series. But we had to remember how to be positive and how to enjoy ourselves and get right back at them.'

Whatever was said in private, publicly the captain was prepared to concede no more than that his side had had a bad game. 'Our batting wasn't good enough,' he admitted, and went on, 'At 100 for 3 in their second innings we had an opportunity to take the game by the scruff of the neck and we didn't.'

Of more immediate concern to Vaughan was what happened to him in the Edgbaston nets two days before the start of the match, when all of his and Fletcher's grand plans for England's revival almost came to nothing. Vaughan was struck on the right elbow by Chris Tremlett so severely that he needed help to remove his batting gloves; and the pain only increased as physio Kirk Russell applied ice to reduce the swelling. The captain was soon on his way to hospital, but when X-rays revealed no breaks the alarm bells were silenced.

The Australians were determined to continue to talk a good game, with captain Ricky Ponting suggesting: 'I wouldn't say we've destroyed their confidence with our performance at Lord's, but we've gone some way towards doing that.'

Glenn McGrath was … well, Glenn McGrath. 'It doesn't matter what they do,' he said. 'If we play our game well, we'll win.' Then he proceeded to fillet the display of the England team at Lord's as follows: 'The only performance we were not expecting came from Kevin Pietersen. Everyone else seemed to stand there, get stuck in the crease and wait for something to happen. But as good a game as he had with the bat, he had a terrible game in the field. To drop guys at the top of the order is something you cannot afford to do at Test level.

'Shane bowled as well as I've seen him for a long time. But I just couldn't comprehend the way the England openers tried to play him by repeatedly padding up. Even for someone like me batting at number eleven, I would think that was a pretty bad option. As for Ian Bell, Shane set him up perfectly with a couple of big-turning leg-breaks followed by the slider. Shane told us exactly the same thing happened when he bowled at Bell in a county match, except in that game it took him two balls.

'Perhaps the most disappointing aspect of England's performance was their lack of resilience. The way the match finished when we picked up those wickets cheaply on the fourth day was a bit too easy, like the fight had gone.'

In other words, one false move in Birmingham, and the Ashes would also be as good as gone.

DAY ONE: ENGLAND 407 ALL OUT

Then, at 9.15 a.m., with little more than an hour to go before the start of play on the first day, one of the greatest bowlers in the history of the game stepped on a cricket ball.

McGrath had been warming up for the action with a spot of tag-rugby. He had noticed the line of cricket balls laid out in preparation for a fielding routine and thought how neat they looked. But when he brought his conversation with reserve wicket-keeper Brad Haddin to an abrupt halt in order to give chase to an oval-shaped one, the next thing he felt was an agonising crunch in his right ankle that told him he was out of the game before he hit the ground. The whereabouts of the ball he stepped on are unknown. Rumours that Vaughan asked McGrath to sign it for his benefit auction proved impossible to substantiate. One newspaper dubbed it 'The ball of the series'.

According to McGrath: 'My first thought was, What can I do to make this unhappen? Can I just go back and rewind the tape? Then you go through every possibility of why it is not going to be as bad as it feels. But deep down I knew I was cooked.'

Michael Kasprowicz was drafted in. 'I turned up expecting to have plenty of coffee and tea and cake,' he said later, 'and ended up playing in a Test match.'

No player takes pleasure in injury to another, and this case was no exception. But the news that the bowler who had tormented them in the first Test

The whereabouts of the ball he stepped on is unknown. Rumours that Vaughan asked him to sign it for his benefit auction proved impossible to substantiate.

was out of the second naturally generated some 'interest' in the England dressing room. Trescothick recalls: 'When some-one told me that McGrath had tripped over a ball and was not going to play, at first I really didn't take too much notice. I was trying to keep calm and focused on my own preparation, and the last thing I needed was a distraction, particularly if the information then turned out to be wide of the mark. Obviously you never wish ill on anybody, but I must admit that when the story was confirmed I sat there in the dressing room and thought, Crikey – this is going to make things a bit easier!'

His opening partner Andrew Strauss recalls: 'When I saw the stretcher come out and I saw the look of absolute agony on Glenn's face I felt for him immediately. But at the same time I did wonder whether this was the point where the luck might be turning our way.'

So everyone at the ground had already had more than enough pre-match drama to keep occupied, but there was more to come …

Having seen his main strike bowler sidelined just an hour before, Ricky Ponting could be forgiven for being in some-thing of a head-spin. However, as he and Vaughan appeared on the pitch for the toss, nobody expected what happened next. Whoever won the toss, the pundits believed, simply *must* bat first. And that applied especially to Australia, who now didn't have McGrath (their best chance of making early inroads) but still had Warne (the best on the planet at bowling out sides batting last on a wearing pitch). The theory was simple: bat England out of any chance of winning, then let Warney loose on them. Win the match, go two up in the series, break English hearts, retain the Ashes. Simple.

> *'I turned up expecting to have plenty of coffee and tea, and cake ... and ended up playing in a Test match.'*
> MICHAEL KASPROWICZ

Admittedly, there was a smidgen of moisture in the pitch. Torrential rain over the previous week had meant Warwickshire groundsman Steve Rouse had not been able to bring the playing surface quite to the boil as he would have liked. He pronounced it a day or two underdone, and the outfield was lush and green. But there seemed no persuasive reason to insert the opposition. Once again W. G. Grace's famous dictum – 'If you win the toss, bat. If you are unsure, consider all the issues, weigh up all the possibilities, *then* bat' – seemed entirely appropriate.

The England players were unanimous. If they won the toss, they wanted first use of the pitch, and they were equally certain that the Australians would do the same. According to Trescothick: 'If someone had offered us first use we would have bitten their arm off. In the dressing room we were watching the toss on TV. Mark Nicholas was poised to thrust his microphone into the face of the captain who won the toss. After Ricky called "heads", Mark went straight towards him and our hearts sank. Having been hammered at Lord's, we needed the chance to hit back hard. If they had scored 400-plus the game would probably have been out of our reach. So when Ricky told him, "We're going to have a bowl," I couldn't believe what I was hearing. I looked around the room to see if anyone had any ideas. Everyone was just standing there open mouthed.'

Vaughan admitted: 'Some people said they saw a little smile wander across my face at that point. My emotions went from wondering how much stick I was going to get from the players for losing the toss to thinking, Well, if Ricky doesn't want to have a bat, that's fine by me.' Strauss said: 'I just couldn't understand Ricky's decision. None of us could.'

As for the bowlers, Steve Harmison wondered whether Ponting was playing mind games. 'Maybe it was the Aussie macho thing, saying, "So what if we've lost McGrath? We're not bothered. We'll win without him."' Matthew Hoggard, who had been preparing for what looked like a hard day's work on a flat pitch, remembers: 'You should have seen my face.'

Ponting later conceded that he may have erred. There were rumours that some of his colleagues thought so at the time. But his explanation for the decision was that the side batting first had won only once in the last thirteen Tests on this ground, and the absence of McGrath had not altered his bowl-first strategy. He had chosen his statistics selectively, however, ignoring the fact that the side batting first in the 2003 and 2004 Tests at Edgbaston had both passed 500!

> *'So when Ricky told him, "We're going to have a bowl," I couldn't believe what I was hearing. I looked around the room to see if anyone had any ideas. Everyone was just standing there open mouthed.'*
> MARCUS TRESCOTHICK

The scene was set and the enthusiastic Edgbaston crowd, bolstered by the Barmy Army, was ready to give whole-hearted support.

Trescothick and Strauss, mindful of the words of their captain and coach, went on the offensive. Rarely can a statement of positive intent have been delivered so resoundingly. Brett Lee, Jason Gillespie and Michael Kasprowicz lacked

McGrath's nagging accuracy, and England's openers thrashed away at numerous short and wide deliveries. The pitch wasn't quick enough for short-pitched balls to have any real impact, a fact that didn't seem to dawn on Ponting or his quicks.

If you are going to receive short and loose deliveries on a slow pitch, the batsman you want at the wicket is Trescothick, for few players in the world are as effective at capitalising on wayward bowling. And when he hit Shane Warne back over his head for six in the leg-spinner's first over, the crowd sensed they were witnessing a truly significant change in the order of things. Strauss, too, loves to hit square of the wicket. It was hard to believe that the team piling on the runs was the one fighting to keep its Ashes hopes alive.

'When we spoke about what we had to do in this Test,' explains Trescothick, 'we realised that if we carried on like we had at Lord's we were going to get badly beaten. So whatever else we did, we had to go at Australia. We said, "Let's play with the same passion as we have done. Let's be positive. Let's run hard, call loud and if you want to whack it, whack it." In the past couple of seasons we had backed ourselves to play like that and take people apart, so why not now? And from the moment we went out to bat we just lashed it. The sighting was good, the pitch was easy-paced and both Strauss and I got into our rhythm very quickly. I had a bit of luck when I was caught off the no-ball, but the crowd picked up the momentum. Every run scored, every boundary hit, was cheered as though it was an event in itself. It was astonishing stuff. And playing Warne was a lot easier than at Lord's because the pitch was slower and he wasn't able to operate with five men around the bat.'

Strauss says: 'Tres and I realised that Warne had been forced to come into the game earlier than he might have liked because the other bowlers were getting a pounding, and we felt it was our responsibility to take the game to him and not let him settle. Then Tres absolutely nailed him back over his head for six! He always seems able to adapt his game to the situation. I saw him eyeing up the ball in question and there was no way he was going to miss it. Beautiful.'

Australia were limited to one wicket in the morning session, when Strauss was bowled by one that ripped back fiercely from Warne. The pair had put on 112, their sixth century stand since coming together at Lord's in 2004, but the departure of the Middlesex man did not interrupt England's flow. Trescothick, who had been caught off a no-ball on 32, and Vaughan went into lunch with the cheers ringing in the ears, amplified after Trescothick's 18 runs off the final over from Lee, including a six over third man. 'I think that over was quite important,' says Trescothick. 'Normally you are just feeling your way towards lunch, making sure you will come out for the next session. But he bowled a couple of hittable balls and I thought, There's no point in throttling back. I'll just trolley them as hard as I can.'

Remarkably, the scoring rate increased after lunch as England stuck to their guns and kept on attacking, even though there was a mini-collapse as the scoreboard went from 164 for 1 to 187 for 4. Trescothick fell 10 runs short of a maiden and richly deserved Ashes Test century when he suffered a momentary lapse of concentration and went chasing outside the off stump once too often, but his was a massive contribution by any standards. Ian Bell lasted just three balls (making 6), and then the England captain became Gillespie's first wicket of the series.

> '... [Lee] bowled a couple of hittable balls and I thought, There's no point in throttling back. I'll just trolley them as hard as I can.'
>
> MARCUS TRESCOTHICK
> WORKS HIS WAY
> TO LUNCH ON THE
> FIRST DAY

As Andrew Flintoff walked out to join Kevin Pietersen the expectation in the air was almost tangible. England's two big hitters with a platform from which to attack. Crash helmets were advised.

The Lancashire all-rounder's first Ashes Test had been a huge disappointment, both from a team and a personal point of view. He'd gone away to Devon for a few days after Lord's with wife Rachael and daughter Holly to try to get his head together. After that break, he worked on his game with Neil Fairbrother, his friend, former county colleague and now manager, trying to recapture some confidence and form with the help of a bowling machine at Old Trafford. Then he concentrated on his mental approach with sports psychologist Jamie Edwards, who helped him 'identify the things I do when I am playing well. Maybe I had just lost sight of those things a little. I'd probably put too much pressure on myself at Lord's, so escaping with the family was just what I needed and it helped me to refocus when I got back to cricket.'

Flintoff then rejoined Lancashire for Twenty20 finals day at the Brit Oval, where his mates ribbed him that sports shops had already cleared their shelves and were pulping replicas of his Woodworm bat and replacing them with Kevin Pietersen's. Duncan Fletcher believed a quick net in the knockabout atmosphere of the occasion might help. Trescothick, there with eventual winners Somerset, saw the benefit of the tactic: 'Fred hadn't looked right at Lord's, but the way he hit a few balls that day, I realised he was going to be OK.'

About the Edgbaston Test, Flintoff says: 'I had a bit of luck before I got off the mark when I chipped the ball over mid-off. After that I just took the attack to their bowlers and it came off.'

Pietersen also had a shaky start, but then he and Flintoff swung the series in England's favour with a spectacular display of big hitting. Between lunch and tea, England added 157 runs in 27 overs. The crowd were in raptures and in fine voice.

Andrew Strauss cheered along with everyone else: 'Fred had done OK in the one-day series, but something just didn't look quite right. He didn't look as confident as he had, was scratching around a bit and when he tried for a big shot he would invariably hole out. Then, in the first Test, it looked like he was battling with himself a bit and we were all a bit worried, thinking, Is he going to come through this? But, as always, it only takes one innings, and that first innings at Edgbaston transformed him. When you watch him batting like that with Pietersen there is absolutely no way you can avoid being a fan. Certainly I can't play like that, and most of the other batsmen can't play like that. So when you watch him do his stuff you are just a bit in awe.'

Pietersen was also enjoying himself immensely, truly coming into his own when Flintoff departed almost immediately after tea (giving Gillespie his 250th Test wicket) and Geraint Jones followed soon after. When Pietersen reached his half-century, it was only the sixth time that an England batsman had begun his Test career with three fifties. He says, 'I don't think Ponting got enough stick for his decision to send us in, to be honest, but we weren't complaining. We knew we had to be positive, but we were helped by the lack of discipline among the bowlers. They missed McGrath massively and after the start we had Fred and I just jumped on the bandwagon. People were slightly concerned that if we batted together, we might try to outdo each other rather than playing the man with the ball in his hand. But the way he was batting, smashing the ball to all parts, I was more than content just to play around him. It was fun. But for me the best thing about the partnership was to see Fred get back into real form. He is such a great player, and now the Aussies knew it too.'

Pietersen's departure, soon after Giles had finally fallen to a Warne LBW shout (the first two had resulted in a ticking-off from umpire Billy Bowden), left England 348 for 8, but the doggedness of Hoggard and big-hitting of Harmison and Simon Jones took England past 400. It was only the second time since the Second World War that England had scored 400 on the first day of a Test (the previous occasion was against Pakistan in 1962), and was their highest first-day total since the 409 for 5 against the Australians at Lord's in 1938.

Flintoff had led the way with five sixes (three off Warne; two off Lee), Trescothick managed two and Pietersen (who lashed Lee over midwicket), Harmison and Simon Jones all cleared the boundary rope, too. Ten maximums against Australia was a record for a single innings. With another 216 runs coming in fours, England had made a clear statement of intent. In the context of a limited-overs game, it would have been impressive. In a Test match that England must not lose, a run rate of 5.13 sustained over 79.2 overs was sensational. The only disappointment was that rain prevented Australia facing a torrid half-hour that evening. Some commentators suggested England might have missed the boat (Geoff Boycott: 'They're 100 short on a plum pitch'), but the England dressing room found such opinions perplexing.

DAY TWO: AUSTRALIA 308 ALL OUT; ENGLAND 25 FOR 1

The newspapers were full of the Flintoff and Pietersen show, and so were the minds of the Australians. Or, at least, that's what England believed. 'I think the Aussies were a little shell-shocked by what had happened the previous day,' says Trescothick. 'When Fred and KP were batting together it was like watching a benefit match. You're just not supposed to be able to do that to Australia, with or without McGrath, and when they came out to bat at first they were a bit gun-shy.'

England knew they needed to crash through the breach they had opened in the Australian wall, and, as they had done on that first morning at Lord's, they flew at their opponents from the start. Justin Langer was hit on the helmet by Harmison, but this time two England players immediately enquired about his well-being. Then, from the first ball of the next over, sent down by Matthew Hoggard, Matthew Hayden fell into a trap that had been prepared painstakingly and was now executed perfectly. 'I loved getting Hayden out, especially as it was the first golden duck of his career,' says Hoggard. 'When we played against them in Australia on the last tour in 2002–03 he was such a bully. He murdered us, taking two steps down the wicket when the bowler was bowling at 90 m.p.h. and smacking him back over his head. He's very, very talented and physically huge when you are bowling at him from 22 yards away. We knew his game was about imposing himself with big, booming drives right from the start. We already had one man on the shot at short mid-off, but Vaughan wanted another a bit wider, at short extra-cover, and, obligingly, Hayden smacked it straight to Strauss.'

Ominously, though, Ponting looked in little difficulty thereafter, and he and Langer moved Australia to 88 without further loss. England needed something to happen and someone to make it happen. This time it was Giles, on his home county ground and under intense pressure in the lead-up to the match, who answered the call. By the time he had finished his work for the day, Ponting, Michael Clarke and Shane Warne had fallen to him, and Australia were subsiding to a first-innings deficit that ultimately proved crucial. The first victim, Australia's captain, paddle-swept one from the left-arm spinner and saw the top-edge dolly straight to Vaughan. Understandably, after the 'better-off-without-him' jibes, Giles was ecstatic, punching the air as he raced across the square before being mobbed by his team-mates. Whatever others may have thought, the team and its supporters left no one in any doubt as to their opinion of his value to the side.

Vaughan's morning got even better when he raced to the ball, grabbed it and spun around in one movement before

Understandably, after the 'better-off-without-him' jibes, Giles was ecstatic, punching the air as he raced across the square before being mobbed by his team-mates.

throwing down the stumps to run out Damien Martyn. Back in the dressing room at lunchtime, one of Vaughan's team-mates (not mentioning any names, Fred) suggested the Ashes must be in the bag if the skipper – not always the most accomplished fielder – could take a catch and perform a run out in the space of twenty minutes. Any team, he reasoned, would be helpless against that sort of miracle.

After the break, with Australia again seemingly weathering the storm, Giles struck to have Clarke caught by Geraint Jones off the faintest edge. Langer's long vigil ended when Simon Jones speared one into his pads to make it 262 for 6; and when Shane Warne momentarily took leave of his crick-eting senses, charged down the track to Giles and was bowled all ends up, Australia were reeling at 273 for 7.

With the ball starting to reverse-swing, one more big push from Simon Jones and Flintoff, who finished the innings with successful LBW shouts against Gillespie and Kasprowicz in successive deliveries, left Adam Gilchrist high and dry on 49 not out. Australia's total of 308 gave England a handy first-innings lead of 99.

As Trescothick and Strauss walked out for the second innings, the noise generated by their supporters was deafen-ing, but the question they almost dared not ask was 'Will it be enough with you-know-who bound to be brought on early?' Their nervousness was not eased when, for the second time in the match, Strauss was utterly bamboozled by Warne, bowl-ing round the wicket into the rough outside the left-hander's off stump. Strauss walked across so far that he left his leg stump exposed, lifted his bat out of the way, then heard the death rattle behind him. At that moment Warne became the first bowler in Test history to take 100 wickets against any side on their home territory.

Strauss recalls: 'Warne had put down a marker by bowling so well against us at Lord's. In the second innings there he made us all look a little stupid. But for me this was worse. Once we had got the technical problem with the Merlin leg-spin bowling machine sorted out, I had worked very hard with it prior to the second Test, in the outdoor nets, getting it to bowl into a rough patch we had kicked up to replicate match conditions. But for some reason, all the work I had done was against over-the-wicket bowling and I hadn't quite sorted out the round-the-wicket angles in my head. When it came to the ball that bowled me, I completely misjudged it. I knew that before the start of the series Warne had been calling me his new "Daryll", after [South African] Daryll Cullinan, whom he seemed to be able to get out at will. During the long walk back to the pavilion that evening, I was wondering whether he was going to be proved right.'

Langer insisted that Warne's delivery to Strauss indicated his side was still very much in the game. 'The more Shane Warne demons we can place in the England dressing room, the better,' he said.

But, if the English batsmen faced a nervous wait for morning, at least one of their bowlers could view the match so far with considerable satisfaction. 'Someone asked me afterwards if I felt I had proved my critics wrong,' says Ashley Giles. 'But it was never about that. I did allow myself a small gloat in the general direction of Dave Houghton, but the important thing to me was that we were in with a real chance of winning the Test match.'

DAY THREE: ENGLAND 182 ALL OUT; AUSTRALIA 175 FOR 8

Warne's demons would have to wait, though, for it was Brett Lee who crashed through the England batting line-up with a blistering assault that turned the match on its head. In nine deliveries, his express pace accounted for Trescothick, nightwatchman Hoggard and Vaughan. A promising position had suddenly become precarious. Trescothick chased a delivery he would have been well advised to leave alone. The England skipper was squared up, stranded on the crease and bowled for the third time in the series. And it might have been even worse if umpire Bowden had detected the faint contact between Lee's delivery and Pietersen's glove the first ball he faced.

But it was a short reprieve anyway. After slog-sweeping Warne for two sixes, Pietersen's luck ran out when he swept at Warne and Gilchrist claimed the catch. The replays showed no contact with bat or glove, but umpire Rudi Koertzen's finger went up all the same. Koertzen was probably wrong again during the next Warne over when the Aussies were granted an appeal for a catch behind off Bell. England, who had started the day aiming to extend their advantage to 400, were instead in some disarray at 75 for 6, a lead of just 174.

Flintoff's impact on the match and the series was every bit as significant as anything produced by the great Ian Botham in his fantastic series of 1981.

No more wickets fell before lunch, but the crowd was hushed when it appeared Flintoff had seriously injured his shoulder driving at Warne. The England physio Kirk Russell rushed on and spent a few minutes manipulating the shoulder before Flintoff could resume. At least it wasn't his bowling shoulder, but he showed signs of real discomfort as he struggled to get through the twenty minutes to lunch. He recalls: 'I thought the shoulder had popped out. It was a short ball and I made a late decision to try to get it through the off side. It's no secret that my bottom hand is the dominant one. I just tried to get the left hand out of the way too quickly and it jarred. It had never happened to me before and it hurt.'

Russell had checked for any restriction to the movement in Flintoff's right shoulder, and, to the relief of all concerned, found no signs of serious damage. He says: 'When I went out there obviously we were all pretty concerned because from the dressing room it didn't look good. But I was able to assess the situation very quickly. I tested the stability of the shoulder by getting him to stretch then move his arm back and forward, and I was happy there was no significant problem. Then, at lunch I was able to see if there had been any effect on his muscles and ligaments.' A couple of painkillers later and the big Lancastrian emerged ready to continue.

As he strode to the wicket, no doubt the England team were hoping to see a bravura performance from the man rated the number-one all-rounder in world cricket. But no one could have foreseen the extent to which Flintoff would dominate the remaining two sessions of play. He simply stamped his authority on both the second Test and Australia. In an effort with bat and ball that was nothing short of immense, he overwhelmed his opponents – officially the best side in the world – with the sheer force of his will. No wonder that, by the end of the day, the crowd were chanting, 'Super, Super Fred ... Super Freddie Flintoff', for in his impact on the match and the series, Flintoff was every bit as significant as anything produced by his great hero Ian Botham in his fantastic series of 1981.

When Geraint Jones fell to Lee with the lead at exactly 200, Flintoff reacted by going all-out on the offensive. However, at 131 for 9, England were still only 230 runs in front when last man Simon Jones came out to join him. After dominating the first two days of the match, a couple of hours of poor shot selection and drifting concentration were in danger of costing England the Test. Strauss, for one, was fully aware of that fact: 'In the back of my mind I was thinking that we had just let a great position slip away through sloppy batting, and that all our hard work might yet come to nothing.'

When the Glamorgan man arrived at the wicket he instantly asked Flintoff what the plan was. Flintoff recalls: 'Simon is an aggressive batsman as well, so I told him, "Whatever you do, do it wholeheartedly. If you are going to defend, leave the ball with commitment. And if you are going to have a 'do', really have a 'do'. Get enough of your bat on the ball so that if you nick it, it'll fly over the slips; and if you get hold of it, it will fly over the rope." And that's what he did. Sometimes when you are batting with the tail you can bat with a lot more freedom and try a lot more things. In the situation we were in, I had a licence to do just that, and those extra 50 runs probably made the difference between winning and losing the match.'

Jones remembers the experience with undisguised glee: 'Myself and Harmison had some decent partnerships with the recognised batters. In the West Indies I'd kept Graham Thorpe and Fred company when they got hundreds, Thorpe in Barbados and Fred in Antigua, and Duncan Fletcher is always stressing how vital it is that we bowlers get as many runs as we can. I fancied I might get a few myself, to be honest, but managed to rein myself in, tried to stick around and let him bludgeon it everywhere because he was seeing it like a pumpkin. I've never seen hitting like it. Kasprowicz was the first to go, and Fred destroyed him. Warne was trying to get into my head to have a dart at him by saying I should swap with Strauss up the order because I was playing him so well. But I wasn't biting. Then Fred put a 94 m.p.h. ball from Brett Lee on to the roof of the pavilion. Incredible! I thought, How the hell has he done that? Then I thought I'd better watch it at the non-striker's end because he was smashing the ball with such ferocity that, had he hit one straight at me, I'm not sure I would have been able to get out of the way.'

Trescothick looked on in awe. 'That was something special. That is why he is a god. When he gets in one of those situations where he has licence to go for his shots, he can hit anyone out of the park from anywhere and he is completely fearless.'

In just forty minutes of this last-wicket partnership, Flintoff and Jones crashed 51 runs in 49 deliveries and effectively put England back in charge. Flintoff was irresistible, belting six fours and four sixes. His fifty came up with a six off Kasprowicz, the second in an over that included three no-balls and brought Flintoff 20 runs. Kasprowicz retired from the fray and Lee was brought back to face the music. He sensibly put nine men on the boundary and invited Fred to go over the top. The crowd went wild as two enormous straight blows sailed over their heads, let alone those of the fielders. A TV camera-man and Graham Gooch on the top tier of the pavilion fetched the ball and threw it back. Lee's over went for 18.

Warne was next to accept the challenge and managed to claim Test victim 599 as Flintoff missed for once and was bowled. The capacity Edgbaston crowd rose as one to offer a standing ovation. His 73 runs off 86 deliveries had revived England's fortunes, and his nine sixes in the match had easily surpassed Botham's record Ashes tally of six. After his 167 here against the West Indies, Edgbaston was fast becoming Flintoff's favourite ground. The cheers continued for Warne, whose 6 for 46 was his eighth five-wicket haul against England. But even the legendary Australian wanted the last word to be congratulations for his opponent. As the crowd's volume crescendoed, Warne shouted towards Flintoff at the top of his voice, fighting to make himself heard. Finally Flintoff turned towards him and heard the greatest attack-ing bowler in the history of Test cricket salute him: 'Well batted, Freddie. Well played, mate.'

When Australia came out to bat on that third evening of the second Test at Edgbaston, to begin their chase to the victory target of 282, there were 44 overs remaining in the day's play. The target was soon reduced to 235 as the openers found little difficulty in coping with the new-ball attack.

'I fancied I might get a few myself, to be honest, but managed to rein myself in, tried to stick around and let him bludgeon it every-where because he was see-ing it like a pumpkin. I've never seen hitting like it.'
SIMON JONES ON BATTING WITH FLINTOFF

Vaughan knew the time had come for decisive action and, to a rapturous cacophony from all round the ground, at exactly four o'clock he threw the ball to Flintoff. The skipper wanted one last effort from a man who had already illuminated the day with the power of his hitting. No one knew how much he would be hampered by the shoulder he had wrenched during his brilliant innings. An ambulance had even been on stand-by all afternoon just in case a trip to the local hospital was necessary. But as he stood at the end of his run-up in front of the Pavilion End to start his spell, Flintoff somehow seemed to sense that one of those rare moments of cricketing destiny had arrived. The crowd, many kept up to speed by their radios, knew that Flintoff was on a hat-trick, so there was a huge groan when Justin Langer survived the first ball. But it was swiftly drowned out by more cheers, louder now than ever. Flintoff recalls: 'I was probably still on a high, buzzing from my batting and the way I had played. I just decided I was going to run in as fast as I could and let the ball go as fast as I could. I felt it was a nice time to come on.'

Lee was brought back to face the music ... The crowd went wild as two enormous straight blows sailed over their heads ...

A TV cameraman and Graham Gooch on the top tier of the pavilion fetched the ball and threw it back. Lee's over went for 18.

Nice indeed.

His next delivery was fast and straight, and climbed a little more than Langer was expecting. It cannoned first off his armguard, then on to his thigh, and finally, crucially, into the stumps. A wall of noise enveloped the arena. No hat-trick then, but three wickets in four balls would do just fine.

Over the course of the remainder of the over to Ponting, the all-rounder proceeded to dismantle the defence of one of the best batsmen in world cricket with five deliveries (one was a no-ball) that left his team-mates awe-struck with admiration, reignited with belief and certain that this series would never be quite the same again. Ponting's first ball swung in late and hit him hard on the pads; a massive appeal had umpire Billy Bowden wondering, but ultimately unmoved.

The Australian captain, clearly ruffled and under pressure after his decision to insert England on the first morning, knew little about his next, but got just enough bat on it to send it safely down towards Ashley Giles at fourth slip.

The next, another sensational in-swinger, smashed into Ponting's front leg but hit him just outside the line of off stump.

Ponting managed to leave the final scheduled ball of the over, but his sense of relief at surviving soon disappeared when he heard the no-ball call that gave Flintoff a bonus opportunity, and there was no mistake this time. Flintoff had saved the best for last. With the seam turned around in his hand to see if the ball would reverse-swing away from the right-hander, it was pitched on a perfect length and line. Ponting was drawn into the shot, the ball jinked away, just as Flintoff had commanded it to, glanced off the outside edge and Edgbaston went wild as Geraint Jones took the catch.

On Channel Four, Richie Benaud hit exactly the right note: 'big leg-cutter, vast edge … What an over. Ponting no score and it's 48 for 2 …'

For shock value, England supporters had not witnessed an over like it since 1992, when the Pakistani swing-king Wasim Akram destroyed their chances of winning the World Cup in Melbourne by bowling Allan Lamb and Chris Lewis in successive balls. Those with even longer memories cast their minds back to Michael Holding's dismantling of Geoff Boycott in the third Test of the 1980–81 series in Barbados. Boycott failed to lay a bat on any of the first five and the sixth bowled him.

Added to his first-innings finale, Flintoff had now taken four wickets in nine balls. After his Herculean efforts with the

bat only an hour or so earlier, even his team-mates were mar-
velling at his ability and resilience to deliver an over that
brought this Test right back into England's grasp. Ponting,
head spinning, never knew what hit him. As he walked past
the wildly celebrating players the expression on his face read:
I'm sorry, I cannot play that.

Marcus Trescothick says it was an experience he will never
forget: 'Every one of those five balls was right at Ponting.
There was just no escape. I remember standing at slip thinking you cannot bowl any better than that. He was bowling at
upwards of 90 m.p.h., every ball in the zone, nipping it in,
then nipping it out. Afterwards I said to him, "That was the
best over you will ever bowl."'

Geraint Jones recalls: 'I could feel the intent building in
Fred with each ball.' Ian Bell, at short leg, says: 'I was lucky
because I was right in the thick of it. I was looking at
Ponting's face, thinking how calm he looked, but with all the
noise and commotion and the way Fred was bowling at him,
inside he must have been churning.' Duncan Fletcher insists:
'His bowling to Ponting was as good as you'll get. That over
was a jewel, and it was vital that we got Ponting quickly and
really put them on the back foot. The way he worked him out
showed thinking, and that is the most pleasing aspect of
Andrew's bowling in the last year: the way he thinks through
his overs.' Michael Vaughan has no doubts: 'That over was
probably the turning point of the series.'

Indeed it was, for the simple reason that Flintoff had
shown both his team-mates and, crucially, their opponents
the weapon with which they could win back the Ashes: high-
quality reverse-swing at devastating pace. Even better,
England knew they had another master of the art, Simon
Jones, ready to work in tandem with the Lancastrian.

Flintoff was typically self-effacing afterwards. When
pressed by reporters from the Australian media over comparisons with Ian Botham, he said: 'I'm just trying my best, trying to make my way. I'm playing in an Ashes series which is

something I've desperately wanted to do for a long time. I've wanted to get involved which is something I feel I have done today, to some degree. As for comparisons with people, I don't see it like that. I'm just playing cricket with my mates and enjoying it. I don't want to put myself under any pressure trying to be someone I'm not. I'm Andrew Flintoff and this is the way I play.

'That over was probably the best I've ever bowled. I was slightly lucky to get Langer, but then I sent down a few decent balls at Ponting. The ball was reverse-swinging, coming back into the right-hander, and I thought I'd just swap it around and see if it went away from him. It did, and it was great.'

Matthew Hoggard says simply: 'He's now bowling 90 m.p.h. on a handkerchief. He's a big, strong lad who puts a lot of effort in and hits the bat really hard. If he is in rhythm and his tail is up, he's extremely difficult to play, as the Australians were finding out.'

> *'That over was probably the turning point of the series.'*
> MICHAEL VAUGHAN

Australia needed partnerships, but Simon Jones, capitalising for the first time on the reverse-swing he was later to employ to such devastating effect, and helped by a marvellous diving catch by Trescothick, got rid of Hayden. Then Hoggard – first ball back – dismissed Martyn. 'Taking a wicket with the first ball of my spell was becoming a habit,' he recalls. 'I did it twice in this match. Maybe from then on I should have asked the captain to bowl me in one-ball spells.'

Australia were 107 for 4 just after five o'clock, and Vaughan began wondering whether he could finish the job that night. The crowd were certainly up for it, and the noise grew louder and louder as the day wore on. Edgbaston had been keen to create a passionate atmosphere, and Flintoff agreed that the noise level was like having an extra man on the field: 'They seemed to know when we needed a lift and they provided it,' he said. Then the celebrations began in earnest when England took 3 wickets for 3 runs, leaving Ponting's team looking like history at 137 for 7.

The first two fell to Warwickshire's own King of Spin, Ashley Giles. Simon Katich was undone by a fine juggling catch at slip by Trescothick. Then came the wicket later nominated by Flintoff as the point when England believed they had finally broken Australia's spirit: Adam Gilchrist attempted to hoist Giles over long-on and was safely pouched by Flintoff himself. On this day, who else could have taken it? He celebrated in style by kicking the ball high in the air, before trapping Gillespie LBW with a full delivery. Gillespie had been scheduled to come in as nightwatchman ahead of Gilchrist, but he hadn't been ready.

The score was now 140 for 7. Vaughan, going in for the kill, requested and was granted the extra half-hour to try to wrap it up. But Warne and Clarke had other ideas. It soon became apparent that the match would go into Sunday, and that these two Aussies at least would not be disappearing without a fight. Momentarily, it looked as if that might be literally true when Clarke objected to a Flintoff full toss and the pair exchanged a few words and stern glances in the middle of the pitch.

Then, with stumps beckoning, Steve Harmison bowled the perfect ball to bring to an end a near-perfect day for England. It was a slower ball from fast-bowler's heaven.

The Durham paceman explains: 'I had been trying to get Warne on strike; first to throw the kitchen sink at him, short and in the ribs, then to attempt to get him with the slower ball. But we just couldn't get him down to my end. So I thought, What the hell, if it feels the right ball to bowl I'll try it on Clarke instead. I set him back on his heels with a couple of bouncers and the next one, fuller, he jabbed down on. Then, on the way back to my mark I said to myself: "If you were going to bowl the slower ball at Warne now, why not bowl it at Clarke?"

'He was on the back foot expecting another short one and

instead I gave him the best slower ball I have ever bowled. I was totally in control and confident I could execute it. The ball had been coming out at about 90 m.p.h. so I put my hand behind it as normal then just as I brought it up before releasing it I just pulled the index finger away and it slowed down nicely to around 60-odd. I couldn't have bowled it any better. Clarke played all round it.

'I thought we had won the game there and then.'

He wasn't the only one. The crowd celebrated as if the urn itself was England's for the taking. With Australia on 175 for 8, still 102 runs behind, with only Warne, Lee and Kasprowicz left to bat, surely the victory that would bring England level at 1–1 in the series was in their grasp.

'I'm just trying my best, trying to make my way ... As for comparisons with people, I don't see it like that. I'm just playing cricket with my mates and enjoying it.'
FLINTOFF ON BEING COMPARED TO IAN BOTHAM

Even Flintoff himself, while trying to remain cautious, said: 'We came out believing we could defend 280 and stuck to the task. We cannot get ahead of ourselves because we still have to take two wickets in the morning. But this was my best day in international cricket and to finish it off will be the sweetest feeling.'

DAY FOUR: AUSTRALIA 279 ALL OUT; ENGLAND WON BY 2 RUNS

The proceedings might have lasted only two balls and been completed by 10.33, but Edgbaston was still packed when Warne and Lee walked out in search of those 107 runs. Surely they had no chance of getting them ... did they?

According to Vaughan: 'I really thought we had done the hard work. The wicket had started to play a few tricks on the Saturday evening, the ball had swung and we assumed that there would be plenty in it for us when we pitched up on Sunday morning. In fact, it was entirely the opposite: the ball didn't swing, the pitch went slower and more placid, and they had two dangerous hitters. It was quite surreal being out there knowing that our chances of staying in the Ashes basically depended on us getting those two wickets.'

Surreal turned to unreal as Warne and Lee, batting like men with nothing to lose, cut the deficit with alarming ease. So when Warne stepped on his wicket with the Aussies still 62 short of the victory target, there was more relief than celebration. Now, though, with Lee likely to carry on hitting out and Kasprowicz a genuine, no-nonsense number eleven, it was surely only a matter of time. That eventually proved to be true, but in the 61 minutes that followed the last-wicket pair whittled away both England's advantage and their sense of well-being.

At times like these the captain earns his corn. Vaughan kept his nerve as Lee hit forcibly through the off side, Kasprowicz fended the ball off his body to leg and England's bowlers strayed and showed signs of panic. Balls frequently popped in the air, but never anywhere near the fielders. England were also unlucky when umpire Bowden was about the only person who did not agree with Harmison's view that he had Kasprowicz plum LBW. As the target diminished, Vaughan decided that Harmison and Flintoff were the bowlers to give him what he wanted, but there was little roaring on of England's strike force this time: the crowd grew progressively quieter as the giant screen displayed the dwindling number of runs required.

The target was down to 20 when Flintoff hit Lee on the hand. Then the batsman sent a Chinese cut to the boundary and scampered a single, having dropped his bat. As the tension rose and fingernails were chewed to the quick, England's chance finally came with 15 runs needed, when Kasprowicz speared one from Flintoff down to third man. Simon Jones, usually as safe as the Bank of Wales, awaited its arrival. Harmison assumed it was all over: 'I had the mortgage on Simon catching it. He has a great pair of hands. He caught a great catch off my bowling to dismiss Graeme Smith in the first Test of the winter tour to South Africa in Port Elizabeth, so I was convinced he was going to take it. The ball was up there for so long and you've got ten players all charging towards you, ready to celebrate. He didn't even lay a hand on it. Funny, but from that moment I felt we were all thinking we *had* to get this last wicket, not only for us as a team but for Simon.'

Kevin Pietersen was equally convinced: 'I'm not one to talk too much about dropping catches, but when the ball was in the air travelling towards Jones I jumped up and thought, That's it. But when it went down I also thought, That's it. Up to that point, I had been convinced we would win. Now I thought, Are we actually going to lose this after all we've done to win?'

Jones himself admits: 'I thought I had lost us the Ashes. It was the kind of chance I would normally snaffle, no problem. I thought it was coming straight to me but then at the last minute it seemed to dip on me. I sort of sprawled forward but it hit me on the thumb and never got anywhere near the palms. In the end I was just grateful it didn't go for four. And I was thinking, I've just done that and now everyone is looking at me in a very strange way. As they got closer and closer, all I could think of were three words: "You absolute prat." I started thinking of what I was going to say to the lads

'I started thinking of what I was going to say to the lads when we got back to the dressing room. Then I realised there wasn't much point because I wasn't going to make it back to the dressing room.'
SIMON JONES ON DROPPING KASPROWICZ

when we got back to the dressing room. Then I realised there wasn't much point because I wasn't going to make it back to the dressing room. But the supporters were fantastic. They were shouting, "Don't worry, catch the next one," and that helped me keep my mind on the next ball, and the next.'

Vaughan also clapped his hands and got everyone ready for the next ball. Deep down, he was now wondering more than ever if his side had blown it, but he clung on to one hope: 'The nearer they got, the more pressure they put themselves under. When they first started they were just batting, thinking that they couldn't win, so it was almost a free-for-all, but once they started getting closer, to 20 or so away, you could sense that they were becoming more nervous. In that situation, once your mindset changes from nothing-to-lose to everything-to-lose, the task becomes appreciably more difficult.'

Certainly, now that the target had become attainable, even to tail-enders, they had to start playing properly. And they did. As Australia's target fell into single figures, the enormity of what a loss would do to this England team became apparent. Many fans were holding their heads in their hands, only lifting them briefly to look at the screen and take a deep breath. Then came the moment they had all dreaded: the target was now 4. A single scoring shot, a lucky edge, one fielding lapse, one brave blow and it would all be over. England's fielders had to be prepared to give everything for the cause. Steve Harmison concedes he was not in the best state of mind or body: 'When they got down to 10 I believed that we had gone, and soon after *I* had gone. I was OK bowling but when I was standing in the field I was shaking. We'd already won the game in our

> '*When they got down to 10 I believed that we had gone, and soon after I had gone. I was OK bowling but when I was standing in the field I was shaking.*'
> STEVE HARMISON

minds. We'd put so much into it. I was thinking that if they won, from here it might be five–nil.' Then, a full toss outside off stump from Harmison was sent flying past the in-fielders by Lee, and millions of television viewers thought the game was over. So did Ashley Giles, fielding at fine-leg: 'I saw the shot and thought, That's that. Then suddenly, from out of my line of sight, Simon Jones appeared on the cover-point boundary. I had no idea he was there because my view had been obscured.'

Jones himself was praying very hard that his hands wouldn't fail him a second time: 'Lee got hold of all of it, and a couple of yards either way and I wouldn't have been able to get to it. If it had bobbled or gone through my legs there would have been a lynching in Birmingham that night.'

Vaughan had set the field for a purpose. Whereas most captains would have been trying to save singles, he wanted to keep the game alive until the last possible moment, as he explains: 'I didn't want them to be able to win it with one shot if I could help it. I just wanted to make it as difficult as possible for them. If they were going to get the runs, I wanted them to face as many balls as possible in doing it.'

His strategy paid off spectacularly just two balls later.

In one final, gigantic effort, Harmison, all but spent, searched deep within himself and found a ball that reared up off a long-dead pitch and crashed into Kasprowicz from just short of a length. The Australian number eleven, tucked up, couldn't quite get his gloves out of the way as the ball went down the leg side to Geraint Jones. There was clear contact and England started to celebrate even before Bowden's famous crooked finger went up. England's euphoria was understandable, and the players danced, hugged, patted, embraced and mobbed each other as almost everyone in Edgbaston went crazy. Lee and Kasprowicz sank to their knees. So close – a last-wicket stand of 59 in 77 balls – but no cigar. Maybe losing by 100 runs would have been easier for them to bear.

Shortly after England's Ashes summer was saved, doubts were cast on whether Mr Bowden had made a correct judgement. There was no doubt that the ball had flicked Kasprowicz's right glove, but some angles showed that his hand was off the bat handle at the time, and he therefore should not have been given out. The England team, who had just won by the smallest number of runs in Ashes history, couldn't have cared less.

Simon Jones was the happiest man on the pitch: 'I couldn't have felt better, because Geraint had got me off the hook bigtime.'

His namesake recalls the moment: 'I think Harmison was a bit in two minds about what ball to bowl. He'd gone at the stumps a lot and had one big LBW shout turned down. But I picked the line of this one quite early. There is something in his action that enables me to see the short ball early and I was able to move into position quickly. Then, when it came off Kasprowicz's glove, it was just perfect for me. I took the ball nice and clean, looked up at Billy and saw him nod, so I knew he was going to give it out. It took him some time to raise the finger, but I think that was because he was waiting for Kasprowicz to look up at him. Then all I can remember is turning and giving some major stick to the Aussies in the crowd who had spent most of the last day giving me loads. All the emotions came out when I celebrated. I think they have developed a chant for me – they flap their arms and miss all the time. I find it quite amusing, but I didn't mind giving some back.'

Harmison thought his head was going to explode: 'I was running round like a mad thing!'

Vaughan was lifted off his feet by Flintoff, but in his moment of triumph England's principal hero then took the time to seek out Lee. The image of big all-rounder consoling his vanquished opponent was one of the most poignant of the summer. Flintoff says: 'I just told Brett he had played unbelievably well and that he should be proud of how he batted. The last three Aussie batsmen stood up to everything we could fire at them. Fantastic.'

Immediately after the match Vaughan was honest enough to admit that losing would have left his young team in tatters. 'I don't think we would have come back from two–nil down against a team like Australia, the number-one side in the world. To get over the line is a real boost. It's fantastic to get back to one-all.'

What the skipper couldn't appreciate at that point was that the whole country had now caught the Ashes bug. As the drama had unfolded, with radio and television news bulletins announcing that England had still not won, the audience had grown until gardens and supermarkets were almost deserted. For only the second time in nine series, England had won a Test while the Ashes were up for grabs.

> '... all I can remember is turning and giving some major stick to the Aussies in the crowd who had spent most of the last day giving me stick.'
> GERAINT JONES

Flintoff, of course, was Man of the Match on account of his 141 runs, seven wickets and two catches. It was probably the easiest choice an adjudicator has ever had to make.

In the immediate aftermath, Trescothick was one of a number of players who complained of feeling nauseous. 'I was sitting there with a can of lager trying to take it all in,' he remembers, 'and I was thinking, I feel quite ill, here.' Hardly surprising, considering the assault on mind, body and spirit they had all just experienced. Indeed, only two of the occupants of the England dressing room appeared unaffected by the fuss.

Harmison explains: 'I brought in my two kids – Emily, who's six, and Abbie, two – and sat them down with a yoghurt and a banana. They seemed to enjoy the atmosphere, but they had absolutely no idea what was going on.'

Second Test, Edgbaston, Birmingham

4, 5, 6, 7 August 2005

Result England won by 2 runs   Toss Australia

Umpires B.F.Bowden (NZ) and R.E.Koertzen (SA)   Match Referee R.S.Madugalle (SL)
Man of the Match A.Flintoff

England First Innings		R	M	B	4s	6s
M.E.Trescothick	c Gilchrist b Kasprowicz	90	143	102	15	2
A.J.Strauss	b Warne	48	113	76	10	0
*M.P.Vaughan	c Lee b Gillespie	24	54	41	3	0
I.R.Bell	c Gilchrist b Kasprowicz	6	2	3	1	0
K.P.Pietersen	c Katich b Lee	71	152	76	10	1
A.Flintoff	c Gilchrist b Kasprowicz	68	74	62	6	5
+G.O.Jones	c Gilchrist b Kasprowicz	1	14	15	0	0
A.F.Giles	lbw b Warne	23	34	30	4	0
M.J.Hoggard	lbw b Warne	16	62	49	2	0
S.J.Harmison	b Warne	17	16	11	2	1
S.P.Jones	not out	19	39	24	1	1
Extras	lb 9, w 1, nb 14	24				
Total	all out, 79.2 overs, 356 mins	407				

FoW   1–112 Strauss (26th ov), 2–164 Trescothick (33rd ov), 3–170 Bell (33rd ov), 4–187 Vaughan (37th ov), 5–290 Flintoff (55th ov), 6–293 G.O.Jones (58th ov), 7–342 Giles (66th ov), 8–348 Pietersen (67th ov), 9–375 Harmison (70th ov), 10–407 Hoggard (80th ov)

Bowling	O	M	R	W
Lee	17	1	111	1
Gillespie	22	3	91	2
Kasprowicz	15	3	80	3
Warne	25.2	4	116	4

Australia First Innings		R	M	B	4s	6s
J.L.Langer	lbw b S.P.Jones	82	276	154	7	0
M.L.Hayden	c Strauss b Hoggard	0	5	1	0	0
*R.T.Ponting	c Vaughan b Giles	61	87	76	12	0
D.R.Martyn	run out (Vaughan)	20	23	18	4	0
M.J.Clarke	c G.O.Jones b Giles	40	85	68	7	0
S.M.Katich	c G.O.Jones b Flintoff	4	22	18	1	0
+A.C.Gilchrist	not out	49	120	69	4	0
S.K.Warne	b Giles	8	14	14	2	0
B.Lee	c Flintoff b S.P.Jones	6	14	10	1	0
J.N.Gillespie	lbw b Flintoff	7	36	37	1	0
M.S.Kasprowicz	lbw b Flintoff	0	1	1	0	0
Extras	b 13, lb 7, w 1, nb 10	31				
Total	all out, 76 overs, 346 mins	308				

FoW 1–0 Hayden (2nd ov), 2–88 Ponting (20th ov), 3–118 Martyn (25th ov), 4–194 Clarke (45th ov), 5–208 Katich (50th ov), 6–262 Langer (62nd ov), 7–273 Warne (65th ov), 8–282 Lee (68th ov), 9–308 Gillespie (76th ov), 10–308 Kasprowicz (76th ov)

Bowling	O	M	R	W
Harmison	11	1	48	0
Hoggard	8	0	41	1
S.P.Jones	16	2	69	2
Flintoff	15	1	52	3
Giles	26	2	78	3

England Second Innings

		R	M	B	4s	6s
M.E.Trescothick	c Gilchrist b Lee	21	51	38	4	0
A.J.Strauss	b Warne	6	28	12	1	0
M.J.Hoggard	c Hayden b Lee	1	35	27	0	0
*M.P.Vaughan	b Lee	1	2	2	0	0
I.R.Bell	c Gilchrist b Warne	21	69	43	2	0
K.P.Pietersen	c Gilchrist b Warne	20	50	35	0	2
A.Flintoff	b Warne	73	133	86	6	4
+G.O.Jones	c Ponting b Lee	9	33	19	1	0
A.F.Giles	c Hayden b Warne	8	44	36	0	0
S.J.Harmison	c Ponting b Warne	0	2	1	0	0
S.P.Jones	not out	12	42	23	3	0
Extras	lb 1, nb 9	10				
Total	all out, 52.1 overs, 249 mins	182				

FoW 1–25 Strauss (7th ov), 2–27 Trescothick (12th ov), 3–29 Vaughan (12th ov), 4–31 Hoggard (14th ov), 5–72 Pietersen (25th ov), 6–75 Bell (27th ov), 7–101 G.O.Jones (34th ov), 8–131 Giles (45th ov), 9–131 Harmison (45th ov), 10–182 Flintoff (53rd ov)

Bowling	O	M	R	W
Lee	18	1	82	4
Gillespie	8	0	24	0
Kasprowicz	3	0	29	0
Warne	23.1	7	46	6

TOP: The Australians gather round Glenn McGrath after he picked up a serious ankle injury while practising ahead of the second Test at Edgbaston. (*AP Photo/Matt Dunham*) ABOVE: After Ricky Ponting's surprise decision to put England in, the England openers took the attack to Australia. Here Andrew Strauss drives Shane Warne. (*Nick Potts/PA*)

Ricky Ponting and Shane Warne look depressed as Andrew Strauss and Marcus Trescothick celebrate their 100 partnership. (*Getty Images, Rui Vieira/PA*)

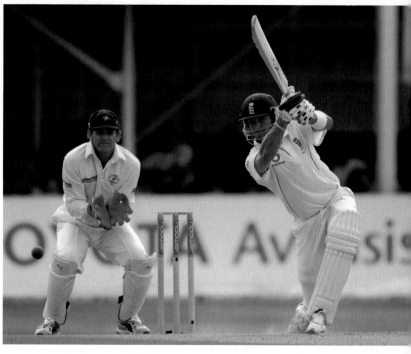

Kevin Pietersen continued his Lord's form with a third successive half-century. (*Empics*)

After England scored 407, Australia needed to get off to a good start, but Matthew Hoggard had Matthew Hayden caught first ball to put the pressure on straight away. (*Empics*)

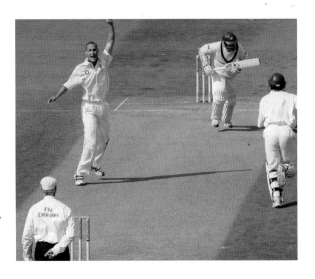

Rudi Koertzen's finger is on its slow journey up, and Justin Langer is LBW to Simon Jones for 82. (*Getty Images*)

Another wonder ball from Shane Warne bowls Andrew Strauss, as the Australians begin their fightback. (*Nick Potts/PA*)

Six! Andrew Flintoff hits Shane Warne out of the ground on his way to a superb 73. (*Nick Potts/PA*)

One of the greatest overs ever bowled: Andrew Flintoff bowls Justin Langer and then celebrates with the team after having Ricky Ponting caught behind. (*Getty Images, Rui Vieira/PA*)

ABOVE, LEFT: Michael Kasprowicz gloves the ball to Geraint Jones as Australia's valiant attempt to win the match falls two runs short. (*Getty Images*) RIGHT: At the end of the closest Ashes Test match in history, Andrew Flintoff consoles a distraught Brett Lee. (*Getty Images*)

Joy and relief all round as Steve Harmison leads the celebrations after taking the last wicket to win the Test. (*AP Photo/Matt Dunham*)

A moment of huge fortune for Michael Vaughan in the Old Trafford Test, after Glenn McGrath bowled him off a no-ball. He then went on to make a commanding 166. (*Phil Noble/PA, Jon Super/AP Photo*)

Ian Bell cuts Shane Warne for four during his gritty knock of 59. (*Getty Images*)

Shane Warne hooks Simon Jones, only to be caught by Ashley Giles when just ten runs short of his maiden Test century. (*Phil Noble/PA*)

ABOVE: Andrew Strauss recovers from being hit by a Brett Lee bouncer, before going on to score a fabulous 106. (*Empics*)

Ian Bell hits Glenn McGrath for six on the way to his second half-century of the match. (*Phil Noble/PA*)

Australia Second Innings

		R	M	B	4s	6s
J.L.Langer	b Flintoff	28	54	47	4	0
M.L.Hayden	c Trescothick b S.P.Jones	31	106	64	4	0
*R.T.Ponting	c G.O.Jones b Flintoff	0	4	5	0	0
D.R.Martyn	c Bell b Hoggard	28	64	36	5	0
M.J.Clarke	b Harmison	30	101	57	4	0
S.M.Katich	c Trescothick b Giles	16	27	21	3	0
+A.C.Gilchrist	c Flintoff b Giles	1	8	4	0	0
J.N.Gillespie	lbw b Flintoff	0	4	2	0	0
S.K.Warne	hit wicket b Flintoff	42	79	59	4	2
B.Lee	not out	43	99	75	5	0
M.S.Kasprowicz	c G.O.Jones b Harmison	20	60	31	3	0
Extras	b 13, lb 8, w 1, nb 18	40				
Total	all out, 64.3 overs, 307 mins	279				

FoW   1–47 Langer (13th ov), 2–48 Ponting (13th ov), 3–82 Hayden (23rd ov), 4–107 Martyn (27th ov), 5–134 Katich (32nd ov), 6–136 Gilchrist (34th ov), 7–137 Gillespie (35th ov), 8–175 Clarke (44th ov), 9–220 Warne (53rd ov), 10–279 Kasprowicz (65th ov)

Bowling	O	M	R	W
Harmison	17.3	3	62	2
Hoggard	5	0	26	1
Giles	15	3	68	2
Flintoff	22	3	79	4
S.P.Jones	5	1	23	1

Close of Play   Day 1 England 407
Day 2 Australia 308, England 25–1 (Trescothick 19*, Hoggard 0*)
Day 3 England 182, Australia 175–8 (Warne 20*)

CHAPTER III

THIRD TEST

OLD TRAFFORD

PREVIEW

Breathless, nerves stretched to snapping point by the incredible finish to the second Test at Edgbaston, the players had just one day to recover. Then they had to haul themselves to Manchester for the next round of what had now become the unofficial super-heavyweight championship of world cricket.

England's mood was unrecognisable from the utter deflation they had felt in the aftermath of Lord's; and their joy at achieving the last-gasp victory in Birmingham was all the more profound because they knew that defeat there would essentially have crushed their dreams of winning back the Ashes. Two down with three to play might be overturned in a few tight golf matches, but not in a Test series against Australia.

As the general public – more than seven million of whom had died more than seven million deaths while watching the climax of the second Test on Channel Four – tried to make sense of their renewed passion for the game, Sunset + Vine, the TV production company, rushed out a DVD of it entitled *The Greatest Test*. Some of the Australian players smiled to themselves and wondered aloud whether this was what happened every time England won a match when an Ashes series was still up for grabs (last time: first Test, Edgbaston, 1997).

The mood was so buoyant in Michael Vaughan's camp that they were impervious to such snidery. But they *were* knackered, both physically and emotionally. A few of them, including Strauss, Trescothick and Geraint Jones, managed to drag themselves around the Belfry for eighteen holes on the Monday, prior to driving up to Manchester. The bowlers mainly just slept. In his column in *The Times* Matthew Hoggard revealed: 'As Test cricketers we are all finely tuned professional athletes and the right preparation for us is crucial. So this week I have been at home in Yorkshire, cutting the grass, playing with the dogs and having a couple of barbecues.'

As relieved as they were that they were still in the contest, Vaughan's men were now growing more confident that they could maintain their winning momentum. Or, in Flintoff's case, super-confident, as his magnificent all-round performance at Edgbaston had confirmed him as one of the great cricketing forces of nature. To most of those pondering how he had turned things around after his below-par performance at Lord's, the name of Jamie Edwards meant nothing, but in the context of Flintoff's – and England's – resurgence, Edwards might just have meant everything. For in three sessions with the sports psychologist (who had previously worked with golfers Lee Westwood and Darren Clarke), Flintoff was transformed.

According to Edwards: 'Fred had been working on his technique and fitness, but he just wasn't himself. I asked him how he felt after the series against the West Indies and he said "ten feet tall". Then I asked him how he felt after the Lord's Test and he said "a shrinking violet". That helped me understand where he was coming from. There are four key areas for a sportsman: before play, at play, between shots and after play. One of these is usually the leverage point of the problem. In Freddie's case it was before play. There had been so much expectation on the team and he had put it all on himself. Now his confidence was low.

'Athletes tend to focus on what is not working and we needed to reaffirm what he does well. The key to Freddie is presence. We talked about how other great sportsmen dominate even before a ball has been played. Elrick Woods becomes Tiger when he goes out to play; Michael Jordan becomes Air Jordan. We needed to turn Andrew Flintoff into Freddie Flintoff. He has a warrior presence and a warrior doesn't walk into the arena with his head down.'

Edwards asked Flintoff what message he would take from a bowler who walked back to his mark with his head down. 'That I've got him,' said Flintoff. Then he asked him what message the bowler would get if Flintoff was standing in his crease with his shoulders back and his head held high. 'That I've got him,' he repeated. Edwards says: 'The message is more important for yourself than the opposition. I've never met somebody of his standing who is so humble. He is *almost* a legend, but he'll go on to be one because he has real skill at the mental game.'

All the players were starting to realise that their efforts were being watched by a significantly wider audience than usual. Steve Harmison learned that when he popped into his beloved St James's Park. 'Even I wasn't prepared for the reaction I got,' he said. 'All the lads wanted to know what it was like to play in such a nail-biting finish. Can you believe it? The Premiership was only a few days away and all the footballers wanted to talk about was cricket. In the past they've always told me what a boring sport cricket was. Now it was everywhere. There was hardly a front page without Freddie or Mick on it all week, and suddenly we were hearing that the Aussies might not be all they were cracked up to be. That they were on the way down, and on the way out. But we felt that if the Aussies were on the way down, it was because that was where we'd put them.'

Andrew Strauss remembers: 'I definitely sensed a change among our supporters. At the Belfry loads of people came up to us and said things like "That was absolutely brilliant. Keep going, you can beat these guys." We looked at each other and thought, Yes … we can. After what happened to us at Lord's it seemed the whole mood of the country had lifted. It was so important to win a match when the series was still alive. We had overcome a massive hurdle in that, even though we had made hard work of it, we had proved to ourselves that we could beat Australia.'

England had long forgotten the controversy over whether Michael Kasprowicz should have been given out from the final ball of the match. But there had been slightly more fuss over what happened to the ball itself. Geraint Jones explains: 'At the end of the match Billy Bowden came up to me and asked if he could keep the ball. He said to me: "Excellent. This is my first Ashes Test. A little memento." Because of everything that was going on and all the excitement of the moment, I just gave it to him without thinking.'

'After what happened to us at Lord's it seemed the whole mood of the country had lifted. It was so important to win a match when the series was still alive.'

ANDREW STRAUSS
ON THE EDGBASTON
VICTORY

When Jones mentioned in passing to an ECB official that he regretted handing it over, Bowden was approached and happily agreed to return it to the keeper. The Board's statement read: 'The England and Wales Cricket Board are to present the ball which dismissed Michael Kasprowicz to clinch England's victory in the second npower Ashes Test to wicket-keeper Geraint Jones. The ball used to take the final wicket will be mounted by the ECB and presented to Geraint Jones, who took the winning catch. Geraint Jones will lend the ball to the Edgbaston Museum, to be put on display for the remainder of the year. Umpire Billy Bowden asked the ECB if it would be possible to retain a ball used in the Edgbaston Test to mark his standing in his first Ashes Test.'

Of more current concern was what kind of pitch the players would find at Old Trafford. Normally Manchester is notorious for helping spin, as if Warne, who by now was on 599 Test wickets and was returning to the scene of his 'ball of the century' to Mike Gatting in 1993, needed any of that. But when England had their first look at the pitch, advance reports that the surface would be hard and abrasive seemed to be correct. Simon Jones and Andrew Flintoff, the kings of the reverse-swingers, liked what they saw.

And, at first, the news seeping out of the opposition camp did nothing to dampen England's optimism. At that stage not only was Glenn McGrath assumed to be unfit for duty, but Brett Lee was now struggling with a knee infection. However, as the England players were checking in to their hotel in Manchester, elsewhere in the city McGrath was summoned to see the Australian management in theirs. He later admitted that he went to the meeting prepared for the worst news: that his final Ashes tour was over. The great fast bowler recalled: 'We had already had one discussion earlier that day, during which our physio Errol Alcott had given me the results of the latest scans, and they sounded bad enough. He told me that I had snapped in half two ligaments under my right ankle; that they had been ripped from the bone; and that I might require an operation. He also said that our trip to London to see the specialist, Dave Connell, the next day would show whether I had suffered a stress fracture. If it did, I was cooked. With a recovery time of six to twelve weeks, I would be on the next plane home.

'So my heart was in my mouth when I went through the door to be told my fate. I didn't know what they were going to say, and, of course, the thought running through my mind was that they were going to tell me I was finished. When I sat down that evening with Errol – and the team manager Steve Bernard – there was a slight change in his mood. He did re-iterate that a stress fracture would spell the end of my series, but he then suggested that if the scans showed no fracture I could have an outside chance of playing again. Not in the fourth Test at Trent Bridge, which had been my optimistic target, but in three days' time, at Old Trafford! Errol wanted to know, if that was the case, just how far I was prepared to go to play and I told him all the way. So the next morning, when we went to London and Dave Connell gave the positive news that there was no stress fracture after all, it was all systems go in an effort to be fit.

'Even when I turned up at the ground unexpectedly to attempt to jog and roll my arm over again, some people present thought I must be trying it on. They were so convinced that I had no real chance of playing – as I myself had been a few days earlier – that this had to be some kind of psychological trick to put thoughts in the minds of the England team. But this was no sleight of hand, no smoke and mirrors. As I told some of my mates, the aggressive treatment Errol had put me through and some taping of the foot so that the ankle was properly supported had helped me prove that there are a couple of ligaments in the ankle that are surplus to requirements.'

Brett Lee's problem came out of the blue, just as McGrath's had earlier. On the day after the conclusion of the second Test he had been admitted into a Birmingham hospital. The rest of the team left for Manchester without him while he was being given antibiotics intravenously and undergoing tests.

In the event, both men made the starting eleven. McGrath's recovery, bearing in mind he had been hobbling around on crutches less than a week earlier, had been especially miraculous. But the England players contented themselves with the fact that the Australians were prepared to risk him even though he clearly wasn't 100 per cent fit. That seemed to suggest a certain amount of desperation.

Whoever they were playing against, however, England knew they were about to face a backlash. How they combated it might well determine the outcome of the series, so they were determined to be as prepared as they could be. Strauss recalls: 'In South Africa last winter we made the mistake of starting the Cape Town Test slowly after an exceptionally draining Boxing Day Test in Durban. Against the Aussies we couldn't afford to make the same mistake.'

With memories of what they had been through in Birmingham so fresh, it was hardly surprising that Ashley Giles kept waking up in the middle of the night thinking about the heart-stopping climax of that Test. Then he started having a recurring dream about it. 'The problem was that the dream always ended with Australia winning the bloody match!' he remembers.

Vaughan had less spooky matters to address. His scores in the series thus far had been 3, 4, 24 and 1, a far cry from his amazing performances on the previous tour Down Under. Whatever he felt inside, though, on the outside he was ice cool as usual, and his sang-froid gave his players renewed confidence. On the eve of the match he told them: 'You should be proud of the way you have fought to get us back into this series. Now we all have to show how strong we are.'

Only Hoggard, Duncan Fletcher and a few lads from Yorkshire's second eleven knew just how hard the skipper had been working at his game.

DAY ONE: ENGLAND 341 FOR 5

Vaughan was keen to keep the momentum going, and winning the toss was an important first step. He had no hesitation in deciding to bat, McGrath or no McGrath. The England captain, whose day had started with an honorary doctorate from Sheffield Hallam University, had walked to the wicket for the toss with Connor Shaw, who two years earlier had had three heart operations, including a transplant, and been given the last rites. Two days before his sixth birthday he was handed the coin as a souvenir.

McGrath might have made it, but Australia soon had to bring on a substitute fielder. Michael Clarke wrenched his back and was forced off the field for treatment. The injury would affect his performance for all five days of this Test. However, Lee showed no signs of his recent knee trouble when he uprooted Strauss's off stump with a slow yorker to collect his 150th Test wicket. The opener had already received treatment after being hit on the face by a bouncer from the same bowler. McGrath's morning would have been a lot better if Adam Gilchrist had held on to a chance when Trescothick flashed outside the off stump.

The scoring rate was not quite as violent as at Edgbasaton, but the Old Trafford outfield was larger and slower, and it was impressive enough. Furthermore, those who had forecast that Vaughan's run drought must soon come to an end took heart from the fact that, by lunch, he was outscoring his partner and friend. The skipper recalls: 'There was a lot of talk that I should have gone and played for Yorkshire between the first and second Tests, playing a four-day game earlier in the season to get in nick, but I have a huge amount of self-belief that I know what is right for me.' His solution had been to take himself off to Headingley between the first two Tests for some intensive technical work with Duncan Fletcher in the Yorkshire nets. His county team-mate Hoggard, who was recruited to help, remembers: 'At that stage there was so much going through his mind: his own form, the fact that we had been hammered in the first Test, and the way we had batted. He didn't want to show it to the rest of the team but naturally he was concerned. There were four of us bowling at him, me and three lads from the Yorkshire seconds, and he looked just awful. Fletch sat him down and said: "Look, Michael, it seems to me that you're trying to do too many things before the ball arrives. Just watch the ball and hit it." To me, he had been taking three steps here and then one back there and was still thinking of what he was supposed to be doing when suddenly the ball was on its way.

'So he said, "Right, I'm just going to react to the ball." The other lads had gone and he could get used to one person bowling. He asked me to bowl half-volleys for ten minutes, then short balls for ten minutes, and it helped him get into some sort of rhythm.'

Vaughan himself recalls: 'I wasn't playing that well after the first game so I went with Hoggard and Fletch and we just worked it out. To be honest, I was disappointed I didn't get a lot more runs at Edgbaston. I thought I was in fantastic nick there but I didn't go on. Then a lot of people said to me before the game in Manchester that they felt the hundred was coming up. It was a nice feeling because I'd been under a lot of pressure and a lot of people had written and spoken what I believed was rubbish. I knew everything mentally was OK, and if I kept going a score would be round the corner. But the great thing for me was that I was able to do it on the first day, which helped us to show everyone that Edgbaston wasn't a fluke.'

Vaughan was still there at tea, just 7 runs short of his century, playing his most accomplished innings of the summer. Few batsmen rediscover their touch as immediately and dramatically as the England captain: from looking like he can't buy a run, Vaughan turns up a few days later and looks a million dollars. Even more remarkable is the pace at which he accumulates runs. There's none of the brutal, powerful hitting of Trescothick, Pietersen or Flintoff, or even Strauss square of the wicket, just exquisite timing and shot selection. Not that it was a perfect innings. On 41, he was relieved to see Gilchrist put down a regulation chance off McGrath that was heading to Warne at first slip. The roar that greeted the keeper's lapse was nothing compared to the noise when McGrath uprooted off stump the very next ball, only to be called for a no-ball by umpire Steve Bucknor. The score was 110 for 1 at the time.

Warne had not bowled in the morning session and had to wait over an hour in the afternoon before collecting the wicket that made him the first bowler to reach 600 in Tests. Trescothick, fresh from being McGrath's 500th scalp at Lord's, completed a unique double when he was caught off the back of his bat, sweeping. Warne celebrated in style. Then, in one of the most moving incidents of the entire series, the blond leg-spinner kissed the wristband given to him by his daughter when he and his wife Simone decided to separate just before the start of the Ashes contest. The band carried a single word: 'Strength'. Warne explained afterwards, 'When my daughter gave me this she told me: "You're going to have to be strong now, Daddy."' The brilliant reflex catch by Gilchrist gave him his 299th Test victim. The 23,000 crowd gave Warne a standing ovation, and another when he led the Australians off at tea.

England's second-wicket stand of 137 between Vaughan and Trescothick had been a new record for Old Trafford, 3 more than Arthur Fagg and Wally Hammond had managed against India in 1936. Vaughan was even more imperious after tea, soon reaching his fourth century in eight Ashes Tests, and his fifteenth overall, with 3 runs through midwicket off McGrath. With just a dozen fifties, Vaughan's conversion rate in Test cricket is currently bettered only by Don Bradman and George Headley.

Jason Gillespie was the Australian bowler most under pressure coming into this game, and there was no respite on the opening day: his 15 overs cost 89 runs. Hard as he tried, he was unrecognisable from the fast bowler who had been a crucial part of Australia's attack during their record-breaking run. Every time it was announced he was coming on to bowl, an ironic cheer rose from the stands. Vaughan picked him off through the on side at will and hoisted a huge six over square-leg. In that spell, four Gillespie overs went for 42 runs, including seven fours and that six. Vaughan, especially after Hayden had dropped him at slip off Warne, looked destined for the double hundred that had evaded him through his golden period in the second half of 2002. He progressed from 100 to 150 in just 39 balls.

Ashley Giles says that the experience of watching Vaughan bat in such a mood is the kind of thing that turns Test cricketers into fans again. 'Fantastic,' says England's spinner. 'You always felt, though, that he was going to do it, that the moment would come when he would get a very big hundred. Because he does, when he gets in. When you speak to him about how he bats he says, "If I get a fifty, unless I get myself out, I'll get a hundred." And that's against the best players in the world. It was a typical Vaughan knock: work to fifty, play some great shots, but then fifty to a hundred just completely professional, never in doubt. Then, when he got to a hundred, he really started to express himself. And the quality of batting was unbelievable. There are moments when you think you're not worthy of playing with these guys, the likes of Vaughan and Fred. But when it's you doing something – you know, when you bowl a magic ball at somebody – you think that's a bit of luck. Yeah, I do find myself being a closet cricket fan at times.'

But suddenly, and unexpectedly, it was all over when a Katich full toss was struck straight to McGrath at long-on. The England captain could not believe what he'd done. After his recent run, a score of 166 was welcome enough, but there's little doubt he felt he had thrown away a golden opportunity

'It was a typical Vaughan knock: work to fifty, play some great shots, but then fifty to a hundred just completely professional, never in doubt. Then, when he got to a hundred, he really started to express himself. And the quality of batting was unbelievable.'

ASHLEY GILES ON HIS CAPTAIN'S 166 IN THE OLD TRAFFORD TEST

unnecessarily. By the close, there were murmurs that England had done the same.

Bell had been quietly going about his business, at one stage remaining on 18 for 37 balls, but Pietersen reacted boldly against the new ball when it might have been better to curb his aggressive tendencies until the next morning. He was caught on the midwicket boundary. Then nightwatchman Hoggard was bowled by Lee off the final ball of the day.

England's promising 333 for 3 had become a merely pretty good 341 for 5, giving Australia hope for the next day.

Vaughan admitted that walking out with the mascot had brought him down to earth: 'I saw this brave lad and thought, What have I got to worry about? This was probably better than my three hundreds in Australia because it is one-all in the series and it really counts.'

DAY TWO: ENGLAND 444 ALL OUT;
AUSTRALIA 214 FOR 7

In spite of the mini-collapse in the evening, England were still well on course to make the 400-plus that they felt would bat Australia out of the game. And their satisfaction was laced with relief that their captain had come good just when he, and they, needed him to. Steve Harmison says: 'Vaughan is a great leader and a great captain. He never once let his batting problems get in the way of how he was with the team. When he finally got those runs the pleasure among the players was huge. You could see how much it meant to us, and how much we were behind him.'

However, Australia made an immediate impact when Bell was given out caught behind after trying to pull a Lee bouncer. The shot might have been considered rash so early on, but positive intent remained the order of the day, and replays suggested the ball had not actually touched the England number four's bat. Bell, whose unhappy game at Lord's had led to some calls for Graham Thorpe to be reinstated, received warm applause for a job well done, and felt a weight lift from his shoulders. 'I could easily see an England team in the past where I wouldn't have got to Old Trafford,' he confesses. 'But luckily the set-up has changed a bit now in terms of sticking with people and giving them a fair crack, and I paid back a bit here. I guess I wasn't a hundred per cent sure what people were expecting from me. Whether they expected me, as a twenty-three-year-old in my first Ashes series, in my first proper Test series, to go out and average 50; and whether it was fair on me to expect that I was going to do that. I wasn't sure, but my goals were to go out and learn, *really* learn, from the fantastic players around me. If I could get some runs it was a bonus. This year I wanted to go out and dig in, get some runs when I could, but not push too hard to succeed and therefore put myself under too much pressure if that didn't happen straight away. Just go out and enjoy it, the experience.

'I'd always hoped that I'd have a bit of time to get my feet on the floor at this level. So I found it a bit harsh when, after one match, people were saying, "Chuck him out!" But the selectors were very supportive. David Graveney rang me to say, "Go out and enjoy it. We believe you can do it. We're backing you. Everyone's backing you." And the way the team have been was just spot on.

'I didn't, to be honest, read

> '*Whether they expected me, as a twenty-three-year-old in my first Ashes series, in my first proper Test series, to go out and average 50; and whether it was fair on me to expect that I was going to do that. I wasn't sure, but my goals were to go out and learn*, really *learn, from the fantastic players around me. If I could get some runs it was a bonus.*'
>
> IAN BELL

the papers much, especially after that Lord's Test when I guess there was a lot of bad press towards me. You can understand it. There had been a big build-up and we got hammered and I didn't score any runs. When I then failed in the first innings at Edgbaston, I'd scored 6, 8 and 6, and all of a sudden I was thinking that's nearly half a series gone and I've got no runs. But I managed to make 20-odd in the second innings there and that was a nice little turning point.

'Then, scoring the fifty in the first innings in Manchester was a huge hurdle for me to overcome. They threw everything at me: McGrath was back and Warne was doing his best to get into my head again. I tried to cope by breaking the innings down and literally taking it ball by ball. So when Warne was bowling I was just focusing on the ball that's going to come down, not the one after that or the ball that's just gone, or who's on at the other end.

'It's a ground special to my heart. I love playing here. I know everyone from the gateman to the dressing-room attendant. I have the same peg in the dressing room for the Test. My corner of the dressing room is usually a disgrace, mind, particularly my locker. But it feels like home.'

ANDREW FLINTOFF
ON OLD TRAFFORD

'A couple of moments stand out. The first was a back-foot shot for four off Brett Lee, when I'd got 30-odd. After battling so hard, that was when I started just to get myself going a bit. I felt a bit more fluid. And then Warne, who had bowled really well at me, dropped one short and I hit a punch shot off the back foot, just wide of mid-on, for four. That took a bit of pressure off as well.'

The setback of Bell's early dismissal on the second day was quickly forgotten as Flintoff and Geraint Jones put England in an even more commanding position. Flintoff had been given a tremendous homecoming after his heroics at Edgbaston, compounded by the fact that he was celebrating his fiftieth Test, but only his third at Old Trafford. There seemed to be at least fifty cut-outs of 'Super Fred' adorning the hospitality boxes at the Warwick Road End. Lancashire's main sponsor, Paul Beck of LBM, had hired a trumpeter for the occasion, who took the crowd through the themes of *The Flintstones* and *Superman*, among others. The all-rounder says: 'It's a ground special to my heart. I love playing here. I know everyone from the gateman to the dressing-room attendant. I have the same peg in the dressing room for the Test. My corner of the dressing room is usually a disgrace, mind, particularly my locker. But it feels like home.'

Flintoff and Jones found the boundary regularly, and even a rain break did not disrupt the flow for long. At 433 for 6, the home side were threatening a huge score, but another loss of concentration towards the end of a session again cost England wickets. Warne made the breakthrough with the seventh-wicket partnership at 87 when Flintoff hit him hard but not quite far enough; Langer took a good catch at long-on. Six balls later, England went in to lunch 434 for 8 after Geraint Jones was bowled off the inside edge by Gillespie. The bowler's first success of the game came one over after he had conceded a century of runs.

England survived for just three more overs after the resumption. Both wickets went to Warne, who finished with figures of 4 for 90. Giles edged the ball straight to Hayden in the slips, while Simon Jones was bowled through the gate. McGrath had failed to take a wicket.

Vaughan had been hoping for a 500-plus total during the morning session, but he remained satisfied that England had retained the initiative they had grabbed, juggled, then just clung on to at Edgbaston. By the close of play, there was no more debate as to who held the initiative in this Ashes series. Two gigantic performances from Ashley Giles, with wily left-arm spin, and more spectacularly from Simon Jones, with almost unplayable reverse-swing, ensured that it was England.

Australia opened up confidently enough, with Langer and Hayden putting on 58 for the first wicket before Bell brilliantly held a sharp chance from Langer at short-leg off Giles. It was England's sole success before tea, but England's spinner had opened a crack in the wall. By stumps, he and his team-mates had stormed right through it. England, roared on by a passionate Mancunian crowd, were on fire again.

During the tea interval, TV viewers' attention was focused on Warne's 'ball of the century', his first delivery in Ashes cricket that had drifted into Mike Gatting, then spun past him to hit off stump. Gatting faced up to England's bowling machine, Merlin, programmed to replicate the exact delivery. This time, knowing what to expect, he managed to avoid the same fate, although it was mentioned that the ball would have to spin a lot further to get past Gatt these days.

Few of those watching could have foreseen that Giles was about to produce a wonderball of his own. But first Ponting fell to Jones, giving Bell his second catch of the day. Then Giles trapped Matthew Hayden in front: 86 for 3. Simon Katich, bewitched and utterly bewildered by Flintoff's pace and swing from round the wicket, shouldered arms and was

> *'I've not taken 600 wickets in Test cricket; I've not taken 600 first-class wickets. To be set against Warne is tough because he is the best who has played the game, but if you look at the team sheet, he's their spinner and I'm ours, so to an extent it is him against me. The trick is not to try too hard.'*
>
> ASHLEY GILES ON DEALING WITH COMPARISONS TO SHANE WARNE

bowled before he knew which way the ball was curving. Then came the oft-ridiculed left-arm spinner's moment of glory when he bowled what some instantly dubbed 'the ball of the twenty-first century'. Damien Martyn played inside the line of a ball pitching just outside leg stump, and it slid past him and flicked the top of off stump.

'That was a moment and a ball I will never forget,' says Giles. 'Warne had just taken his 600th Test wicket in the first innings, so I suppose people were looking at me to see how I might respond. I try not to compare myself with anyone, especially not Warne, who is a genius. I've not taken 600 wickets in Test cricket; I've not taken 600 *first-class* wickets. To be set against Warne is tough because he is the best who has played the game, but if you look at the team sheet, he's their spinner and I'm ours, so to an extent it is him against me. The trick is not to try too hard.

'Then this ball happened. To be perfectly honest, I'd bowled exactly the same ball before and it missed the off stump by inches. You try to get these things right and you practise them time and again. Some people might not believe me, but I'm always trying to spin the ball, always trying to get the ball past the bat, and if everything works at the same time, you're in business. It was like the ball with which I bowled Brian Lara the previous year. People ask me, "How did you do it?" and I say, "I needed him to come down the wicket; I needed him to play a shot; I needed the ball to spin. And that was that: I knocked out middle stump."'

Michael Clarke, still nursing his injured back, had not been expecting to bat that evening. But when Giles struck and Australia were 133 for 5, he received the call to get down to the ground from the hotel room where he was trying to keep as still as possible.

It might have been curtains for Australia that night, but Gilchrist was dropped twice in the space of four deliveries off Flintoff, who was touching 93 m.p.h. with nearly every ball. Both chances were difficult, but far from impossible. A diving

Bell was only able to parry the ball at point when the Australian danger man was on 13. Then Pietersen made it four dropped Ashes chances in a row when he could not hold on to a low drive to his left at cover.

Cue Simon Jones, ready and willing to confirm his growing reputation.

Gilchrist was the first to fall to the Glamorgan man's mastery of 'Irish' bowling, caught behind for 30. Then Clarke, clearly in pain, did not last long with Hayden as his runner, holing out to mid-off. The score was now 201 for 7.

The tourists finally trudged off after adding another 13 runs, still 34 short of saving the follow-on – something they had not been asked to do since 1988. Overnight England knew their main obstacle now was Warne, unbeaten and already top scorer on 45.

Australia had expected anything but three wickets each for Giles and Simon Jones. 'It was bloody terrible. Everyone talks about Harmison and Flintoff, but then these two rabbits come in and do that,' said coach John Buchanan.

And Jones the rabbit was not finished yet, although he was about to be rudely interrupted.

DAY THREE: AUSTRALIA 264 FOR 7

Poor weather was forecast, and it duly enveloped Old Trafford to create a day of English frustration. At one stage it looked likely that no play at all would be possible. Desperate to finish off Australia and give themselves the option of asking the world champions to bat again, England were forced to sit and wait, and wait, and wait, until finally, after heroic efforts from groundsman Peter Marron and his team, the players emerged at 4 p.m., with a possible 38 overs left in the day.

Somewhat bizarrely, the deficit had been reduced by 4 runs even before the start of play. Steve Bucknor had neglected to signal 'four' the previous evening when Simon Jones had bowled a full toss that bounced in front of Geraint Jones on its way to the boundary. Bucknor had signalled 'no-ball', had a word with the bowler, and forgot about the four.

During what little play there was, Warne didn't need any more help from the officials as he crashed and carved his side past the follow-on target. Infuriatingly, though, England gave the buccaneering leg-spinner two lives. And at the close of play one man in particular had cause to wish the rain had washed out the whole day's proceedings. Exactly a week earlier Geraint Jones had safely pouched the catch to dismiss Michael Kasprowicz for one of the most dramatic victories in the history of Test cricket. In that instant the delirious Kent wicket-keeper, so staunchly supported by coach Duncan Fletcher against a rising tide of criticism of his inconsistent glove-work, had punched the air and roared his defiance to those Australian supporters who had spent much of the series taunting him. Now he was reminded that there is no hiding-place for the man with the gloves. First, with Australia still 14 short of the follow-on target of 245, Warne was lured down the track by Giles, and the instant the ball passed the bat the left-arm spinner was convinced he had his man. But Jones couldn't gather the ball cleanly for what would have been a regulation stumping.

> 'It was the lowest point of my England career; probably the worst I've ever felt ... in the dressing room I just sat in my chair – stunned. The lads were great and tried to say things to cheer me up, but I couldn't hear a word.'
> GERAINT JONES ON FAILING TO STUMP AND CATCH WARNE

Later, Warne, now on 68, edged one from Flintoff. This time England's keeper failed to pick up the line of the ball and, with all Old Trafford waiting to let loose a roar of celebration, he let the chance literally slip through his hands.

Unsurprisingly, the snide remarks began again. One commentator suggested that not only would the great Lancashire keeper George Duckworth have held on to the second chance, but so would Vera. The joke doing the rounds that night was: 'What do Michael Jackson and Geraint Jones have in common? Both wear gloves for no apparent reason.'

But Fletcher continued to support his man afterwards, saying: 'If you go for the option of a batting keeper, then mistakes are going to be made. I'm sure Geraint has the character to handle it.'

Jones himself admits the whole experience left him in pieces: 'It was the lowest point of my England career; probably the worst I've ever felt. If I am down, I try not to show it too much to the other boys, but in the dressing room I just sat in my chair – stunned. The lads were great and tried to say things to cheer me up, but I couldn't hear a word. And I could barely speak. I was just thinking: This is going to explode now. This could be it for me. I could be history.

'I knew the stumping was coming because of the way Warne had shown such intent all the time, but it all happened so quickly. I saw the ball reasonably well, but it came through quickly and bounced. My gloves were getting there, but just not quick enough. And with the extra bounce, sometimes those balls can go into the webbing and stay there, but this one had the pace to go through. But the catch, for me, was the real kick in the teeth because it was straightforward. I don't think I still had the stumping on my mind. What I did have on my mind was that I was struggling to pick up the pace of the ball because the atmosphere was a bit hazy. I don't want to make any excuses because I think I should catch and take everything, but I remember at the end of the over really straining to work out how quick the ball was coming out of Fred's hand. I've watched the replay and in a way it looks like I'm not watching the ball. I look in good position to take the ball, but I really remember searching for it and thinking,

Where is it? How quick is it coming? Catches like that, you know, you just can't afford not to catch them. If you can't catch them, it's "Where do we go from here?" time.

'Fred was fantastic. At the end of the over I said sorry to him and he was good as gold. He said, "Don't worry about it." But in the dressing room I was gone. I knew it was time for the pencils to be sharpened again. So I was sitting there in the chair and I thought, There are two ways I can go here. I can either go up to my room and just churn through what happened over and over again and make myself feel even worse, if that's possible. Or I can attack the feeling.

'There was talk of some of the lads going to the greyhound races at Bellevue in Manchester, to watch Freddie's dog, Ouseam. I was asked to go and I was umming and aahing, but then I thought, Oh sod it. What's happened has happened, and it's not going to unhappen just because I feel so bad about it. And tomorrow's a new day. I've got to go and do something. There were going to be punters out there, people who may well have watched the cricket, and I felt it might give me a chance to face the music before the papers mashed me the next day.

'The turning point for me came when Fred's dog won. Everyone had lumped on it. But one person decided it was too good a thing to be true and he backed another dog. Me. That's when I realised things couldn't get any worse. I decided there and then that if I was going to be judged as not up to the job at some point in the future, I was going to play until that moment on my own terms, play my way and let others decide whether that was good enough.'

DAY FOUR: AUSTRALIA 302 ALL OUT; ENGLAND 280 FOR 6 DECLARED; AUSTRALIA 24 FOR 0

By the time the players reassembled at Old Trafford for the fourth day, both Jones boys were in a positive mood. Simon was fired up to take out his frustration at the previous day's lack of action, while Geraint was ready to respond to the barrage of criticism that he knew would hit him full on. He had successfully managed to avoid reading the papers, but could not shut himself off entirely. However, when he heard Bob Willis give a radio interview in which he called for Jones to be dropped, the former England captain's words merely strengthened his resolve.

In the event, the keeper had little time to dwell on what had gone before as Simon Jones bagged the last three Australian wickets in short order to leave the tourists with a first-innings deficit of 142. Jones's figures of 6 for 53 were his best in Tests and the best Ashes bowling figures at Old Trafford since Jim Laker's 10 for 53 in 1956. More important to him was that they were also the best by a Welshman, surpassing both Robert Croft's 5 for 95, and, more poignantly, his father Jeff's 6 for 118 against Australia.

'My dad has been through everything with me,' says Jones. 'He's my best mate as well as my father and he was absolutely chuffed for me. It brought back strong memories to all of us of the lowest point of my career, on the outfield in Brisbane on the last tour. When I did my knee it took him right back to all those years ago when he was forced to finish his career at twenty-five through injury. When he saw me go down that day on television he was so upset. He told me he thought the family must be jinxed. There I was thinking I might never be able to play again and he was back home thinking the same thing. It must have been so hard to bear.

'Throughout my comeback he was so supportive. On the days when I was fed up and felt I was never going to get anywhere near playing again he kept faith and kept me going. So finally to go past all his records was a special moment for me because we both knew it might never have happened.

'As for the reverse swing – I always like to get the old ball in my hand. Moving it the other way is something I just do naturally. I'm used to doing it at Sofia Gardens with

Glamorgan, where the ball gets scuffed up, and here at Old Trafford the surface was so abrasive that the ball started to reverse after about twenty overs. I felt I was in great rhythm on the second evening and I would have loved to have carried on bowling all night. But when we pitched up that Sunday morning it felt just the same. It was important that we got Warne out because he was playing sensationally well, like he was on a personal mission. And finishing them off quickly meant that we still might have enough time to turn our superiority into the win we all wanted so badly.'

On the dressing-room balcony Duncan Fletcher was revelling in what he was seeing. 'We always knew Simon could bowl but what surprised me was how quickly he has come through to the point where he is now so dangerous. It wasn't that he wouldn't put in some great performances for England, but we thought there would be some bad ones along the way as he took time to find consistency. But he proved me wrong by the way he bowled not from time to time but every time he grabbed the ball this summer.

'He's always had great ability and it must have been so frustrating for him to have suffered so many injuries. After that terrible injury in Australia few thought he would get back to anything like full pace; certainly no higher than 80-odd m.p.h. But he bounced back and we now have three bowlers who can bowl 90 m.p.h.-plus consistently.'

According to Vaughan: 'That was an incredible spell of bowling. As a captain, you have to judge the situation and try to gauge when the ball is going the other way. Once you know it's reverse swing, you have to click into gear and get your fields right and get your lines right and get your bowling right. It's easy saying it, but having the bowlers who can do it is another thing entirely, and that's what we've got at the moment. We've got bowlers who can create opportunities in the field because they can reverse the ball, they can swing it traditionally and put the ball in the right areas. When the ball starts reversing it is almost like having another player turn up.'

Warne looked devastated to have fallen for 90, just 9 short of his highest Test score and 10 shy of what would have been a truly extraordinary century. Australia had hoped to bat at least until lunch to reduce the time they would have to endure in the fourth innings, but Trescothick and Strauss (the latter's right ear bandaged after another clout from Lee) had extended the lead to 169 by the end of the first session. Then England added 102 runs off 27 overs between lunch and tea. It was steady rather than spectacular progress: a launch pad for a full-on assault in the final session. Trescothick provided the early momentum before being bowled by McGrath, his 45 runs taking him past 5,000 in his 65th Test. Only four of England's batsmen have reached the milestone quicker, and it's hard to think of a better list: Hobbs, Hammond, Hutton and Barrington. On this occasion Trescothick was somewhat unlucky to see his defensive shot bounce back and dislodge a bail. Vaughan was the other wicket to fall, leaving Strauss and Bell with a golden opportunity to stamp their mark on this amazing Ashes series.

'We always knew Simon could bowl but what surprised me was how quickly he has come through to the point where he is now so dangerous.'
DUNCAN FLETCHER
ON SIMON JONES

Strauss took charge, despite blood still oozing from his ear. The Middlesex left-hander had taken a lot of stick from Warne, who had bamboozled him twice at Edgbaston, but this time he dealt with the leg-spinner and the rest of the Aussie bowlers confidently. He went on to make his sixth Test century, his first of the summer and his first on any English ground aside from Lord's. The fans were brought to their feet with a stunning pull off McGrath to bring up the hundred.

'A lot of things were said, but it goes with the territory in an Ashes series,' insists Strauss. 'It's tough, which is why when you do well you can be proud. I'd now learned my lesson not to try to hook Lee too early in my innings. He hit me twice in this match, though this was less painful than the one that got me in the first innings. The Aussies were telling me that the patch over my left ear didn't do too much for my street cred and they were right.'

Some of the crowd were worried that Strauss and Bell were going too slowly immediately after tea, but before long they accelerated impressively to silence the doubters. According to Strauss: 'Batting from the platform of a first-innings lead to set up a declaration is generally a good position to be in, but it's also a position where you can lose wickets stupidly by almost not caring enough about getting out. Tres and I realised it was important to get off to a decent start again.

> '... as has been the case all summer, Tres was just smoking. He was spanking them after lunch and that took a lot of pressure off me.'
>
> ANDREW STRAUSS ON HIS OPENING PARTNER

That Edgbaston game was still in the back of our minds: we'd sort of let it slip from the position of a first-innings lead and so nearly paid the price.

'We were expecting it to turn quite a lot so there was still a lot of pressure going out there to bat. I think we felt we had to get through to lunch first of all, then push on after lunch. But it was pretty tough. Old Trafford's a skiddy, quick wicket and Brett Lee was bowling pretty quick. Certainly I had a bit of luck nicking one through the slips, but then, as has been the case all summer, Tres was just smoking. He was spanking them after lunch and that took a lot of pressure off me because we got to 60 or 70 very quickly. And by the time I got to 30 I felt pretty comfortable.

'Then Ian Bell came in and did really well. The coach has got to take some credit for making sure Belly didn't feel the pressure of not having scored many runs. A lot of what's said when someone's out of form and struggling only adds to the problem because it makes them feel as though they're out of form and struggling because you're talking to them about it. It's a vicious circle.

'One thing I've always tried to do with Belly is try to be as relaxed as possible out there in the middle. Just say, "Come on, let's enjoy this and have a good time." But I've never had the impression from Belly that he's been overawed and nervous; he's quite a chirpy and very confident bloke. I haven't seen him showing any sign that he was struggling despite the fact that he hadn't got many runs before that Test. But it was massive for him to get that fifty in the first innings, and he grafted really hard for it. I think that impressed everyone. The second innings was a bit easier. By the time he got to 20-odd the pressure was really off us. We had enough on the board: if everyone chipped in a bit we were going to get up to around a 400 lead. But he still played beautifully and showed that he's

---

'It was just in the slot and I watched it sail over square-leg for six. At that point I was thinking, I'm happy with that. Go on, Vaughany, declare.

'He took a bit of time. Then, just as McGrath reached the end of his mark to turn and bowl again, and before the cheers had died down, he called us in. Perfect timing, Skipper. I walked off the field feeling as tall as a house, and that feeling stayed with me for the rest of the game. He knows what he's doing, that Vaughan.'

GERAINT JONES HITS MCGRATH FOR 6 — THE LAST
BALL OF THE INNINGS

---

got an array of shots – like hitting McGrath back over his head for six. With every ball he said he gained a little more confidence.

'Belly and I pushed on quite hard after tea. At teatime I think the instructions were: "Right. Let's bat for an hour and then we can go at it for an hour. We need to have wickets in hand." But I was in the 70s and 80s and was feeling pretty confident, and Belly was playing shots, so we were scoring sixes in that first hour anyway. Then Geraint Jones came in and got 27 from 12 balls, and suddenly we were where we wanted to be.

'As for declaring earlier, I think you've got to back yourselves to bowl a side out in a day and a bit. I don't think we could have pushed much harder to give ourselves more time. And at one stage they looked like they might have a chance of chasing down that total anyway.'

Geraint Jones had been as good as his word to himself: don't leave anything in the locker. 'Vaughan said to me, "Go out and hustle them and run them ragged," and I was utterly determined to stand tall, be aggressive and be myself. I hit the first ball down to Matthew Hayden and pushed for two from the off when it would have been easier to settle for one. So I took a risk from ball one and that got me started. From then on I felt so comfortable at the crease. And when I got the chance to go for it I hit Glenn McGrath for six, four, six in one over. I had scored a few twos off him and he went round the wicket to try to cramp me for space. The first ball was just on or outside the line of leg stump, I shimmied down and clipped it over midwicket. At first I wasn't sure if I'd got enough bat on it but it just kept going and going. I was into McGrath's head now and I thought the next ball was going to be short because when I had done something like that to him in previous matches that was how he had reacted. It was. I threw the lot at it and just managed to hoist it over the slips for four. Now I was sure he would bowl me a fuller-length ball to try to york me, so I walked across my stumps to lever it to leg. It was just in the slot and I watched it sail over square-leg for six. At that point I was thinking, I'm happy with that. Go on, Vaughany, declare.

'He took a bit of time. Then, just as McGrath reached the end of his mark to turn and bowl again, and before the cheers had died down, he called us in. Perfect timing, Skipper. I walked off the field feeling as tall as a house, and that feeling stayed with me for the rest of the game. He knows what he's doing, that Vaughan.'

McGrath had taken advantage of England's crash-bang approach to collect another five-wicket haul, but he was in no mood to celebrate. Vaughan's declaration left Australia 423 to win. The target was reduced to 399 by the close without the loss of a wicket, although Vaughan's occasional spin caused one or two awkward moments. As only three teams (Australia in 1948, India in 1976 and the West Indies in 2003) had ever scored 400 runs to win a Test, few gave the tourists a chance. The real question was: could England take ten wickets or would Australia be able to hold out and avoid back-to-back Test defeats?

After Edgbaston, the country was following this battle closely, and Lancashire's offer of £10 tickets at the gate (£5 for kids) ensured there would be no lack of atmosphere on the final day.

DAY FIVE: AUSTRALIA 371 FOR 9; DRAW

Just how much the country was caught up in this Ashes drama was revealed on that final morning. *Early* on that final morning.

Despite the bargain-basement ticket prices, nobody could have anticipated the scenes that awaited those arriving at Old Trafford. The gates were closed at 8.30 a.m. because the ground was already full. The authorities had expected about 15,000 to turn up, but the fans had started queuing at 3 a.m.

For every one of the 23,500 inside, there was another disappointed cricket lover locked out or advised in advance against making the journey from the city centre to the ground.

The last time there had been anything remotely comparable at an English cricket ground had been at The Oval in 2000 when a mere 5,000 could not get in on the final day. Attendances at Old Trafford had broken the 100,000 barrier for the first time in a Test match. ECB plans to set up a giant TV screen in Manchester's Albert Square were vetoed by the police on safety grounds: they were worried that too many people would want to watch it. The England players took over an hour to complete what was normally a ten-minute journey from their hotel at Worsley. Some thought there had been a bomb scare and the ground had been evacuated because so many fans were milling around outside.

Steve Harmison was forced to ignore the rules of the road to ensure he got there on time: 'I was stuck in traffic and so late getting to the ground that I ended up driving down the wrong side of the road for about a hundred yards; otherwise I might have missed the start. This bloke on the gate came towards me waving his arms, saying: "You can't do that, you can't do that." Then, when I wound down the window and he saw who I was, he said: "Oh, you'd better come in, then."'

Other members of the squad were using their mobiles to warn each other of the jams around the ground, but there was no escape from the crowds, even inside. Vaughan's players had never done their warm-up in front of a packed ground before. If there were any lingering doubts about the importance of this day, the roars that greeted hamstring stretches and back twists blew them away.

Once play started, and Matthew Hoggard produced the perfect delivery with his first ball of the day, the roof came off. Justin Langer was the Australian batsman most likely to bat his side to safety, so when he edged to keeper Jones, England's joy was unconfined. One down; nine to go.

Harmison recalls: 'Our emotions were being pulled this way and that. I'm not sure I drew a breath all day. When Hoggard got Langer out first ball I convinced myself that we were going to run through them; that it would all be over by lunch!'

In this series? No chance!

Hayden and Ponting dug in and dug deep. The edges from Hayden's bat were flying everywhere but to the fielders. Try as they might, England's bowlers couldn't seem to extract anything from the Old Trafford wicket. So, in that no-nonsense way of his, Flintoff simply took all other factors out of the equation, hurled the ball as fast as he could at the burly left-hander and comprehensively bowled him around his legs: 96 for 2. Eight to go.

At lunch the Test was still in the balance. Australia were happy to be only two down after Langer's early exit; England were content to have removed both openers, and would have taken that at the start of play.

In the afternoon, every time England got a wicket and a home win became favourite again, the Aussies dug in. Then, every time the Aussies got a partnership going and a draw looked more likely, another wicket would fall. Throughout all this tension and these swings of fortune, Ponting was a rock. The phrase 'captain's innings' is wheeled out every time one makes a fifty in a tight situation, but this was the real deal. Ponting had been vilified back home for the Edgbaston loss after putting England in to bat; and rumours emerged at Old Trafford that all was not well in the Australian dressing room, too. Irrespective of whether the stories were true, Ponting's team had their backs to the wall here, and someone had to play a special innings to find a way out. The skipper did just that.

He lost three more partners before tea. Damien Martyn was unlucky to be adjudged LBW off Harmison after getting an inside nick, but superb bowling from Flintoff – fast, on line and length, and swinging both ways – accounted for Simon Katich. Apparently totally in the dark as to whether the ball would be cutting into him or darting away, Katich prodded tentatively outside off stump and turned to see Ashley Giles snaffle a superb catch at fourth slip. Gilchrist, equally flummoxed, then spooned one to Bell in the inspired field placing of second gully. Kevin Pietersen, at first gully, hoisted Bell high into the air in celebration.

At 182 for 5 with only half the overs gone, England were now clear favourites. Just five wickets to go; and one of them was McGrath's, so make that four and a half ... surely. The old ball was reversing beautifully but England still took the new one when it became available. The thinking was that Harmison or Flintoff might well crash through the remaining Aussie batsmen with it. Even if they didn't, the abrasive pitch was bringing reverse swing into play far earlier than under normal circumstances, and there were still plenty of overs left in the day. However, England's initial failure to make in-roads had the crowd peering nervously at the giant screen, which was counting down the overs. As the partnership between Ponting and Michael Clarke progressed, the distant possibility of an Australian win crept into view. Then it disappeared for good as Simon Jones made the breakthrough with a crackerjack delivery: Clarke attempted to pad up as the ball swung past him and smashed the unprotected off stump clean out of the ground.

It was one of Jones's favourite moments of the series: 'The best feeling ... I was standing at the end of my mark geeing up the crowd. I just turned to have a look behind me and they were going berserk. Then I ran in and bowled the perfect reverse in-swinger. He shouldered arms with his bat high above his head and the stump went spinning out of the ground. What a sight that was! I was so pumped I thought my heart was going to burst.'

At 263 for 6 there were now just four to go. Then England saw a most unexpected sight: walking out to the wicket was not Shane Warne, the hero of Australia's first innings, but Jason Gillespie. The conclusion was inescapable: Australia

*'The best feeling … I was standing at the end of
my mark geeing up the crowd. I just turned to have a
look behind me and they were going berserk. Then I
ran in and bowled the perfect reverse in-swinger. He
shouldered arms with his bat high above his head and
the stump went spinning out of the ground. What a
sight that was! I was so pumped I thought my heart
was going to burst.'*

SIMON JONES BOWLS MICHAEL CLARKE

were no longer going for the win. For the first time in an
Ashes series for as long as anyone could remember, they were
setting their sights, stretching their sinews and busting their
guts merely to survive. Warne confirms: 'Jason has probably
got one of the best defences at just blocking the ball, and he
went in there to do that for as long as possible.' He lasted five
balls.

'That was a serious moment,' recalls Hoggard. 'Gillespie
can be a stubborn individual but he was so plumb it was
unbelievable. He almost walked. Now I really thought, We've
got a big chance here.'

The crowd had no doubts: 264 for 7 and 31 overs to get the
last three wickets. Surely England *must* win from here.

But Ponting was still there, having already reached his 23rd
Test century (his fifth against England). And now, as if
England's supporters hadn't had enough agony in the emotional spin-dryer, the Australian skipper found the perfect
partner in Shane Warne, who was proving to be as much of a
thorn in England's side with the bat as he had always been
with the ball.

Flintoff, bowling like a man possessed, threw all he had at

his opponents. A big appeal for LBW against Ponting was turned down by Billy Bowden. Warne then fended one off his body but Flintoff just couldn't reach the ball for the return catch. 'We were trying so hard,' he recalls. 'We all knew how close we were and what victory would mean not just for us, but for the whole country. When you looked around the ground you could not help but be lifted. We all wanted to win so much it hurt.'

But when the final 15 overs began captain and vice-captain were still there: 314 for 7. Then came an incident that many feared would haunt Kevin Pietersen for the rest of his days. Warne shovelled a full toss from Jones at catchable height just to the right of Pietersen at short midwicket. He dived and looked certain finally to break his catching duck. Instead, his drop all but broke England. 'Has he dropped the Ashes?' asked Mark Nicholas, commentating for Channel Four. Every other cricket fan in the country was probably asking the same question.

A little later, the grimace on Simon Jones's face was more than mere disappointment at seeing another chance go to ground off his bowling. He was struggling with cramp. 'I was in the most pain I had experienced for some time,' he says. 'It felt like someone had shot me. I couldn't bend my leg, but I was so disappointed that I had to go off because I really fancied being there to help finish them off. I had tried to run it off but as I ran in from the boundary to field a ball off Warne I just couldn't make it. I said to Vaughan: "Sorry, mate. I've got to go off. I'm no use to anyone out here." There was just nothing I could do about it. Watching the rest of the match from the dressing room was just horrible.'

Still, the hope returned with just under ten overs to go when Flintoff got rid of Warne through a brilliant reflex catch by Geraint Jones. This was not your traditional keeper's dismissal: the ball bounced off second slip Strauss's hands and thigh before Jones dived in front of Trescothick to take the rebound in his right glove inches off the ground.

Strauss recalls: 'Just before Fred ran in, Tres turned to me and said: "Right, he's nicking this one. Be ready. It's coming to you. Be ready." And sure enough there was a big nick and it came straight to me. I saw it all the way and then I missed it completely! My first reaction was: how the hell did I not catch that? The ball thumped into my thigh and could have gone absolutely anywhere. In fact, I had no idea at all where it had gone, but then I heard everyone cheering and saw Jones

---

'Just before Fred ran in, Tres turned to me and said: "Right, he's nicking this one. Be ready. It's coming to you. Be ready." And sure enough there was a big nick and it came straight to me. I saw it all the way and then I missed it completely! ... then I heard everyone cheering and saw Jones with the ball in his gloves ... Thank God, he's got me out of jail.'

ANDREW STRAUSS

---

with the ball in his gloves, and my feeling went from the despair from dropping the catch to thinking, Thank God, he's got me out of jail.'

Jones says: 'I do practise a few rebounds from time to time, mainly with Matthew Hoggard and a tennis ball because it bounces more, just for awareness more than anything else. But that one was pure instinct.'

Flintoff was ecstatic, and went from flat on his back to his feet in one acrobatic movement. Steve Harmison was impressed: 'I've only ever seen him do that before when he's been on the sauce!' he said. 'Not bad for a bowler nearing the end of a workload of twenty-five overs for the day.'

Flintoff was focused and back to his mark as Brett Lee

walked out. England knew all about Lee's stubbornness after Edgbaston, but they were also well aware of McGrath's general ineptitude with the bat. So Vaughan was not alone in thinking that one more wicket would inevitably lead to two. With 9.4 overs left, there seemed to be enough time, as long as Flintoff and Harmison could keep going.

Substitute fielder Stephen Peters almost ran out Lee, but then Harmison took an even more prized scalp when he ended Ponting's brave resistance. Australia's captain appeared incredulous that all his hard work could be for nought when he gloved a delivery down the leg side to Geraint Jones. He had been at the wicket for just under seven hours for his 156 off 275 balls. It was his tenth Test 150. There had been some sterling support, but none of his team-mates had even passed 40! Just one more to go, with the score at 354 for 9.

'When Ponting went I thought, It must be ours,' says Harmison.

Strauss, though, had other ideas: 'I had a horrible feeling in the back of my mind that the gods weren't going to be kind to us two matches in a row. Ponting had played a magnificent innings and his dismissal should have been it. Twenty-four balls sounds a lot, but you're straining so hard that with each ball you bowl when the wicket doesn't fall you can't help thinking, That's another one gone. We needed to be bowling at McGrath but we just couldn't get him down the business end enough.'

Flintoff, running on empty but bowling on sheer will, had an over at Lee before Harmison could target McGrath. He finally got one past Lee's defences, saw it crash into the batsman's pads and roared for LBW. Watching in the field, Harmison felt sure Lee was 'stone dead'. The ball would certainly have smashed straight into the stumps, but Steve Bucknor rightly gave the batsman the benefit of a slight doubt because it might have hit him just outside the line.

For the final over of a pulsating match, Harmison could run up to the wicket but scarcely had the energy to do any more. Nevertheless, there was always a chance while McGrath was facing. But once he got off strike by scampering a single with three balls to go, that was pretty much it. Lee, defiant to the end, not only denied Harmison and England but hit the exhausted Durham man's final full toss for four.

'It was another great game and it had everything: hundreds, sixes, a 600th wicket, a close finish, the lot,' said Vaughan. 'I don't think the fact that they hung on for a draw will matter one iota come Trent Bridge. We've dominated four days against the number-one team in the world. Three weeks ago we were being written off. We were even better here than in our win at Edgbaston.'

Ponting, though, was equally positive: 'It was probably one of my best knocks. I tried to play instinctively and it is satisfying to put your hand up when it matters as a batsman and leader. We've come away with a draw after being outplayed, so there's a good mood in the changing room right now. It was a long, hard, tough day of Test cricket.'

'Look over there at the Australian dressing room ... Australia are celebrating a draw. Just think what that means.'
MICHAEL VAUGHAN

The packed Old Trafford crowd, who had lived every agonising second of it, couldn't agree more. At Edgbaston, the nail-biting had ceased just after noon. Here it lasted all day, with the lunch and tea breaks merely heightening the tension. But the fans had just witnessed a cricketing day to remember for the rest of their lives. And they were now convinced that England's resurgence in this Ashes series was no flash in the pan.

There were plenty of remarkable aspects about this game, one of them being the simple fact that it ended in a draw. The last drawn Ashes Test had been seventeen matches before, when a storm had prevented Australia winning on Alec Stewart's tour in 1998.

Vaughan was determined that, no matter how physically drained his men were, they would leave the arena mentally strengthened by their performance. 'Look over there at the Australian dressing room,' he told them in a huddle on the pitch at the end of the match. 'Australia are celebrating a draw. Just think what that means.'

Third Test, Old Trafford, Manchester

Result Match drawn

Umpires B.F.Bowden (NZ) and S.A.Bucknor (WI)   **Match Referee** R.S.Madugalle (SL)
Man of the Match R.T.Ponting

England First Innings		R	M	B	4s	6s
M.E.Trescothick	c Gilchrist b Warne	63	196	117	9	0
A.J.Strauss	b Lee	6	43	28	0	0
*M.P.Vaughan	c McGrath b Katich	166	281	215	20	1
I.R.Bell	c Gilchrist b Lee	59	205	155	8	0
K.P.Pietersen	c sub (B.J.Hodge) b Lee	21	50	28	1	0
M.J.Hoggard	b Lee	4	13	10	1	0
A.Flintoff	c Langer b Warne	46	93	67	7	0
+G.O.Jones	b Gillespie	42	86	51	6	0
A.F.Giles	c Hayden b Warne	0	11	6	0	0
S.J.Harmison	not out	10	13	11	1	0
S.P.Jones	b Warne	0	7	4	0	0
Extras	b 4, lb 5, w 3, nb 15	27				
Total	all out, 113.2 overs, 503 mins	444				

FoW 1–26 Strauss (10th ov), 2–163 Trescothick (42nd ov), 3–290 Vaughan (75th ov), 4–333 Pietersen (87th ov), 5–341 Hoggard (89th ov), 6–346 Bell (93rd ov), 7–433 Flintoff (110th ov), 8–434 G.O.Jones (111th ov), 9–438 Giles (112th ov), 10–444 S.P.Jones (114th ov)

Bowling	O	M	R	W
McGrath	25	6	86	0
Lee	27	6	100	4
Gillespie	19	2	114	1
Warne	33.2	5	99	4
Katich	9	1	36	1

Australia First Innings

		R	M	B	4s	6s
J.L.Langer	c Bell b Giles	31	76	50	4	0
M.L.Hayden	lbw b Giles	34	112	71	5	0
*R.T.Ponting	c Bell b S.P.Jones	7	20	12	1	0
D.R.Martyn	b Giles	20	71	41	2	0
S.M.Katich	b Flintoff	17	39	28	1	0
+A.C.Gilchrist	c G.O.Jones b S.P.Jones	30	74	49	4	0
S.K.Warne	c Giles b S.P.Jones	90	183	122	11	1
M.J.Clarke	c Flintoff b S.P.Jones	7	19	18	0	0
J.N.Gillespie	lbw b S.P.Jones	26	144	111	1	1
B.Lee	c Trescothick b S.P.Jones	1	17	16	0	0
G.D.McGrath	not out	1	20	4	0	0
Extras	b 8, lb 7, w 8, nb 15	38				
Total	all out, 84.5 overs, 393 mins	302				

FoW   1–58 Langer (16th ov), 2–73 Ponting (21st ov), 3–86 Hayden (24th ov), 4–119 Katich (33rd ov), 5–133 Martyn (36th ov), 6–186 Gilchrist (49th ov), 7–201 Clarke (53rd ov), 8–287 Warne (77th ov), 9–293 Lee (81st ov), 10–302 Gillespie (85th ov)

Bowling	O	M	R	W
Harmison	10	0	47	0
Hoggard	6	2	22	0
Flintoff	20	1	65	1
S.P.Jones	17.5	6	53	6
Giles	31	4	100	3

England Second Innings

		R	M	B	4s	6s
M.E.Trescothick	b McGrath	41	71	56	6	0
A.J.Strauss	c Martyn b McGrath	106	246	158	9	2
*M.P.Vaughan	c sub (B.J.Hodge) b Lee	14	45	37	2	0
I.R.Bell	c Katich b McGrath	65	165	103	4	1
K.P.Pietersen	lbw b McGrath	0	3	1	0	0
A.Flintoff	b McGrath	4	20	18	0	0
+G.O.Jones	not out	27	15	12	2	2
A.F.Giles	not out	0	4	0	0	0
M.J.Hoggard						
S.J.Harmison						
S.P.Jones						
Extras	b 5, lb 3, w 1, nb 14	23				
Total	6 wkts dec, 61.5 overs, 288 mins	280				

FoW 1–64 Trescothick (16th ov), 2–97 Vaughan (26th ov), 3–224 Strauss (54th ov), 4–225 Pietersen (54th ov), 5–248 Flintoff (60th ov), 6–264 Bell (62nd ov)

Bowling	O	M	R	W
McGrath	20.5	1	115	5
Lee	12	0	60	1
Warne	25	3	74	0
Gillespie	4	0	23	0

Australia Second Innings

		R	M	B	4s	6s
J.L.Langer	c G.O.Jones b Hoggard	14	42	41	3	0
M.L.Hayden	b Flintoff	36	123	91	5	1
*R.T.Ponting	c G.O.Jones b Harmison	156	411	275	16	1
D.R.Martyn	lbw b Harmison	19	53	36	3	0
S.M.Katich	c Giles b Flintoff	12	30	23	2	0
+A.C.Gilchrist	c Bell b Flintoff	4	36	30	0	0
M.J.Clarke	b S.P.Jones	39	73	63	7	0
J.N.Gillespie	lbw b Hoggard	0	8	5	0	0
S.K.Warne	c G.O.Jones b Flintoff	34	99	69	5	0
B.Lee	not out	18	44	25	4	0
G.D.McGrath	not out	5	17	9	1	0
Extras	b 5, lb 8, w 1, nb 20	34				
Total	9 wkts, 108 overs, 474 mins	371				

FoW 1–25 Langer (12th ov), 2–96 Hayden (30th ov), 3–129 Martyn (43rd ov), 4–165 Katich (50th ov), 5–182 Gilchrist (58th ov), 6–263 Clarke (76th ov), 7–264 Gillespie (77th ov), 8–340 Warne (99th ov), 9–354 Ponting (104th ov)

Bowling	O	M	R	W
Harmison	22	4	67	2
Hoggard	13	0	49	2
Giles	26	4	93	0
Vaughan	5	0	21	0
Flintoff	25	6	71	4
S.P.Jones	17	3	57	1

Close of Play Day 1 England 341–5 (Bell 59*)
Day 2 England 444, Australia 214–7 (Warne 45*, Gillespie 4*)
Day 3 Australia 264–7 (Warne 78*, Gillespie 7*)

CHAPTER IV

FOURTH TEST

TRENT BRIDGE

PREVIEW

On the eve of the fourth Test at Trent Bridge the *Daily Mail* printed a selection of quotes from what they called the 'motormouth' of Glenn McGrath. Emphasising in less than complimentary fashion the habit of Australia's pace spearhead and cheerleader of talking the talk prior to walking the walk, the paper recalled some of his less ambiguous pronouncements, as in: 'My prediction for the Ashes? Five–nil to Australia,' etc. The paper even advised the England team to cut out the list and pin it on their dressing-room wall for motivational purposes.

But, in that regard, no words of McGrath in printed form could compare with the one he himself uttered at around 9.45 a.m. on Thursday 25 August. For, with forty-five minutes remaining before the start of a match England had to win to keep alive their dreams of Ashes victory, their chief tormentor and the bowler they currently regarded as more of a threat than Shane Warne told Australian physiotherapist Errol Alcott: 'No.'

When reports of a problem with McGrath's right elbow first emerged from within the Australian camp in the aftermath of their two-day match against Northamptonshire, most observers swallowed them with a large helping of the salt they had poured on suggestions that he might be fit enough play in the third Test a mere week after ripping two ligaments in his right ankle. After all, in the five overs he had sent down at Northants' young batsmen in the final session the previous Saturday, McGrath appeared to have rediscovered the rhythm for which he had been searching since the first Test at Lord's. With Jason Gillespie's place under threat, the Northants match had been billed as a bowling shoot-out between Michael Kasprowicz and Shaun Tait for the right to replace him, and all eyes were on them. Five more overs the following morning had confirmed the impression that McGrath was fit, ready and raring to resume his favourite pastime: hunting Poms. Even when he pulled up sharply after sending down a bouncer as the first ball of the sixth over in that spell, most believed the incident was worth little more than a mental note. His later trip to hospital for a scan was put down to natural and justifiable over-caution on the part of the Aussie management, just checking that the tingling he had felt in his right arm was nothing serious.

McGrath, though, knew better; or rather, from his and his colleagues' perspective, worse. Unbeknown to anyone else, almost from the moment he experienced a sharp pain in his elbow and forearm, he had a fair idea of what had happened and felt a sinking feeling. 'By the end of that sixth over, when I realised the pain had grown progressively severe with each subsequent ball, I knew it was pretty serious,' he said. 'Then, when I tried to throw the ball in from the boundary, that was no fun at all. I never like to say I'm not fit until I've given myself every chance, but by the eve of the match I was already ninety-nine per cent sure I was out.'

The truth of McGrath's predicament became clear for all to see as the two sets of players prepared to begin again the titanic struggle for the 2005 Ashes. The greatest fast bowler of his type in the modern game first sent down half a dozen deliveries with his right arm; then, for the benefit of the cameras, a couple with his left. Both were arrow straight on the line of off stump and just back of a length, of course, but his involvement in the series was again, temporarily at least, halted. 'It couldn't have happened at a worse time,' he said. 'Having got through the original injury I was exactly where I wanted to be and feeling great. Someone with a voodoo doll was out to get me and they were doing a pretty good job.'

Mike Atherton suggested McGrath might be paying the price for playing at Old Trafford, that trying to bowl when clearly not 100 per cent fit might have led to a referred injury in an area of the body required to do too much to compensate. At the time some considered the former England captain was having trouble identifying his ankle from his elbow, but McGrath later accepted the possibility: 'I'd probably put it down to going in at Old Trafford with a dodgy ankle. Maybe because it was not as supportive as usual I might have changed my action by one or two per cent and that indirectly affected the elbow. Or maybe it happened because I bowled a lot around the wicket, which is unusual for me. I don't think we were too worried about me bowling a first spell, but coming back again would have been hard.'

> 'The Aussies have been lording it for eighteen years, crowing about how good they are and suggesting that maybe the Ashes were a waste of time. Now they are trying all kinds of psychological claptrap to hide the fact that they've been outplayed.'
>
> GEOFFREY BOYCOTT

Shaun Tait, the 22-year-old from South Australia whose

previous experience of bowling in England was short and eminently forgettable (two games for Durham in which he had conceded 176 runs in eighteen overs, including an analysis of 12–0–113–0, overstepping for 21 no-balls), had already been selected to replace Gillespie. So Australia turned again to the man who had come in for McGrath at Edgbaston, Michael Kasprowicz.

Tait was doing his best to emulate McGrath in the sound-bite department: 'I don't set out to kill anyone,' he said, 'but you do need to hit a few. I want to hit their batsmen and if there's blood, that should frighten off the others watching from the balcony. Now I can get at England. If I hit them, it will hurt.' This was no idle threat: the previous weekend he had seen to it that Northants' Tim Roberts needed five stitches above his left eye. (Tait's team-mate Justin Langer had been less impressed when he hit him with a low full toss in the nets …)

For the fourth Test in a row, England were unchanged. Pictures appeared in the papers of the last side to remain so for an entire Ashes series: Arthur Shrewsbury's, which beat Australia 3–2 in 1884–5. In the final Test at the MCG, which England won by an innings and 98 runs, Shrewsbury became the first England captain to score a Test century. The selection meetings were rather shorter on that tour, though, as the squad totalled only eleven (plus a management of two). But the self-confidence expressed by David Graveney when naming the same line-up camouflaged an injury concern for England, too. Simon Jones, excellent with the ball all series but particularly penetrative at Old Trafford because of his ability to bowl reverse-swing, had been forced to miss the climax of the extraordinary final day in Manchester due to an attack of cramp. Some observers considered his absence at the crucial moment might have cost England victory. After the match Jones was sent for precautionary scans, and when these were first viewed by the medics the prognosis was not good. In fact, they were so bad that both Jones and coach Duncan Fletcher

ABOVE, LEFT: Thousands had to be turned away from Old Trafford on the final day, when England needed to bowl out Australia to win the match and take a 2–1 lead in the series. (*Getty Images*) RIGHT: Ricky Ponting set himself to bat out the final day and to take whatever came his way. (*Getty Images*)

Michael Clarke shoulders arms to Simon Jones's reverse swing and loses his leg stump. (*Martin Rickett/PA*)

Andrew Flintoff can't control his excitement after Shane Warne was the eighth man to fall after almost 100 minutes of resistance. (*Getty Images*)

Ricky Ponting's mammoth innings of 156 is ended as Steve Harmison has him caught behind. In scenes of incredible tension, England now had four overs to take the last wicket. (*Getty Images*)

TOP: The big screen says it all … (*Getty Images*)

ABOVE, LEFT: … but Brett Lee and Glenn McGrath survived to hold out for a draw. (*AP Photo/John Super*) ABOVE, RIGHT: Michael Vaughan reminds his dejected team how close they had come to another famous victory, and that there would be all to play for at Trent Bridge. (*Getty Images*)

ABOVE, LEFT & RIGHT:
Andrew Flintoff hits out in the
first innings at Trent Bridge.
He is congratulated by Geraint
Jones on his maiden Test
century against Australia.
Together they put on 177 for
the sixth wicket. (*Getty Images*)

Geraint Jones cracks Shane
Warne through the covers
on the way to making 85.
(*Getty Images*)

Ian Bell is congratulated by Matthew Hoggard after he has caught Justin Langer for 27. (*Rui Vieira/PA*)

Andrew Strauss's catch of the series to dismiss Adam Gilchrist for 27. (*Getty Images*)

Simon Jones salutes the crowd after dismissing Brett Lee to complete his five-wicket haul. (*Getty Images*)

ABOVE, LEFT: Durham super-sub Gary Pratt is lofted high after his direct hit ran out Ricky Ponting. (*Empics*) RIGHT: Simon Katich (right) and Michael Clarke held England at bay for nearly 50 overs as they put on a century partnership to help give Australia a fighting chance of setting England a total. (*AP Photo/Max Nash*)

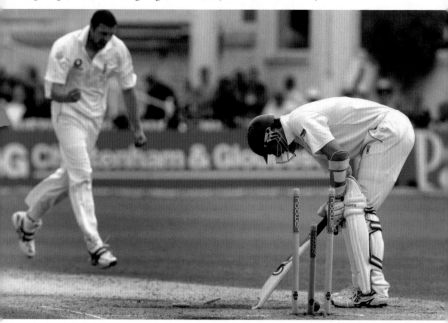

Steve Harmison celebrates after Shaun Tait walked across his stumps to be bowled, leaving England just 129 to win. (*Gareth Copley/PA*)

Michael Vaughan falls to Shane Warne for 0, and a brief rally by Kevin Pietersen soon came to an end when he and Andrew Flintoff both fell to the pace of Brett Lee, as the Test built up to a third successive nailbiter. (*Getty Images*, *Getty Images* and *AP Photo/Jon Super*)

Ashley Giles raises his bat as he and Matthew Hoggard make the crucial runs to secure England's three-wicket win. (*Empics*)

With England 2–1 up in the series with one to play, Kevin Pietersen, Andrew Flintoff, Andrew Strauss, Ian Bell and Simon Jones celebrate on the balcony. (*Rui Vieira/PA*)

Michael Vaughan leads his victorious team on a lap of honour round Trent Bridge, and looks forward to the decider at The Oval. (*Gareth Copley/PA*) were told to prepare for the probability that he would miss the fourth Test. Thankfully for them, a second set of scans gave the Glamorgan man the all-clear.

Blissfully unaware of this drama, the pundits were in fine form, as were one or two of the protagonists. In the red and white corner, Geoffrey Boycott claimed: 'The Aussies have been lording it for eighteen years, crowing about how good they are and suggesting that maybe the Ashes were a waste of time. Now they are trying all kinds of psychological claptrap to hide the fact that they've been outplayed.' On behalf of the baggy green, Richie Benaud countered: 'I think the media here, the public and maybe the England dressing room have started to write off Australia. If so, that would be their second mistake. Their first was not taking the last Australian wicket at Old Trafford.'

Shane Warne agreed. Responding to claims from Nottinghamshire groundsman Steve Birks that his pitch would be largely unresponsive to spin, he said: 'He should keep his mouth quiet and just worry about preparing a good pitch.' Nothing could make the spinner follow similar advice, mind. 'England will be kicking themselves they didn't declare earlier at Old Trafford,' he continued. 'That's just one of the little things that have not worked out for them. The pressure is on them. They have to win one of the last two Tests to regain the Ashes, simple as that. They'll want to play the same way as they have done in the last two matches but they have the added pressure that they have to win. It will be in their minds that they have outplayed us twice but the series is all square. We haven't done the business in the last two matches but I can guarantee this team will deliver in the next two Tests.'

Some of the sports pages featured Kevin Pietersen's fielding practice in the National Academy at Loughborough after rain forced the cancellation of outdoor work. They had picked up on the fact that, after missing Gilchrist and Warne at Old Trafford, the energetic young star had now dropped all five chances that had come his way. Of more interest in the England dressing room was the *Sunday Times*'s feature of England's cricketers, their partners and houses. Many were jealous of Geraint Jones's gaff. So was he: the wicket-keeper had never set eyes on the glorious country pile that the paper had claimed was his home sweet home.

There was rain all over England: six inches had fallen since Monday and the Notts groundstaff stayed until midnight on Wednesday to clear an outfield that had been left underwater by a late deluge. However, the considered opinion was that batting would be more fun than bowling for at least three days, and that conditions would not be conducive to the reverse-swing with which England's attack had tormented the Australian batsmen on the rough playing surface in Manchester.

As a result, the toss seemed vital. Michael Vaughan duly won it, and had no hesitation in making first use of a white-faced pitch that looked full of runs. He knew that his team had to make the most of it. If England could take a 2–1 lead to The Oval for the final Test, their chances of regaining the Ashes after sixteen years would be greatly improved but they simply had to avoid defeat.

If Australia could manage to win in Nottingham, it would be at least another fifteen months before the Ashes were coming home.

DAY ONE: ENGLAND 229 FOR FOUR

The match started amid some confusion when, having placed the bails carefully on top of the stumps, one of the two umpires attempted to balance a beer can on them, too. The capacity crowd watched with mounting curiosity as the duo then proceeded to practise a few exaggerated signals. All finally became clear when another pair of officials, Steve Bucknor and Aleem Dar, walked through the pavilion gate towards the square. The security guards appeared momentarily unsure as to which couple required escorting from the field, but finally made the correct choice. The impostors were later charged with aggravated trespass.

Perhaps the incident helped to relieve some of the tension for England's opening pair, Marcus Trescothick (wearing a black armband in memory of a young fan, Stuart Dove, who had succumbed to cancer the previous week) and Andrew Strauss. It certainly did not distract them as they raced to their seventh century stand in eighteen Tests at a scorching rate of five runs per over. When he reached 31, Trescothick became England's highest scorer (876 runs) against Australia without making a century.

Strauss recalls: 'We didn't necessarily say it, but, after having come so close at Old Trafford, we felt it was vital to get off to a good start just to maintain our positive momentum. With McGrath failing his fitness test and the wicket playing well, we knew there would be scoring opportunities and, although Tait was pretty awkward to face with his slingy action, Marcus just banged the ball everywhere. Suddenly he had reached fifty, we were a hundred for none off twenty overs, and away.'

That is until Strauss, attempting to sweep Shane Warne, was caught off his boot by Matthew Hayden at slip. At first sight it looked as though he had hit the ball into the ground, but the Aussies were united in claiming a catch, with Warne at his most appealing. Bucknor and Dar conferred before signalling to the TV umpire, Mark Benson, and the replays were clear. 'I was very frustrated at getting out to Warne after starting well,' says Strauss. 'I said to myself prior to the match that if I got in I should make sure I went on. I suppose I was trying to get a little bit cute in trying to manipulate the field.'

From the moment he came in, Vaughan struck the ball as sweetly as he had done at Old Trafford. The Aussie bowlers did themselves no favours, bowling eighteen no-balls in the session, including one from Brett Lee that Trescothick (then on 55) chopped on to his stumps. 'We had set ourselves a target of not bowling one,' mused Aussie coach John Buchanan that night. England weren't complaining.

But while the Aussie bowlers could not contain them, the Nottingham weather did the job instead. The dark rain clouds that had been predicted arrived at lunchtime. Trescothick and Vaughan added only 5 runs in the 3.1 overs that were possible after the afternoon session got under way an hour late. Tea was taken early and when play resumed at 3.55 with a scheduled 42 overs left in the day, the sun had long since disappeared and so had England's sparkle. Indeed, when Tait claimed his first two Test wickets in quick succession to leave England on 146 for three, they were in danger of wasting their fine start. Trescothick, on 65, was comprehensively bowled by Tait's full-length in-swinger four balls after coming back out. Ian Bell's less-than-positive forward prod gave Adam Gilchrist his 300th Test victim (the fourth wicket-keeper to reach that mark). Australia had a real opportunity to break through, but first Kasprowicz dropped a return catch from Pietersen, then, nine balls later, Hayden put down Vaughan. He also missed a chance to run out Pietersen.

However, just when it seemed England were riding their luck, their captain looked appropriately disgusted with himself when his opposite number, Ponting, at best a part-time bowler, dismissed him for 58. It was the first time Vaughan had failed to convert a fifty against Australia into a hundred. The score was 213 for four. Ponting, having taken just his fifth wicket in ninety-two Tests, then almost caught Flintoff on the hop with one that cut back.

England may not have taken advantage of a great start, but the Australians had not fully capitalised on the weather or the home side's later carelessness as the best side in the world might have been expected to do.

DAY TWO: ENGLAND 477;
AUSTRALIA 99 FOR FIVE

Listening to Andrew Flintoff's loud but not particularly tuneful rendition of his favourites from the Frank Sinatra songbook just as the Australians were taking the field on the second morning, his team-mates were left in no doubt as to his frame of mind. According to Strauss, 'Fred was relaxed, confident and keen to take centre stage.'

Flintoff himself confessed that the excruciating tension of the final day at Old Trafford and the twenty-five overs he sent down (the most he had ever bowled in a single day's cricket) had left him shattered, physically and mentally. Just as well, then, that prior to reporting for duty in Nottingham he had managed to get away from cricket and switch off, taking his wife Rachael and daughter Holly for a short break in St Tropez. 'I really enjoyed getting away from everything for a few days,' he said, 'particularly to a place where no one was remotely interested in cricket. I suppose it's going to happen when you're on the front pages of papers. And I guess being six foot four I am quite noticeable, but I am shy by nature and I do find it quite strange when people come up and start talking to me. The only person who recognised me in France was a bloke wearing a Preston North End shirt!'

At the end of a week in which he had been named in both the one-day and Test Rest of the World squads for the ICC Super Series matches against Australia in October, the refreshed Flintoff did indeed step even more firmly into the spotlight. He produced an innings that confirmed his status as the most complete all-rounder currently playing the game. His first Ashes century (in a partnership of 177 with Geraint Jones) could certainly be termed a match-winner, and possibly even a series-decider.

Duncan Fletcher recalls: 'The extraordinary thing about Fred is that even though so much is expected of him, he seems able to play as though he doesn't feel the pressure. When we really needed him to come up with a solid and mature innings that might have made all the difference, he did it. It was down to those two, Fred and Geraint Jones; they were the only ones left who could do it. I believe it is close to one of the best partnerships that I've seen in terms of its importance. More than likely, it won us the Test.

'Fred has periods when his technique might be a little rusty or out of sync and his sheer power will get him through. But if anyone thinks he is a slogger they are crazy. He always wants to prove that he can play an innings that requires real thought, and here he did. And the pressure Geraint was under after all the criticism he had received for his keeping … You just cannot believe the character that was shown by those two guys.'

Flintoff said: 'After Edgbaston, where I tried to hit myself back into form, things really happened for me here. Everything just seemed to click and I was doing what I was last year when I was playing well. Geraint came in and played brilliantly. We have the kind of relationship on and off the field where we instinctively know when one of us is about to do something daft and we can calm each other down. Usually there is plenty of chat between us at the end of each over, but this time we were so focused. We both knew what we had to do.'

> '… if anyone thinks he is a slogger they are crazy. He always wants to prove that he can play an innings that requires real thought, and here he did.'
> DUNCAN FLETCHER ON ANDREW FLINTOFF

Jones, who made 85, agrees: 'I knew it was time to really stick my hand up and contribute. And again it was a situation for the team where it could have been 300 all out, along those lines. Afterwards I sat there thinking I should have got another fifteen runs and that would have really topped it off, but I was really pleased to have "put in". We just really like building partnerships together. Because we're both so attacking and we hit the ball in such different areas, we don't give the bowler much margin for error. Fred is so powerful hitting straight and then if they give me any width, I'll try to cash in. They've got to be changing what they do all the time rather than bowling to their patterns.'

It's clearly a system that works: this was the fourth time the Flintoff–Jones combination had added three figures together.

Flintoff brought up his fifty with a six off Warne into the Fox Road Stand. He was not so confident facing the same bowler on 99, surviving a clutch of nervous deliveries and a maiden over from the leg-spinner before pushing the single that allowed the Trent Bridge crowd to erupt in joyful celebration. The Australians had had no answer to his controlled aggression, his 102 coming off 132 deliveries, with fourteen fours and a six. For the first time in his career, his Test average was higher with the bat than with the ball.

Jones, whom the Aussies were convinced had been caught behind off Lee the first ball after lunch, more than held his own, and looked set for his second Test century when he was well caught and bowled by a diving Kasprowicz. Warne then claimed the last three wickets, including the stumping of Harmison, who fell over in a heap after trying to heave him over square-leg. Hoggard and Simon Jones added 23 for the final wicket to increase Australia's frustration as England made 477, their highest total in a Trent Bridge Test for sixty-seven years.

But a great day for England was only half over: Australia were in tatters by the close, with Matthew Hoggard enjoying his best day of the series thus far. The Yorkshire swing bowler had not been at his best, but he had nevertheless picked up some valuable wickets during the earlier Tests. On this day the conditions were ideal for him, although he admits he felt under a tad more pressure thanks to Simon Jones, who had told the press that Trent Bridge would be right up his colleague's street. Hoggard utilised every ounce of the assistance offered him by the pitch and atmosphere, dismissing Langer, Hayden and Damien Martyn in a devastating final session that left Australia 99 for five at the close. According to the man dubbed by the Barmy Army 'The King of the Swingers, an England VIP': 'It was a massive relief when the first ball went down and it swung because it opens up a lot more ways for me to get wickets than if the ball is just going straight on. Getting the two openers was sweet, especially Hayden, because all I can remember from the last tour to Australia was that he just murdered us.'

Australia's batsmen were certainly getting the worse of the close umpiring decisions, but they could not deny they were also struggling to cope. Hayden's miserable Ashes continued. Ponting's faint inside nick when given out LBW off Jones was picked up only by the super-slow-mo camera, not by the umpire. Martyn, too, was given out LBW after hitting the ball. The three fell in just eleven deliveries. Langer's resistance was ended by another fine Hoggard effort that was taken by Bell at short square. Then, to England's undisguised delight, Steve Harmison, for the third time in the series, ended the day's play with a wicket when Michael Clarke was the fourth Aussie to be adjudged LBW.

After play, Gilchrist admitted his team were coming second: 'England are showing the world they are a very good, dangerous cricket team at the top of their game,' he said. 'We are facing the ultimate challenge at the moment and we are under pressure. It is a vicious cycle for us. England are doing to us what we have done to teams for years. This is the best Test attack I've faced in my Test career, working together and hunting in a pack.'

DAY THREE: AUSTRALIA 218 & 222
FOR FOUR (FOLLOWING ON)

Steve Harmison was the man chosen to give the morning pep talk. It was not quite what his colleagues were expecting: instead of cajoling them to give maximum effort, he offered the bowlers a carrot. The Durham man explains: 'Fred was late arriving at the ground because he had had to have some treatment in the hotel and as a result the lucky sod missed the warm-ups. I told the lads the real reason he was late was that he had been allowed to sleep in after scoring a hundred the day before. "Nice to see you out of bed," I told him in the huddle, "perhaps if one of us poor bloody bowlers gets a five-for, we might be allowed a lie-in as well."' Simon Jones surely did enough to earn such a reward, but his day would later go from the highest high to the lowest low.

Australia may have been in the mire, but Simon Katich and Gilchrist went on the offensive. Hoggard, especially, took a battering as 58 runs were added in forty minutes, with the final 41 coming off just three overs. Then, at 157 for five, Vaughan threw the ball to Jones. By the time he had finished the first part of his day's work, the England captain was in a position to ask the Australians to follow on for the first time in seventeen years and 191 Tests.

When Katich edged Jones's second ball to Strauss at second slip, cricket fans were rather perplexed by the Glamorgan man's celebration. He patted both hands on his head in a gesture known as the 'Ayatollah'. Welsh rugby fans had seen Grand Slam skipper Gareth Thomas make a similar gesture as he ran under the All Blacks' posts for the British Lions in Wellington a few months earlier. But the celebration had its origins at Cardiff City Football Club, where it started in the 1980s as a celebration that mimicked the way Iranians paid tribute to the Ayatollah Khomeini.

When the booing that greeted Shane Warne's entrance

turned to cheers next ball after he spooned a leading edge to Bell in the covers, the great leg-spinner was said to be deeply unimpressed when Jones also 'Ayatollahed' him back to the pavilion. One newspaper erroneously suggested it was a comment on Warne's heavily publicised recent hair regrowth programme, but Jones found out later that Warne was upset because he thought the gesture was intended to indicate that the bowler now believed him to be his rabbit. Jones recalls: 'I'd had a miserable time during the past week because I was so disappointed at having to leave the field with cramp at such a crucial stage of the last Test. I felt as though I had let the boys down. It was lucky that I was able to switch off and chill out with my mates and family back home because it wouldn't have been nice to be on my own brooding about what might have happened had I not left the field.

'When I got to Trent Bridge I felt I had some unfinished business. First, I wanted to make up for what had happened; and also I wanted to prove I wasn't a one-trick pony because some people had said that I was only any use if the ball was reverse-swinging. So I was delighted to have success with conventional swing this time. After the two wickets in two balls I suddenly realised I was on a hat-trick, in an Ashes Test. Somehow it just didn't seem real. In the event I bowled a poor ball to Brett Lee. I should have bowled it a lot fuller and given it the chance to swing. But my next wicket, bowling Michael Kasprowicz, was my favourite ball: it pitched on leg stump and hit off. Beautiful.'

The fourth wicket of the spell that sent Australia tumbling from 157 for five to 175 for nine belonged to Flintoff. The way it happened belonged to the world of fantasy cricket. Patrick Eagar's photograph of the moment when Andrew Strauss took the catch to dismiss Adam Gilchrist belongs in a gallery. And anyone who saw England's second slip leap full length and then some to his left and cling on to the ball one-handed now believes a man can fly. Strauss remembers: 'It was just one of those freaky things. It didn't actually come that quick because it was a defensive shot. You just see it and dive and hope it sticks when it hits your hands. It almost hit me too much in the palm and as I was falling I was thinking, This could easily just bounce out as I land. So I tried to sort of to shield it into my body as I hit the deck and, fortunately, it just stuck. It was quite incredible really. As a fielder, it's great when you get catches that come along like that because you've almost got nothing to lose on them. Maybe it is the kind of catch that you can only take when the level of intensity is as high as it was for us then and it gives everyone that extra percentage that enables things like that to happen. You're just so committed to any chance you might get. And, of course, you know you've caught it a split second before anyone else, a split second when you think, I can't believe I've got it. And then you hear the roar and you realise what has happened. I sort of lost track of reality and I was running around like an idiot. I've seen the pictures and you do think: Was that me?'

When Jones bowled Kasprowicz with his brilliant away-swinger, England were anticipating a first-innings lead of around 300. Brett Lee had other ideas. In less than half an hour, Australia went from 175 for nine to 218 all out, with Lee belting three sixes in his 47 off 44 balls. Two of the sixes were huge hits off Harmison over midwicket, one travelling out of the ground and the other landing on the bonnet of the Nottinghamshire chairman's silver Audi. Frustrated as England were by the last-wicket stand, they never appeared rattled, although it took a fine running catch by Bell on the boundary to end the onslaught and give Simon Jones his second five-wicket haul of the summer – 'the first Welshman to do that in Test cricket', he said – and his third in all. Jones (five for 44, including four for 22 in 32 deliveries that morning) raised his arm in salute, and as Vaughan gathered his team into another huddle before they left the field, he shrugged off the slight tightening he had started to feel in his ankle. 'I'd felt it towards the end of their first innings,' he explains. 'The pain had been getting progressively worse, but it was nothing I couldn't deal with. In any case, the wickets kept me going, no problem.'

Well, no problem yet, at least.

Strauss remembers his captain calling the team together towards the end of the Australian innings. The topic under discussion was whether to enforce the follow-on. 'We had a little chat about it when we took the ninth wicket and, as they were still only 175 and so far off, and we'd probably only bowled about forty overs, it just seemed obviously the right thing to do. Although a little bit of the wind got knocked out of our sails by the fact they'd put on fifty-odd for the last wicket and Brett Lee kept spanking it, I think Michael's mind was probably made up already. When he brought us together at the end of the innings to confirm what we should do he did get the bowlers round to say, "Look, are we up for this?" and "Are you guys all feeling fresh and healthy?" and they all went, "Yeah." But I think Simon Jones was getting his hat from down on the boundary or something at that moment, so I don't think Vaughany knew that he was carrying an injury there, which I suppose might have made a bit of a difference in the end. If he'd known that, he may have chosen not to enforce the follow-on.'

In the event, Jones managed to bowl just four overs before limping from the field in agony, just after two o'clock. After treatment in the dressing room he made one attempt to return but it was useless. 'I was gutted when I realised I couldn't carry on,' says Jones. 'All the boys were trying to get me going, saying, "Come on, we need you to bowl," but physically I just couldn't do it.' He was sent to hospital for X-rays at teatime, came back in a surgical boot and took no further part in the proceedings that day. However, simply by being absent, Jones (or, more precisely, his replacement) would have a profound influence on the game and the series.

Before that, Flintoff's first over brought the initial break-through, and he should have had a second when Strauss fumbled a straightforward chance off Langer in the slips. Giles was asked to bowl for the first time in the match at three o'clock on the third day. Ten minutes later, Australia came off for tea at 115 for one, still 143 short of making England bat again.

No one could deny there was massive tension in the Nottinghamshire air, but Vaughan's players were still nonplussed by Ricky Ponting's reaction to being run out after the restart. The tourists were 155 for two at the time (Langer having departed to a glove/pad catch by Bell at short-leg off Giles). Martyn pushed the ball into the covers and called his captain for the run. There was always a chance of a run out with a direct hit and that's exactly what happened when Simon Jones's substitute, Gary Pratt from Durham, nailed the stumps. Umpire Dar nodded to the appeal, but called for the third umpire to confirm, which Mark Benson did after a couple of replays. Ponting was clearly agitated, even before the giant screen declared, 'OUT'. But none of the players was prepared for what happened next. Kevin Pietersen recalls: 'We were all together, waiting for the verdict and preparing to have a drink when Ricky just started effing and blinding at us. We had absolutely no idea what he was on about. It was astonishing.' Hoggard remembers: 'After the TV decision came up I saw him having a word with Aleem Dar and as I went past him I basically told him he had better get off the field because he was out and that was the end of it. Then, when he finally dragged himself away, he had a right blast at Duncan Fletcher. We all thought, What is his problem?'

Fletcher was inside the dressing room at the start of the incident and wandered on to the balcony only when he heard someone say, 'What's Ponting up

> *'We all thought,*
> *What is his problem?'*
> MATTHEW HOGGARD
> ON RICKY PONTING'S
> OUTBURST

to?' 'I could see he was having a go at me,' said the coach, 'but I couldn't hear what he was saying.'

Later it emerged that Ponting was expressing his anger at England's use of substitute fielders, believing their system of allowing bowlers to come off the field for quick 'comfort breaks' after a bowling spell, while within the laws, was against the spirit of the game. Fletcher and his players completely rejected the claim. According to the coach: 'I was surprised at the way Ricky reacted and why. Basically we thought they were making a mountain out of a molehill. There was never a concerted plan to rest bowlers, or who to replace them with. Of course, we want good fielders to oper-ate as twelfth men but they are rarely on for more than an over. As for the bowlers coming off for a rest, they probably spend more energy running up and down the steps to the dressing room to relieve themselves and get back again than just walking down to third man at the end of an over.' In any case, the man Pratt was on for was by this time on his way to hospital.

England had been aware that the pressure was mounting on Ponting as Australian skipper ever since his decision to bowl first at Edgbaston. That blunder had given England the opportunity to seize the initiative and they had been running with it ever since. And, as Fletcher commented afterwards, 'If you want to try to take a single when the ball has been hit straight to the cover fielder and get run out, whose fault is that?'

Flintoff said simply: 'Jones was off the field so we're not going to get the worst fielder in the country to replace him, are we?'

'Had I been on the field, I probably would have run him out by yards anyway,' said Jones.

'I've seen our guys run off for a pee and get back on in the space of five minutes,' said Hoggard. 'So if Ricky thought we are all going off for a rub-down he was mistaken. It just shows what pressure can do to a bloke. He didn't like the fact that his side were losing, so he lashed out.'

'You don't go off on one like that if you are calm and in control,' said Strauss. 'We kind of laughed when we saw him shouting at Fletcher. To us, the substitute-fielder thing was just such a minor issue. They lost a wicket through their own stupidity. There is no doubt about it, Australia were feeling the pressure and it was refreshing to see.'

Ponting's fury at getting out would have been exacerbated by the belief that he could have repeated his match-saving innings at Old Trafford, something he alluded to in an official apology to the umpires issued at close of play. By that stage, Australia were 222 for four, still 37 runs short of making England bat again. He said: 'I am very disappointed with my dismissal, given that it was at a crucial stage of the game and I had worked very hard to get to that position. I no doubt let myself down with my reaction, and for that I apologise to those who see me as a role model. My frustration at getting out was compounded by the fact that I was run out by a sub-stitute fielder, an issue that has concerned us throughout this series.' But Ponting knew his public expression of regret might not be enough to save him from disciplinary action from match referee Ranjan Madugalle, who had the power to issue immediate bans.

England ended the day still confident they could press home their advantage, but without Jones in their armoury they knew they needed to take every chance that was offered. In that regard, wicket-keeper Geraint Jones had another moment to forget. 'After having made a contribution with the bat, I was in a position finally to silence the doubters,' he says. 'But then I missed a stumping chance to get Michael Clarke off Ashley Giles, and I had to ride the rollercoaster again. I was feeling good, relaxed. I felt that things were click-ing and then this happened. On TV it looks like it's straight-forward because Clarke's tumbled down the wicket, but I didn't pick it until very late. Ashley bowled it outside leg stump and quite full and Clarke had tried to hit it through the leg side, but it went between bat and pad. So I'm here looking for the ball, expecting it to pass the outside edge, and it's come from in front of his pad in a flash. I was in a great position again but my hands were a fraction too low and it just hit the top of my gloves. And from then on I'm thinking, Well, he's a fairly crucial batsman, how much is this going to cost?'

DAY FOUR: ENGLAND WON BY THREE WICKETS

Vaughan wanted quick wickets, and the priority outlined in the discussions in the hotel the night before was to get at Gilchrist before the new ball was due. But England's skipper was worried. He was a bowler short and was just as concerned about the Aussies scoring at five an over. A couple of sessions of Clarke, Gilchrist and Warne at that rate and England's victory target would no longer be a formality. The official news that Jones was out was no surprise to the home dressing room. The Welshman had been talking positively the previous night, but as he was simultaneously hopping around in a big surgical boot it was clear his Test was over, at least as a bowler. Jones recalls: 'I had spent a pretty painful night and when I woke up in the morning at first I couldn't walk to the toilet. I knew then that was that for my bowling. But I also knew that if it came to it I would go out and bat, whatever the consequences.'

England's bowlers did not make an early breakthrough, but they did ensure that the tourists worked hard for their runs. The crowd grew restless when nobody made an impact with the new ball, but took comfort from the fact that the scoreboard was moving more slowly than it had all series. Nevertheless, a wicketless morning session would have boosted Australian morale and given them a platform from which to accelerate after lunch. Then Hoggard brought the crowd to life just before the break when Clarke went fishing outside off stump once too often. Once again, Vaughan's patient captaincy and England's consistent probing had earned their reward.

Clarke and Katich had put on exactly 100 runs for the fifth wicket, only the second century stand from the Aussies in the series and the first since Lord's, highlighting how well the tourists' much-vaunted batting line-up had been restricted by the England attack. The 48 runs scored before lunch were the fewest in a completed session during the series. Vaughan was more than satisfied that his bowlers had been able to keep Australia in check, and was also relieved that the wicket was not showing any signs of bad behaviour.

However, once play resumed he was less happy. The Australians managed to bat through the whole afternoon session and set England a three-figure target to win. Mistakes in the field were the problem, with the wicket-keeper and England's new star batsman once again the principal culprits. Kevin Pietersen could not hold on to a catch off Kasprowicz at midwicket. It was his sixth drop out of six chances in the series. He remains at a loss to explain his record, but Duncan Fletcher believes, 'At the moment he seems just too pumped, too excited. There may be a slight technical thing as well but the main thing is that he has to learn to settle down and relax.' Then came two Geraint Jones errors. First he dived across Trescothick and put down a catch off Brett Lee that was heading straight to the first slip. Soon after he inadvertently broke the wicket in the process of collecting a throw from Strauss that might have run out the Aussie paceman. The keeper had to watch along with the 15,000 crowd as the error was replayed on the giant screen.

'The first one was instinct, pure instinct,' he says. 'I dived for it because it was right in between Marcus and me and the worst thing would be if we both left it to each other. As for the run out, I was up for a huge appeal off Ashley at the time and I was so convinced it was out that I must have stopped concentrating for an instant. The next thing I knew Strauss had come from nowhere and gone for the run-out. I made to take the ball but just clipped the stumps instead. It doesn't rain. It bloody pours.'

Gilchrist's poor series with the bat continued thanks to more accurate bowling from Hoggard, but Katich and Warne took Australia past 300 before Katich was unluckily adjudged LBW to Harmison. Whether it was going over the top was debatable, but the ball had definitely pitched outside leg stump. Katich was furious at Steve Bucknor's decision and his verbal reaction earned him an appearance alongside his skipper before the match referee later that evening.

Then Warne, with five fours and two sixes, and Lee gave Vaughan more cause for concern before Geraint Jones made amends by stumping Warne off Giles (his first stumping of the year) and catching Kasprowicz off Harmison. When Tait took two crazy strides to the off side, tried to whip the ball through the leg side and was comprehensively castled by Harmison, England faced a victory target of 129.

In the absence of Simon Jones, the England bowling quartet of Flintoff, Hoggard, Harmison and Giles linked arms and took the applause as they led in the side. The smiles on their faces suggested they thought the hard work had been done. Time for a quick shower, a rub-down and a relaxing afternoon in the dressing room before starting the celebrations.

Warne and Lee had other ideas.

The Trent Bridge crowd was already jubilant in advance of what would surely be England's waltz to the winning post. After the nerve-racking finales to the Edgbaston and Old Trafford Tests, the Barmy Army were relieved that this was one match that could be enjoyed without severe risk to physical and mental health. Vaughan, though, knew better. He was grateful for the tea interval between innings to allow his players to focus on the task ahead.

As at Old Trafford, the giant screen came to the aid of those struggling with mental arithmetic and counted down the runs from the very beginning. After five overs, 32 runs had been scored and the target was under three figures. Strauss recalls: 'Before the start of the innings the talk in the dressing room was "Just play the ball and not the situation; don't try to do anything you wouldn't normally do." Then, suddenly, within five overs Trescothick is on 27. I think it was just an adrenaline thing. Even though you've got five sessions to win the match there is something in the back of your mind; you feel that you're so close to victory that anything that's slightly loose you go after. Certainly I felt a bit eager to score; more so than I'd normally be. But as I was still on 1 when he got out I don't suppose anyone could accuse me of getting carried away!'

When Ricky Ponting threw the ball to Warne, the crowd was already chanting, 'Easy, easy ...'

'Then,' Strauss continues, 'when Marcus got out to Warne's first ball, it was like, hold on a second, is there another script here that reads: "Warne comes in and takes a wicket with his first ball and bowls us out"? And when Vaughan got out next over for nought trying to force the ball into the gap Warne had left for him at midwicket and he had taken two wickets for no runs in seven balls and we are 36 for two ... Oh my God. Lee started bowling exceptionally quick, they were giving it everything they'd got, but I'd reached 23 and was just starting to feel comfortable at the crease when I got out.'

> '*When Trescothick played a straight drive for four off Brett Lee at the start of our innings, I thought, This is all right – I'll put my feet up.*'
>
> ANDREW FLINTOFF

When the ball travelled to Michael Clarke off Warne, the Aussies were ecstatic, but initially Strauss stood his ground. The batsman gestured as openly as he felt he could that he wasn't sure the ball had carried. The Aussies didn't like it, but Strauss was not leaving without the umpire's say-so. Aleem Dar consulted with his square-leg colleague Bucknor, and Mark Benson was called into action again. Replays of catches close to the ground are rarely conclusive, and this was no different, but Strauss was soon on his way. The crowd booed when the slow replays were shown on the big screen, but most observers felt the catch looked good at the time.

Pietersen joined Bell. With Flintoff and Jones to come, Bell seemed just the man to provide the anchor for England's innings, so nobody could quite believe it when the Warwickshire man hooked the very first ball of Lee's next over straight down Kasprowicz's throat. The batsman himself felt exactly the same way. He wandered back to the pavilion utterly distraught with the scoreboard reading 57 for four as the crowd worked out that England were not even halfway to their target. 'Watching Trescothick blaze away, we were thinking, We're going to coast this,' he says, 'but the one lesson I have learned above all else from this series is that Australia never give up. That is the reason why they have been number one for so long. And they weren't going quietly now. I was disappointed with the way I got out. If it had been a decent nut then I wouldn't have minded so much, but I felt I'd let people down a little and I started to imagine the reaction to the shot if we went on to lose the match.'

The sight of Super Fred walking out convinced England supporters that while the situation was serious it was not yet critical. 'When Trescothick played a straight drive for four off Brett Lee at the start of our innings, I thought, This is all right – I'll put my feet up,' said Flintoff. 'But it all started unravelling when Warne came on. He is a magician. Brilliant. He looked dangerous every ball. I was a little nervous when I went out to bat, although it's miles better being in the middle than watching from the balcony.'

England's latest sporting superhero was given another noisy welcome but, for once, the fans were not praying for fireworks from him and Pietersen. They were more than happy to watch them run seventy-two singles. The order of the day was sensible shot selection and nothing fancy, and that was precisely the way they played it for three-quarters of an hour. Even Flintoff's hoisting of Warne over wide long-on was carefully controlled.

The giant screen continued to count down the runs required. A huge cheer went up when England passed the halfway point; another when the target was down to 50; and the loudest yet when England reached 100 for four. Surely Vaughan's men were now home and dry. There was no need to take risks; another half a dozen overs of pushing three or four singles an over and the job would be done. But Pietersen had other ideas. Just as Australian heads were dropping, he chased a wide delivery from Lee and was caught behind. That inspired the bowler, who was hurling the ball down at around 95 m.p.h., to find one of the deliveries of the series, a ball that cut back and hit the top of Flintoff's off stump. Lee's reaction, a human starfish roaring with delight, was almost equally impressive. 'He did me all ends up with a ball that beat me for pace and nipped back as well,' recalls Flintoff. 'It would have got me out every day of the week and twice on a Sunday.'

At 111 for six, the nightmare (or dream, depending on your loyalties) was fast becoming a reality.

Ashley Giles joined the last recognised batsman, Geraint Jones, but watched in horror when the keeper advanced down the track and attempted to smack Warne over Kasprowicz. Jones's mood was not improved when some of the crowd let their disappointment get the better of them. He recalls: 'I had felt pretty comfortable against Warne and had used my feet to get to the pitch of the ball with some success in previous innings. Everything felt good about the shot but I

'I just thought: Oh God, if I can have one free rewind in this life, please let me have it now.'
GERAINT JONES IS OUT FOR 3, SECOND INNINGS

just didn't quite get to the ball and sliced it. Had the shot come off, it would have brought the target under 10. But when I saw Kasprowicz under it I knew it was curtains and I just felt desperate. All that had been in my mind was "be there at the end". But all my feelings and thoughts turned to dread. One or two of the crowd got stuck into me big time. "What did you think you were doing?" shouted one. "Don't you realise he's the best bowler in the world?" That made it ten times worse. You feel like saying, "Do you think I don't know that?" I just thought: Oh God, if I can have one free rewind in this life, please let me have it now.'

When Matthew Hoggard walked out to join Giles, 13 were still required and the mood inside the England dressing room was unlike anything the players had felt before: a mixture of chaos, frenzy and excitement laced with panic and near hysteria. Flintoff, sick with tension, did not know where to put himself. At first he tried the showers, next to Vaughan. Neither man could bear to watch and both were kept informed of events by Simon Jones. When Flintoff finally emerged he sat down next to Strauss and began punching and squeezing the opener's leg so hard that the Middlesex man was left with a cluster of bruises after the match. He was saved from further punishment only when Vaughan asked him to strap on his pads to run for Jones if required.

The Welshman, preparing to go out and swing off his good leg, was left in no doubt as to who would be in charge. 'Posh lad Strauss came up to me and said: "Now, Jones, you listen to me. I'll do all the calling. You just hit the ball, see, and whatever you do, don't try to run." I said, "No worries, chief. I can't actually walk."'

Strauss was rather less composed than he seemed. 'It was the recipe for disaster. All I could think was: What if we need a single to win and I cock it up?' Steve Harmison was so nervous that his knees were pumping up and down like steam pistons. There was nothing left of his nails. Kevin Pietersen had almost chewed through his wristband. Geraint Jones said: 'No matter how I felt personally, I knew I had to get out on the balcony to support the lads. But when I got out there I found it almost impossible to watch.'

Harmison was due to be the next man in. Television pictures showed him apparently close to nervous meltdown. 'I think if it had got down to me, we might have been struggling,' he admits. 'First they might not have been able to get me out of the dressing room. Or if they had, I might have got to the bottom of the stairs and turned right into the car park rather than left on to the field.'

For an hour, England fans had been fearing the worst. Now they were preparing for it. In the series so far Giles had scored a grand total of 8 runs off Warne and lost his wicket four times. Hoggard, it was said, had been working hard at his batting. Most of his colleagues wondered what on earth for. On the field the Yorkshireman was simply relieved to be in the action at last, though not many shared his enthusiasm. 'I just knew that we wouldn't do it with only one or two wickets down. But I didn't think it would be me out there at the end. I had spent the rest of the time in the back of the physio's room sat behind the curtain. I was dreaming up all sorts of ailments that needed treating so I wouldn't have to watch. It was appalling. But when I got out to the wicket I thought, This ain't too bad. Thirteen to win? I can stay here until tomorrow and get 13.'

> ' ... *everyone around me was smiling: Katich, Ponting, Warne. On the outside I was smiling, too. But inside I was churning.'*
>
> ASHLEY GILES FACES SHANE WARNE IN THE FINAL OVER AT TRENT BRIDGE, NEEDING 2 RUNS TO WIN

Giles recalls: 'For us, there was no thought at all of anyone batting after us. There was no thought of getting out, just of 13 runs.'

Every one of those runs was greeted as though it was the winning one, especially the two no-balls signalled by Bucknor when Lee overstepped the front crease. But the crowd knew that Warne and Lee were still on fire and feared that either was capable of finishing this match with a hat-trick. Then, with 8 needed, out of a glorious, clear blue sky, came the moment Hoggard will carry with him for the rest of his days: a cover drive for four off Brett Lee made in tailenders' heaven. 'I was thinking: If the ball is straight, I might get an inside edge and squeeze it away for a single. If it's short, I'm not playing it. And if it's wide, I'm not playing it either. Then he bowled me this wide full toss and I forgot everything I had told myself. I just brought the bat down on it and bunted it off to the boundary.'

At the other end, Giles looked on in awe. 'I have never seen Hoggard play a shot like that. To cover-drive a guy bowling 90 m.p.h. in-duckers. Extraordinary.' Then he heard himself saying: 'Just 4 more to go now. Come on mate, do it again. Let's get this over with. Save me.'

But nothing could save Giles from facing the next over from Warne. At the start of it, England needed just 2 more runs. To Giles, it felt like 200. 'We came together before the over started and I said I would try to play a maiden against Warne because both of us felt slightly more confident that we could use Lee's pace to nick a couple. Or rather Warne was bowling so well that neither of us had any confidence whatsoever that we could survive against him. I'm convinced Shane was trying to set me up for an LBW shout. He brought up deep square-leg and deep midwicket into the ring of fielders saving one, challenging me to try to slog the ball over them. But I was determined to resist. Then he bowled me a full toss just outside leg stump and my eyes lit up.' Giles connected cleanly and, up on the dressing-room balcony, skipper and close friend Vaughan thought that must be the match. He raised his fist, ready to punch the air, then collapsed in a heap as the ball hit short-leg Simon Katich on the foot.

'Prior to that ball, the tension was unbearable,' says Giles. 'But after it everyone around me was smiling: Katich, Ponting, Warne. On the outside I was smiling, too. But inside I was churning. Next delivery I had a drive at him and, in the moment I missed the ball, I was convinced I was out – bowled. I was waiting for the sound of the ball hitting the stumps. I just *knew* it would come. But there was no sound, nothing. The replay came up on the big screen and I had to watch it to convince myself I hadn't been bowled. Somehow the ball had missed the wood by a fag-paper.

'And then it happened. Warne just over-pitched a ball on my leg stump, and I got enough bat on it to send it past the fielders. There was a slight delay before I set off and I knew it was going for four, but I thought we'd better run the two anyway, just to make doubly sure.

'What do I remember about the rest of the day? The look on people's faces, the joy. Harmison wrestling me to the ground when I got back to the dressing room. Seeing my mum afterwards in floods of tears: she reckoned she cried for about twenty minutes. Sometimes you just don't realise what those around you are going through. My wife Stine reckons I am a nightmare at home when the pressure is on. But seeing what this meant to her meant so much to me.'

For Strauss, 'The relief, the absolute relief, when Giles hit that ball through midwicket was incredible. I think it was felt by everyone in the country.'

'I actually got a hug from Duncan Fletcher,' recalls Hoggard. 'Now *that's* what you practise your batting for!'

And if anyone needed reminding what victory meant to England's players, one look at the expression on the face of Flintoff would have provided it. Simon Jones had the best view. 'I've never seen a guy so emotional as he was in that moment,' he said. 'There was so much within him and it was all over his "Fearsome Freddie" face: wild, berserk, almost scary. It was as though he were in a trance; it all meant so much to him.'

All the England team were soon down on the field for the post-match ceremony. The crowd cheered every utterance from first Ponting and then Vaughan. Flintoff, inevitably, was the Man of the Match, and the fans went eerily silent so they could hear every word as he was interviewed by Michael Atherton. The England backroom team, led by Duncan Fletcher, stayed out on the balcony and clapped along with everyone else.

After the formalities, Vaughan's team went on a lap of honour, primarily to applaud the fans who had been through the mill once again. 'Being in the dressing room was much tougher than being out in the middle,' says the captain. 'It's easier when you are out on the pitch. Watching in the dressing room was very hard, very tense and nerve-racking because you can't control how the batsmen play. On the pitch, you are in your own little bubble. After the character the guys had shown and their efforts over the previous few days, I would have hated for them not to get there. Andrew Flintoff had become a real sporting hero, we were playing good cricket, but it was too early to say if we would win the Ashes. The final Test looked certain to be another epic game because neither team could go out and play for a draw, even if they wanted to.'

Every England player hugged Hoggard, and England's swing bowler was so determined to enjoy his moment as a batting hero that he didn't leave the dressing room until ten o'clock. The players were in such desperate need of a steadying beer or two that Flintoff used his teeth to remove several bottle tops.

Ricky Ponting was defiant afterwards about his side's chances of retaining the Ashes at the Brit Oval and about his attack on England's use of substitutes. The ICC match referee, Sri Lankan Ranjan Madugalle, docked him 75 per cent of his match fee (around £3,400). Had the series not been in the balance and such a humdinger, Ponting might even have been suspended because of his behaviour. Katich also got off somewhat lightly, being fined half his match fee. But none of this could detract from another amazing Ashes Test.

England, 2–1 up, were in unfamiliar Ashes territory. So were Australia, of course. 'I've never been in this situation before,' admitted Ponting, 'when we're going into the last Test having to win to draw the series. It might not be a bad thing for us, to tell the truth, just to go out and play the brand of cricket we've played for a long time. There's a bit of pressure now.'

He could say that again.

Fourth Test, Trent Bridge, Nottingham

25, 26, 27, 28 August 2005

Result England won by 3 wickets   **Toss** England

Umpires Aleem Dar (Pak) and S.A.Bucknor (WI)   **Match Referee** R.S.Madugalle (SL)
Man of the Match A.Flintoff

England First Innings		R	M	B	4s	6s
M.E.Trescothick	b Tait	65	138	111	8	1
A.J.Strauss	c Hayden b Warne	35	99	64	4	0
*M.P.Vaughan	c Gilchrist b Ponting	58	138	99	9	0
I.R.Bell	c Gilchrist b Tait	3	12	5	0	0
K.P.Pietersen	c Gilchrist b Lee	45	131	108	6	0
A.Flintoff	lbw b Tait	102	201	132	14	1
+G.O.Jones	c & b Kasprowicz	85	205	149	8	0
A.F.Giles	lbw b Warne	15	45	35	3	0
M.J.Hoggard	c Gilchrist b Warne	10	46	28	1	0
S.J.Harmison	st Gilchrist b Warne	2	9	6	0	0
S.P.Jones	not out	15	32	27	3	0
Extras	b 1, lb 15, w 1, nb 25	42				
Total	all out, 123.1 overs, 537 mins	477				

FoW   1–105 Strauss (22nd ov), 2–137 Trescothick (31st ov), 3–146 Bell (35th ov), 4–213 Vaughan (56th ov),
5–241 Pietersen (65th ov), 6–418 Flintoff (104th ov), 7–450 G.O.Jones (113th ov), 8–450 Giles (114th
ov), 9–454 Harmison (116th ov), 10–477 Hoggard (124th ov)

Bowling	O	M	R	W
Lee	32	2	131	1
Kasprowicz	32	3	122	1
Tait	24	4	97	3
Warne	29.1	4	102	4
Ponting	6	2	9	1

Australia First Innings

		R	M	B	4s	6s
J.L.Langer	c Bell b Hoggard	27	95	59	5	0
M.L.Hayden	lbw b Hoggard	7	41	27	1	0
*R.T.Ponting	lbw b S.P.Jones	1	6	6	0	0
D.R.Martyn	lbw b Hoggard	1	4	3	0	0
M.J.Clarke	lbw b Harmison	36	93	53	5	0
S.M.Katich	c Strauss b S.P.Jones	45	91	66	7	0
+A.C.Gilchrist	c Strauss b Flintoff	27	58	36	3	1
S.K.Warne	c Bell b S.P.Jones	0	2	1	0	0
B.Lee	c Bell b S.P.Jones	47	51	44	5	3
M.S.Kasprowicz	b S.P.Jones	5	8	7	1	0
S.W.Tait	not out	3	27	9	0	0
Extras	lb 2, w 1, nb 16	19				
Total	all out, 49.1 overs, 247 mins	218				

FoW   1–20 Hayden (10th ov), 2–21 Ponting (11th ov), 3–22 Martyn (12th ov), 4–58 Langer (20th ov), 5–99 Clarke (31st ov), 6–157 Katich (40th ov), 7–157 Warne (40th ov), 8–163 Gilchrist (43rd ov), 9–175 Kasprowicz (44th ov), 10–218 Lee (50th ov)

Bowling	O	M	R	W
Harmison	9	1	48	1
Hoggard	15	3	70	3
S.P.Jones	14.1	4	44	5
Flintoff	11	1	54	1

Australia Second Innings

		R	M	B	4s	6s
J.L.Langer	c Bell b Giles	61	149	112	8	0
M.L.Hayden	c Giles b Flintoff	26	57	41	4	0
*R.T.Ponting	run out (sub G.J.Pratt)	48	137	89	3	1
D.R.Martyn	c G.O.Jones b Flintoff	13	56	30	1	0
M.J.Clarke	c G.O.Jones b Hoggard	56	209	170	6	0
S.M.Katich	lbw b Harmison	59	262	183	4	0
+A.C.Gilchrist	lbw b Hoggard	11	20	11	2	0
S.K.Warne	st G.O.Jones b Giles	45	68	42	5	2
B.Lee	not out	26	77	39	3	0
M.S.Kasprowicz	c G.O.Jones b Harmison	19	30	26	1	0
S.W.Tait	b Harmison	4	20	16	1	0
Extras	b 1, lb 4, nb 14	19				
Total	all out, 124 overs, 548 mins	387				

FoW 1-50 Hayden (14th ov), 2-129 Langer (34th ov), 3-155 Ponting (45th ov), 4-161 Martyn (47th ov), 5-261 Clarke (95th ov), 6-277 Gilchrist (99th ov), 7-314 Katich (108th ov), 8-342 Warne (113th ov), 9-373 Kasprowicz (120th ov), 10-387 Tait (124th ov)

Bowling	O	M	R	W
Hoggard	27	7	72	2
S.P.Jones	4	0	15	0
Harmison	30	5	93	3
Flintoff	29	4	83	2
Giles	28	3	107	2
Bell	6	2	12	0

England Second Innings		R	M	B	4s	6s
M.E.Trescothick	c Ponting b Warne	27	24	22	4	0
A.J.Strauss	c Clarke b Warne	23	68	37	3	0
*M.P.Vaughan	c Hayden b Warne	0	8	6	0	0
I.R.Bell	c Kasprowicz b Lee	3	38	20	0	0
K.P.Pietersen	c Gilchrist b Lee	23	51	34	3	0
A.Flintoff	b Lee	26	63	34	3	0
+G.O.Jones	c Kasprowicz b Warne	3	25	13	0	0
A.F.Giles	not out	7	30	17	0	0
M.J.Hoggard	not out	8	20	13	1	0
S.J.Harmison						
S.P.Jones						
Extras	lb 4, nb 5	9				
Total	7 wickets, 31.5 overs, 168 mins	129				

DNB S.J.Harmison, S.P.Jones

FoW 1–32 Trescothick (6th ov), 2–36 Vaughan (8th ov), 3–57 Strauss (14th ov), 4–57 Bell (15th ov), 5–103 Pietersen (25th ov), 6–111 Flintoff (27th ov), 7–116 G.O.Jones (28th ov)

Bowling	O	M	R	W
Lee	12	0	51	3
Kasprowicz	2	0	19	0
Warne	13.5	2	31	4
Tait	4	0	24	0

Close of Play   Day 1 England 229–4 (Pietersen 33*, Flintoff 8*)
Day 2 England 477, Australia 99–5 (Katich 20*)
Day 3 Australia 218 and 222–4 (Clarke 39*, Katich 24*)

FIFTH TEST
THE OVAL

PREVIEW

On the morning of Thursday 8 September, the first day of the final Test of the 2005 Ashes series, the *Daily Telegraph* told its readers: 'After 47 sessions, 5,334 minutes, 4,693 runs, 7,306 balls and 152 wickets, watched by a TV audience of 100 million, one match will decide who wins a four-inch trophy … The Ultimate Test.'

At the other end of Britain's media spectrum, in pride of place on page one of the *Sun*, Andrew Flintoff pledged on behalf of 'England's Heroes': 'I promise all *Sun* readers that every drop of sweat we have in our bodies will be left at The Oval. We will give everything we have and more to win back the Ashes.'

For the first time in decades (or possibly ever), cricket featured on the front page of every other national newspaper, too. After urging, 'Come Urn England!' the *Daily Mirror* claimed it had discovered the centre of the universe. A grainy, long-range aerial photograph showed it to be The Oval's Test strip.

So no pressure there then, lads.

At breakfast in the restaurant of their hotel, the City Grange overlooking the Tower of London, the mood among the players was subdued but resolute. Michael Vaughan, as usual, had slept soundly. Some of his colleagues had not: Matthew Hoggard admitted to being 'on and off'. In the team meeting the previous evening the captain had stressed: 'This is what we have prepared for. This is what we have waited for. Enjoy it.'

As they say in sport, that was a tough ask. For no matter how they tried to approach the next five days as just another Test match, assuredly it was not. For example, a two-bedroomed penthouse flat with grandstand views of the ground from a decked terrace had just been let for an astonishing £23,000 for the five days. With every seat for the match sold out for months, wealthy cricket fans had forked out that sum to watch the action from the best seat *outside* the house. Another flat in the same block in Oval Mansions, formerly owned by Lambeth Council, was rented for a snip at £8,000, though that price reflected the restricted views on offer. According to the letting agent: 'Flats like this would normally fetch no more than £500 per week.'

Cricket fever even spread to Whitehall, possibly for the first time since John Major's election defeat in 1997. Tony Blair sent a goodwill message, while Home Secretary Charles Clarke was planning something more practical: he hinted that he would use his discretion to override technical objections to Duncan Fletcher's fourteen-year struggle for a British passport. The principal technicality was that Fletcher had not spent enough time in the country because he was generally engaged every winter on England's overseas tours, which seemed to show something of a lack of logic on the part of the Immigration Service.

> '*This is what we have prepared for. This is what we have waited for. Enjoy it.*'
> MICHAEL VAUGHAN
> SENDS HIS TEAM OUT FOR
> 'THE ULTIMATE TEST'

Fletcher's footballing equivalent, Sven-Göran Eriksson,

under fire after England's 1–0 World Cup defeat by Northern Ireland the previous evening, had been due to attend, but he sent his apologies. One look out of the window of his Regent's Park home at the posse of photographers swarming around and he'd thought better of attending his first cricket match. David Beckham, the man formerly known as the biggest name in British sport, conveyed his best wishes to one England team that seemed to know how to win no matter what the opposition.

The build-up had begun from the moment the teams had left Nottingham eleven days before. Hoggard, prior to this series a household name only in his own home, discovered the true meaning of fame when the staff in his local Burger King refused to let him pay. 'Win the Ashes and you can have free burgers for life,' they told him. Now there's an incentive.

Meanwhile, in a desperate battle to be fit for the final Test of a series in which he had become England's 'overnight sensation', Simon Jones was spending between two and three hours a day in a compression chamber. 'It was like being in bloody *Top Gun*,' said the Welshman. 'Stuck in there with a pilot's mask shoved on my head, sitting in pressure equivalent to being sixty feet underwater with your nose going and your ears popping. The bloke in charge told me that when they send some guys down to fifty metres they go completely bonkers. The oxygen and pressure are supposed to promote the repair of soft tissue, but it was bloody horrible. Name, rank and serial number, though – that's all they got from me.

'Seriously, I was in a bit of emotional turmoil, wondering, Am I going to be fit?'

Jones was named in the squad on the Sunday morning, as were Paul Collingwood and James Anderson, as cover in place of regular twelfth man Chris Tremlett. Chairman of selectors David Graveney explained: 'Chris's involvement with the Test squad has meant limited opportunities for him with Hampshire in recent weeks, and as a consequence we feel that he is not at the top of his game at present.'

Ian Bell, who had collapsed at the wicket with severe cramp in Warwickshire's defeat by Hampshire in the Cheltenham & Gloucester Final at Lord's the day before, was passed fit to play. Jones, in the end, was not, but he still had a defiant message: 'They won't beat us. Not in the form we are in and with the confidence we've got.'

Every man and his dog was asked for his opinion on whether England could finally, after all the years of pain, win back the urn. Among them were the four English captains who had managed to do it, and were still around to be interviewed. Each, in his own way, offered views that demanded to be taken seriously.

Mike Gatting said: 'At Trent Bridge, England were in charge from the very first ball. For the third Test, we dominated the Aussies. The strength of the team is that every player contributed. Matthew Hoggard had a huge performance, taking key wickets. I was chuffed for Matthew and Ashley Giles as they have had a fair amount of criticism.

'There is not much that hasn't been written about Freddie; another powerhouse performance from the best all-round cricketer in the world. Simon Jones will be bitterly disappointed. He has had a great series and we will all sweat on his fitness. If he doesn't make it, I think Paul Collingwood deserves his chance.

'The argument about the use of substitute fielders has the ring of a team who are struggling for form. It is within the letter of the law and England are entitled to continue with this policy. The Australian team need to tighten up on their discipline and focus on the final Test rather than the smaller side issues.

'I will be the happiest man in the ground if I can finally hand the mantle of the last England captain to win the Ashes to Michael Vaughan!'

Mike Brearley offered: 'Michael Vaughan's England have the look of a serious hunting pack. Their pleasure in each other's success is palpable. There seems to be a respect for each other so that each person's moment in the sun is enjoyed all round; no one feels his nose out of joint if he is not for the time being in the limelight.

'Vaughan has shown himself to be an assured tactical captain, willing to experiment in exciting ways. Let us celebrate a Test series against Australia in which we are winning not only the man-to-man duels but also the overall tactical battles.'

According to Ray Illingworth: 'England have to make a major decision for The Oval Test. Do they go for a draw or a win? They will be making a mistake if they settle for the former. Everything should be geared to winning this one. That way they can maintain the positive momentum they have established in the first four Ashes Tests.'

Finally, David Gower believed: 'The hardest thing for England will be to isolate the game from its context. At no stage must they allow themselves to think, the Ashes are at stake. The players must stick to the positive approach that has got them to this point and believe in it because it is working.

'What makes England's performances in this series so special is that after their heavy defeat in the first Test at Lord's so many people must have feared they had blown their chance. But the tension at times has been almost unbearable in the last three Tests for two reasons: first, because so much has been riding on each result; and second, because this Australian team is so good that you know it is a case of kill or be killed.

'The England attack has not allowed Australia's top six to perform. Whereas in the past England captains have sometimes changed the bowlers but the bowling hasn't changed, now the variety and quality of the bowlers mean they all offer something different.

'What will it mean if England win the Ashes? You've got to understand that there are twenty-five-year-olds out there asking, "Have we *ever* won the Ashes?" So I could be sitting in the Sky studio trying to interview people knowing I'm the only sober man in England!'

The news from Glenn McGrath, in his regular Sunday

paper column, was that he would 'definitely play'. However, the Australian management refused to be quite so upbeat about the champion fast bowler. They were cautiously optimistic but insisted no decision had yet been taken on the fitness of his elbow.

Matthew Hayden was the first to bang the Aussie drum. After making 150 retired against Essex at Chelmsford he announced: 'What's gone before means nothing. The Ashes are on the line. The pressure is off us. We can just go and play our game now and if we play how we can, it will be better than England. No doubt about it.'

Shane Warne appeared on a late-night BBC TV chat show hosted by the flamboyant comedian Graham Norton and also featuring American comedienne Ruby Wax and model Jerry Hall. Wax spent most of the evening belittling him, while the leg-spinner's on-air suggestion that he and the former Mrs Jagger should meet after the show seemed not to elicit the desired response. Richie Benaud, prior to commentating on his final Test in England, preferred an afternoon session with Richard and Judy.

Back to serious business the following day, Warne warned: 'The numbers have been pretty good, but however well I've been batting and bowling, that's irrelevant. Now everything comes down to one match, and these are the situations I thrive on.'

On the eve of the match William Hill's spokesman said £50 million had been wagered since the start of the series. He added: 'All cricket betting records have already been smashed. Tomorrow will be the single biggest betting day that cricket has ever seen.'

As if all that were not enough hype, news then came from the Marylebone Cricket Club that, whatever the result at The Oval, the tiny, delicate, irreplaceable Ashes urn would be flown to Australia during England's winter tour of 2006–07. There it would be exhibited for only the second time since 1882. Virgin boss Sir Richard Branson insisted the Ashes would be well looked after on one of his planes: 'The urn will be given the full, award-winning Virgin Atlantic Upper Class service on its way to Australia, with complimentary limos to and from the airport and our famous in-flight entertainment. I'll even ask our beauty therapists to give it a full rubdown and polish.' Steady on!

All that remained was for the umpires, Billy Bowden and Rudi Koertzen, and ICC match referee Ranjan Madugalle to be scrupulously searched by one of the 500 security guards on duty as they made their way into the arena to officiate in probably the most important cricket match ever played in Britain. Just as, according to the *Evening Standard*, Warne had been after he had inadvertently set off an alarm on the way out of a high-street shop the evening before. (An assistant had forgotten to remove the tag on an item he had bought.)

By the time Vaughan spun the coin for Ponting to call, the 23,000 inside the ground and the millions watching on TV or listening to *Test Match Special* were already on tenterhooks. Everyone was experiencing the same nerve-tingling mixture of anticipation and knife-edge tension that had forced millions to watch the climax to the Trent Bridge Test either from behind the sofa or through cracks in their interlocked fingers. So when Channel Four's Mark Nicholas thrust his microphone towards the home captain first, the roar that greeted the news that he had won the toss told its own story. A nation joyously celebrated that round one, or maybe just the weigh-in, had gone to England. Then celebration turned to relief that the anxious wait was finally over.

One match to decide who wins the Ashes. The Ultimate Test.

DAY ONE: ENGLAND 319 FOR 7

In the week before the final Test began at The Oval, Stine Giles, the Norwegian-born wife of everyone's favourite unsung hero Ashley, had a premonition. 'She woke up in the middle of the night,' recounts the spinner, 'and said she had just had this really weird dream. She said, "All you lot were on top of a bus, waving." I told her: "Well, that's the plan, apparently. If we win the Ashes, they're talking about us going on an open-top bus ride through the centre of London." She went a bit quiet and then said: "I had absolutely no idea."'

Mind you, at least one member of the team had had quite enough of predicting the future. According to Andrew Flintoff: 'It was getting a bit much, to be honest. I know the ECB had to start thinking ahead because you can't just pull these things out of thin air, but it was as though the press and the public thought we'd already done it. All the discussion about these plans being made, the bus ride and such like, it didn't really help us at all.'

The same thought had occurred to quite a few observers, which is why, alongside 'open', 'top', 'bus', and 'celebration', the word of the moment was 'hubris'. Dictionary definition: 'arrogant pride or presumption'. And it's anyone's guess what the players truly thought of the frantic attempts to encourage everyone in the country to stand up and sing 'Jerusalem' before the start of play.

But while some of England's supporters might have been getting carried away, there was absolutely no danger of that feeling spreading to the dressing room. The team knew that to overcome Australia they would almost certainly have to carry on beating them until the very last ball of this very last match. Their first target was clear cut: having won the toss, they had to do their utmost to bat Australia out of the game.

When Marcus Trescothick and Andrew Strauss made their way to the crease that morning they may have been trying to put out of their minds the context of the game. But how was that possible? After all, it was universally agreed that this was not only England's most important Test match since 1953, but the greatest sporting event in the country since the 1966 World Cup Final.

Strauss admits: 'It was kind of scary, knowing that this could be it. Knowing that if we batted well enough as a side we could have the Ashes in our hands. Try walking out there without that thought crossing your mind. With each game our nerves had become a little more frayed. At least our task was well defined. In fact, it couldn't have been clearer.

'We had had success against Australia by taking the game to them, being positive and trying to put them under pressure. By looking to draw a game you are only applying pressure on yourselves. We were in a similar situation in South Africa in that final Test at Centurion and it almost did us in. We had learned our lesson.'

Indeed they had. From the moment when Glenn McGrath, finally restored to 100 per cent fitness, sent down the first ball, the openers calmed all England's nerves with some scintillating stroke-play. It was business as usual for a pair who, since managing just 10 for the first wicket on the opening day at Lord's, had consistently set solid platforms for the side with two century stands and two fifties. Here they appeared to be cruising. On a flat pitch and under bright sunshine, they moved serenely past 80 after just 17 overs; not bad for a one-day county match, let alone for the most important, nerve-rackingly tense and mind-blowingly significant Test either of them would probably ever play in. The crowd was in festive mood, but Australia suddenly decided to dampen it.

Little more than an hour had gone before Ricky Ponting was once again forced to throw the ball to Shane Warne on the first morning of a Test. And nobody cruises against the greatest leg-spinner the world has ever seen, 'twilight years' or not. During the next sixteen overs, he transformed the match as perhaps only he could. Despite his dozen years in the Australian Test team, despite his 600-plus wickets, despite working the miracle time and time again, every new challenge is presented as the one that will finally defeat him. Yet those new challenges invariably bring out the best in him and keep him on the top of his game.

His first over went for 9 runs, but then he found his rhythm. Trescothick was well caught at slip by Hayden, 6 runs short of becoming the first batsman in world cricket to reach 1,000 Test runs in 2005. Vaughan was caught at short mid-wicket by Michael Clarke, unable to resist the carrot Warne had dangled in front of him. Bell was trapped LBW again, this time for his first Test duck. After the unrestrained euphoria that had developed during the opening stand, a deathly quiet had descended over The Oval. Three wickets had gone for 22 runs, and 104 for 3 was nothing like the score that England had anticipated.

Vaughan says of Warne: 'He is a thinking bowler with a great cricket brain. The way he changes the field, the way he changes the angle of delivery, opens you up then bowls a tad faster. You know you need to score off him or you can just get stuck, so he gives you opportunities to do so. But those opportunities also carry a risk. He is a wily old fox.'

Warne made it four wickets in 26 balls for 22 runs (131 for 4) when Pietersen, sporting £50,000 diamond earrings under his freshly retouched white streak, tried to squirt a full delivery through midwicket and was bowled. This was Warne at his brilliant best, tempting the ever-aggressive Pietersen, challenging him to rise to the bait. When the ball passed the bat and crashed into the stumps, the look on Pietersen's face as he momentarily stood his ground suggested he couldn't believe he'd fallen for it. But his admiration for his Hampshire colleague and friend is just as deep as Vaughan's: 'He was sensational throughout the series – a true legend. If it hadn't been for him, we would have won the series by Trent Bridge.'

This was the first time in his 128 Tests that Warne had taken the first four wickets to fall, and England's situation was now serious. Enter Flintoff to join Strauss, who had just reached his fifty.

The secret of England's batting success all summer was that they never tried to defend. Even when in trouble with wickets falling, the team kept the scoreboard ticking over. Strauss had been in the England side for fifteen months, but this was the first time he had ever batted with Flintoff, who was hit on the head by Lee early on. Nevertheless, the pair had no problem communicating or putting England back in a comfortable position. The Oval crowd were roaring again as the runs kept flowing, with Strauss scoring just as quickly as Flintoff. They eventually took their fifth-wicket partnership to 143, England's second highest of the series. En route, Strauss reached his seventh Test century by clip-

> '*He is a thinking bowler with a great cricket brain. The way he changes the field, the way he changes the angle of delivery, opens you up then bowls a tad faster ... He is a wily old fox.*'
> MICHAEL VAUGHAN
> ON SHANE WARNE

ping Lee to the midwicket boundary, then set a new high-jump record for international cricket as he swished his bat through the air. Only Don Bradman (twelve), George Headley (ten) and Arthur Morris (nine) have scored more hundreds in their first nineteen Tests. Strauss was also the first player to hit two hundreds in this series. Flintoff cantered to his fifty with three boundaries off Warne before heaving him into the new £25-million OCS Stand at the Vauxhall End.

At 274 for 4, a total of 400-plus looked well within reach. Once again England's supporters began dreaming their and Stine's dream. But while Flintoff and Strauss had hauled England clear of immediate danger in just over two and a half glorious hours, the early clatter of wickets had left them vulnerable should they suffer another wobble. And they did: McGrath made the breakthrough when Flintoff was caught behind.

In came Paul Collingwood, the Durham all-rounder preferred to Lancashire swing bowler James Anderson to replace Simon Jones. He admits he was not in the greatest shape: 'There were nerves leading up to the match because of the uncertainty over whether I would be playing,' he recalls. 'I had tried so hard in the nets to show the management I was up for it. I was desperate to play. The tension eased briefly when I was told I was in, but then you start running through all the possibilities of what might happen, good and bad. Then, when the tickets for wives and friends were handed out and the name on my envelope was "Eleventh man", I managed a bit of a cackle.

'I think I slept all right the night before, although I had been paparazzied for the first time, photographed on a pavement café with the skipper! But when I got up in the morning I just wanted to get on to the field, get into the game somehow. In the event we won the toss and I had to wait my turn, and as the day wore on the feeling within me got worse and worse. I had sweaty palms. I couldn't catch my breath. Just waiting around and watching, I was an absolute mess. As much as you tell yourself, "Calm down, come on, you can cope with it, you're going to do well," stuff like that, it was a horrible feeling, under my ribs and in my stomach, and it just wouldn't go away. And I was yawning all the time …

'I've never been so nervous in my life. The thing is, I knew how crucial it was and maybe I felt it more than the other guys because, whereas they had been involved, I had had to suffer it all on TV. I could see from the pictures how the public were reacting and living every moment, and sometimes you don't get that feeling when you're actually involved in the games. All I knew was that this was going to be the biggest thing in my life.

'After all that, when I finally got out in the middle, I was fine. Or, at least, I *thought* I was. Before I went out to bat I was talking to Duncan Fletcher about facing Shaun Tait, and he said: "He bowls a good yorker." He must have thought I was a candidate because he told me the same thing four or five times!

'I'd certainly been listening to Fletcher, but it's one thing listening and another playing a ball like that. It did reverse-swing a lot and obviously I was trying to keep my foot out of the way, but it still managed to hit me on the toe. It was disappointing to be given out. Looking at the replays, it probably wasn't going to hit the stumps, but that didn't make me feel any better. I was trying to warrant a place in the side. I was trying to prove to people that I should be playing. So I was gutted not to have made more of a contribution in that vital situation.'

Worse was to follow for England, when Strauss fell before stumps. He had batted beautifully and commandingly, but he became Warne's fifth victim when Katich dived forward for a spectacular bat/pad catch. Strauss had been in for seven minutes short of six hours and had hit seventeen boundaries.

Warne showed the ball to The Oval crowd to celebrate his ninth five-wicket haul against England and his thirty-first in all. Five days before his thirty-sixth birthday, he bowled thirty-four overs in the day. Australia took the new ball, but no further wickets. The nation reflected on a good day that might not be quite good enough.

Strauss, though, felt he had more than stood up to Warne's early-season assertion that he was his new 'Daryll'. 'That is all part of Shane's kidology,' stresses the Middlesex man. 'He tries to put pressure on you with the way he bowls and some of the stuff he says. It's important you put it out of your mind and try to concentrate on your batting, and I did that. Warne was awesome all series and it was no different here. It was a fantastic effort to take five wickets on the first day. In terms of importance, though, this was probably the best innings I've ever played.'

DAY TWO: ENGLAND 373 ALL OUT; AUSTRALIA 112 FOR 0

England failed to make it to 400, but 373 wasn't too shabby after Geraint Jones had been bowled by Lee early on the second morning. Once again the home team had cause to thank

Ashley Giles for his contribution with the bat. Heroic amid the carnage of that potential Hammer Horror show at Trent Bridge, here Giles batted for two hours for his 32 and was disappointed to be given out LBW by umpire Bowden from a heavily spun Warne ball that appeared to be turning well past the off stump. England's spinner scored 17 runs in his ninth-wicket stand of 20 with Hoggard (who took 30 balls to get off the mark), but Harmison played the dominant role in their final partnership, scoring 20 out of 28, including four boundaries which Lee found frustrating and the crowd thought hilarious. Giles's wicket gave Warne 34 in the series, equalling his record tally from 1993, but the Englishman was entitled to feel he had done more than his bit.

'Perhaps I was riding on the confidence I'd taken from Trent Bridge,' says Giles. 'I'd been disappointing with the bat, generally, at the beginning of the series, but I actually felt all right and just played. The key was to edge the score up as high as we could. Hoggard was great – he gets them so frustrated – and then Harmison just took over at the end. He said to me, "If they pitch it up, they'll get me out. But if it's short I'm going to have a go at it." He did and it came off, and in that situation every single run is absolutely priceless.'

Then, just when Australia needed to most, they reminded everyone present why beating them at cricket is about as straightforward as pouring water uphill. For the first time in the series, Justin Langer and Matthew Hayden batted like England fans had feared they would from the very start: brilliantly. From the time they came in, seven overs before lunch, their plan was chillingly obvious: take the sting out of the England attack on the best batting wicket in the country, lay the foundations for a total of between 500 and 600, cry, 'Havoc!' and let slip the dogs of Warne. They would not be parted until tea the following day. However, with unsettled weather promised, some critics believed not all the time they took to amass their runs was well used.

Prior to 2005, Hayden had a reputation for massive hitting.

If there is such a thing as 'intimidatory batting', he was the master of it. But this series was different. Plans for having him caught driving early in his innings or LBW to Hoggard's inswing had worked so well that his top score going into this final game was just 36. Langer, on the other hand, had become the top-order wicket England most cherished, and here he showed why by hitting two big sixes off Giles's first over and scoring twice as fast as his partner. Then, out of nowhere, with Langer on 53 and poised to push on, England finally created a chance to break the partnership.

Collingwood recalls: 'The ball wasn't doing that much. I was talking to Vaughan after every delivery. He was asking whether it was reversing, whether it was going conventional, and I was saying, "It was doing a little bit of reverse at the start and then one went conventional," so we didn't really know what the hell was going on.

'I was just trying to get the ball down the other end at a decent pace and I remember he'd missed the one before on a shorter length than I was actually looking for. He went for a cut and it was a bit too close to him. So I thought, Well, let's see if he'll chase it again. I bowled pretty much the exact same ball, he got the edge and I was so excited. I thought, Well, that's out, because it was going to Trescothick, who has great hands. Then I saw it pop out of his hands. He dived but he hadn't really seen it.

'The skipper obviously wasn't as impressed as I was, because after my four-over spell was up, he never let the ball anywhere near me for the rest of the match. Gutted!'

As they came out to begin the final session of the day, it seemed inevitable that Australia would make England rue that error. They were on 112 for no wicket and in a perfect position to accelerate. The clouds had descended and it was a bit gloomy, but conditions were far from unplayable. Nevertheless, the umpires felt obliged to go through the motions of offering Langer and Hayden the light. To the amazement of everyone in the ground, the Aussies accepted and trudged off. England's supporters, normally enraged when play is interrupted by anything less than a plague of locusts, began cheering. Sure, they had paid good money to see some cricket, but if no cricket helped England regain the Ashes, no problem.

Later, Langer attempted to explain why he and Hayden had denied their side valuable time to push past England's total. He said that if a wicket had fallen then, a new batsman would have had to enter the fray in fading light with England fired up. Maybe so, but surely the light was not going to improve enough to make waiting a better option.

The rain was on its way, but it didn't appear for another seventy-five minutes. Australia, with their best opening stand of the summer (beating 56 at Old Trafford) still intact, never got back on. Their decision was all the more bizarre because the forecast for the Saturday was even worse. The openers had asked Ponting what to do if the light was offered and were told to treat it just like any other Test match. The whole cricket world, and a few more, were watching. They all knew that this was not 'any other Test match'. Giles summed up the mood: 'We didn't need to be out there [to win the game], so it was a bit of a surprise when the Australians took the light. That was Ricky Ponting's decision and we hoped he'd live to regret it. But there were three days left and nobody could afford to cloud watch!'

> *'We didn't need to be out there [to win the game], so it was a bit of a surprise when the Australians took the light. That was Ricky Ponting's decision and we hoped he'd live to regret it.'*
> ASHLEY GILES

Warne commented tersely: 'I had my time as Australian captain and thoroughly enjoyed it. Ricky takes advice from certain senior players. It's up to him how he uses it. That was a decision where I thought we maybe had to stay out there

Needing a good start in the decisive Test at The Oval, Marcus Trescothick is first to fall with the score on 82. Shane Warne would soon pick up three more wickets. (*Getty Images*)

ABOVE & RIGHT: Andrew Strauss, however, continued on to make 129 and share a crucial partnership of 143 with Andrew Flintoff, who played yet another vital innings. (*AFP/ Getty Images, Rui Vieira/PA*)

For the first time all summer, Justin Langer and Matthew Hayden made a big opening partnership of 185, with both eventually going on to score centuries, but many were surprised when they chose to take the offer of bad light on the Friday. (*AP Photo*)

Australia started the fourth day on 277 for 2 and in a very strong position, but then came Freddie. First out was Damien Martyn, caught by Paul Collingwood. (*AP Photo/Matt Dunham*)

Matthew Hoggard then got in on the act, here having Adam Gilchrist LBW. (*Getty Images*)

Matthew Hoggard and Andrew Flintoff leave the field comparing bowling figures after helping to dismiss Australia for 367, six runs short of England's own total. (*Getty Images*)

The England fans put up their umbrellas, while the Australians try to sunbathe: English weather comes to the aid of Vaughan's side on the fourth evening. (*AP Photo/Matt Dunham*)

A crucial moment as Shane Warne drops Kevin Pietersen early in his innings. (*Sean Dempsey/PA*)

Paul Collingwood is yet another victim for Warne, after battling it out for over an hour, but England were now 186 for 6 and a sudden collapse could let in the Australians. (*Chris Young/PA*)

ABOVE, LEFT & RIGHT: Kevin Pietersen decided the best form of defence was attack, and in a whirlwind innings, under the greatest pressure, made the game safe. Here he hits Brett Lee for six, and celebrates his century. (*AP Photo/Matt Dunham, Rui Vieira/PA*)

Ashley Giles played a superb supporting role, batting for almost three hours to make his highest ever Test score of 59. (*AP Photo/Matt Dunham*)

The England team celebrate being presented with the Ashes after the most dramatic series anyone could remember. (*Rui Vieira/PA*)

Duncan Fletcher and Michael Vaughan pose with the Ashes. They had worked together so closely to create the opportunity for England to win them back. (*Tom Shaw/PA*)

The families of the players celebrate in the stands. (*Sean Dempsey/PA*)

Kevin Pietersen and Shane Warne, Hampshire team-mates, personify the great spirit that existed between the two sides. (*Getty Images*)

Holly and Andrew Flintoff, Kevin Pietersen and Michael Vaughan, and a little urn, on the bus during the parade through London on 13 September. (*Getty Images*)

LEFT: Huge crowds lined the roads to see the side that won back the Ashes after 18 years. (*AFP/Getty Images*)

LEFT & BELOW: The England team line up in Trafalgar Square with their victorious female counterparts, where more than 30,000 had crammed in to see their heroes. (*Getty Images*) because of the time and the situation of the game. But [coming off] was the decision that was made.'

DAY THREE: AUSTRALIA 277 FOR 2

Rain delayed the start by half an hour. Hoggard, as he did on the final morning at Old Trafford, appeared to have given his team the perfect start by trapping Langer in front of his wicket. Billy Bowden was about the only person at The Oval who did not think it was hitting. That became the story of the day for England: several good appeals got no response from the umpires. The morning session was divided into two spells of 35 and 25 minutes, with Australia adding another 45 runs. Langer was the man in form and he had moved on to 91 by the break, but he faced only 26 balls to Hayden's 59 in this session.

After lunch Langer soon completed his fourth century against England (his twenty-second in all), off just 142 balls, with a steer down to the third-man boundary. His next four took him to 7,000 Test runs, the eighth Australian to reach that milestone.

Vaughan sensed that, having weathered the early excitement, the Australian batsmen were finding batting a little too comfortable. As they progressed to 185 for no wicket, an uneasy feeling had been growing among the crowd, and the captain was concerned it might spread to his players. Where were the life and the energy that had brought them to the brink of triumph? Where was the spark?

Giles explains: 'As a captain, Vaughan very rarely shows his annoyance or shouts and screams. He has blow-outs, quietly, but they are not huge by any means. But the thing he hates above all else is when, as a team, we are flat. If you bowl a bad ball, get out to a bad shot or drop a catch, as long as you get yourself up and ready to go again, he loves it. What he can't stand is having to pander to players when things are not going their way, having to lift people, get their chins up and get them back on their feet. He doesn't like it when our confidence levels and intensity drop, and maybe he saw that in us at this moment.'

Vaughan collared Steve Harmison and urged the Durham paceman to put some devil into his bowling, stick it to Langer and Hayden, fast and short. As with most of Vaughan's actions this summer, his intervention had an immediate effect. Langer, having been largely untroubled for over a day, was hurried a fraction and chopped the ball on to his stumps.

Vaughan would have relished the chance to crack on after that breakthrough, but then the rain started to fall. With Australia still 188 runs behind England, an early tea was taken. England's skipper knew a key moment in the series had arrived. The weather might be disrupting England's rhythm just as much as their opponents', but he needed his team to refocus fast.

Andrew Flintoff, for one, would not be found wanting. 'Before the Test started I had talked in my column in the *Sun* about not leaving anything behind,' he says. 'That wasn't just words. Sometimes at press conferences you find yourself saying things without thinking too much about what you are saying, but I really, truly believed that, having come so far as a side, and given everything we had achieved, we had to go all the way. We had to give it one last big push. We owed it to everyone who supported us and we owed it to ourselves.'

After the resumption, Ian Bell was convinced that he had taken a brilliant bat/pad catch to get rid of Ponting off Ashley Giles, but the Australian captain was given a life by umpire Bowden. Hayden, like Langer, went on to make his fourth century against England, off a pedestrian (for him) 218 balls. His struggle had been evident all summer, and the Test players' union proved to be alive and well when he received a cuddle from Flintoff during his celebration. But while the big all-rounder was happy to see a fellow professional overcome a career-threatening loss of form, he was in no mood to dole out any favours. He was starting to generate frightening pace again, and Australia knew it. With the tourists on 243 for 1 from 65.5 overs, the players headed for the pavilion again. When they returned there were 18.1 overs scheduled to be bowled.

Late afternoon. Time for Flintoff.

First he collected his twentieth wicket of the series when he made a ball stand up and talk at Ponting; Strauss took a good catch. Soon afterwards the Lancastrian made another one rear up at new batsman Damien Martyn, but neither bowler nor keeper seemed to notice that the ball slid off the face of the bat to Geraint Jones. Both eventually joined in the appeals of the other fielders, but did so half-heartedly at best. Unsurprisingly, umpire Rudi Koertzen was unconvinced and gave Martyn the benefit of the doubt.

The day closed with the Australians still 96 runs short of England's first-innings total and with Flintoff champing at the bit to continue what he had only just begun. He recalls: 'Somehow we found something extra in that last session. It was very important for us to keep them down. We'd scrapped for this for a long time. We were going to have to come up with another special performance over the next two days. We had two more days to give every ounce of energy, and everything we had left needed to be left out there in the middle. The character and strength this side had shown was going to be called upon again. There was so much at stake at this stage and there weren't too many people complaining about being tired. Our attitude was that, whatever the circumstances, we would be out there fighting for the two days. We had to keep fighting to the end. Anything less and the Australians would find us out.'

DAY FOUR: AUSTRALIA 367 ALL OUT; ENGLAND 34 FOR 1

The person who responded to Flintoff's Churchillian call to arms was the man himself, who delivered one of the most heroic bowling performances ever seen at The Oval. He did not finish the spell he had started on Saturday night until the job was done just before tea on the Sunday. In eighteen unchanged overs of unrelenting pace, power and sheer physical courage, he took four more Australian wickets to add to his overnight capture of their skipper, as Hayden, Martyn, Clarke and finally, to general ecstasy, Warne (for a ten-ball duck) felt the full force of his will. It was astonishing, match-changing and unforgettable. It was Flintoff at his magnificent, massive best.

Hoggard was the perfect supporting act with the ball swinging, especially as the umpires decided that after a Saturday in which they had given nothing, Sunday was a day to be generous.

Martyn went early on, spooning the ball to give Collingwood a simple catch at midwicket. At 323 for 3, Hayden, Clarke and the Aussie dressing room still had high hopes of getting 100-plus ahead of England. But then Hayden was undone by a ball that darted back at over 90 m.p.h., while Katich also fell LBW in Flintoff's next over. All eyes were on Freddie now, of course, but it was Hoggard's removal of Gilchrist on the stroke of lunch that truly scuppered any chance of a substantial Aussie advantage. Three of the four morning wickets to fall had been LBW. All three had looked plumb.

Then, to everyone's amazement, England gained a first-innings lead of 6 runs as Flintoff and Hoggard completed the rout that accounted for Australia's last 7 wickets for 44 runs in 90 balls. Hoggard claimed three of the last four to fall, with Flintoff, despite Vaughan's best efforts to make a meal of a simple catch, removing Warne. Super Fred's figures were 5 for 78 off 34 overs, but they reveal only a fraction of the significance and value of his extraordinary effort. It was a display of outstanding character and stamina, as well as class, with never a hint that he was tiring or wanted a break. If anything, he looked stronger as the day wore on. Once Flintoff had got hold of the ball, he wasn't going to give it up. For him, this was the end of a very long and sometimes uncertain journey, back from the injury that had forced him home early from the winter tour to South Africa.

He explains: 'That spell is the reason I worked so hard and did all that work in the gym during my rehab; for a moment like that, when I have to draw on every ounce of energy and I've got to do something. And that was what this team is all about. Although Australia were in command, we knew we could get back into that Test match but that someone had to do something there and then. Fortunately, it was me.

'When you are two—one up against Australia and on the verge of something special, you don't seem to feel tired; your body doesn't ache.'
ANDREW FLINTOFF

'I found a nice bit of rhythm, and, at the other end, how good was Hoggard? Even after I dropped Clarke for him he kept coming in. Unbelievable. Even though it had been a long, hard summer not one of the lads complained that they were tired or said, "This is hard work." They just got on with the job and this was my turn. When you are two—one up against Australia and on the verge of something special, you don't seem to feel tired; your body doesn't ache. You just want to be involved and make a difference.

'People have said that what helped me in the long run in terms of being able to bowl that length of spell was the rest I had before and after surgery, because that helped my body properly switch off before all the hard work I had to do to get really fit and build up my reserves of stamina. I have a lot to thank my physio Dave Roberts for, and others like Rhiannon Jones, the chiropractor who worked with me in the hydrotherapy pool at Blackburn Rovers. Dave was the one who gave me a kick up the backside when I needed it and kept me on the straight and narrow when I needed it as well.

Everyone knows I enjoy a pint or two, but when it came down to business Dave was brilliant at sorting out my head and my focus. He was the one who came with me on the 7 a.m. runs on the moors, and he was the one who heard me complaining that I was bored with the waiting and told me where I could shove those complaints.

'Halfway through the rehab programme I got frustrated and I got down. I'd just played in a pre-season friendly at Lancashire for Mark Chilton's eleven against Stuart Law's eleven and hit a century. I was feeling really good about things and gagging to crack on in a game for Lancs second eleven. I thought I was going to be playing in it, then Gary Yates, the club's second-team coach and captain passed on the message that I wasn't playing. I remember having a rant and rave at Gary because he hadn't put me in the side. At the time I didn't realise it wasn't his decision, that the order had come from the England management, and I have to admit that what I thought of as a slow rate of progress was starting to get to me. But being able to bowl a spell like I did that day shows other people knew more about it than me. Bowling those overs on the Sunday morning made everything worthwhile.

'The fact is that although everyone was telling us how tired we must be, I didn't feel that way.'

According to Duncan Fletcher: 'What we saw this summer from Flintoff was the emergence of a genuine world-class talent. I would suggest that if you were picking a world eleven now the first two names on your list would be Flintoff and Warne, then you would build a team around them. It's amazing to me that he kept on producing because with every success the pressure and expectation increased. But every time he rose to it. He is a seriously good cricketer.'

Close friend Harmison is certainly convinced: 'The only problem with Fred is his appalling taste in music. If it's not bloody Sinatra, it's bloody Elton John and bloody "Rocket Man". By the time we got to The Oval we all knew the bloody words to bloody "Rocket Man": "And I think it's gonna be a long, long time …" And the fact that he carries on like an idiot in the dressing room sometimes, running around with no clothes on and the like. Give it a bloody rest, man …

'But on the field with a ball or a bat in his hand, what a player! Phenomenal. Not that you'd ever want this to happen, but if anyone else in the team was injured, you could probably find a replacement for him without the team suffering too much. But how would you, could you, replace the irreplace-able? It is unbelievable how important that bloke is to English cricket at the moment.

'I was quite disappointed in him actually, if I'm honest, because after about six overs in his spell I was trying to say, "Come on, big lad, give me the ball, my go now." But he was just not having it. And when he got his tenth over I saw that look in his eye and I was thinking, He's either going to fall down and hurt himself, and that's the only way I'm going to get the ball, or he's going to bowl this lot out. And that is what he did. It was just a phenomenal effort. He said at the end of the last day at Trent Bridge, when Simon was injured, "It's between me, you and Hoggy, and we're going to have to bowl all day. Forget what's happened, forget how tired your body feels, to win the Ashes we've got to bowl all day." And at the end of the day he did exactly the same again at The Oval.

> *'The only problem with Fred is his appalling taste in music. If it's not bloody Sinatra, it's bloody Elton John and bloody "Rocket Man". By the time we got to The Oval we all knew the bloody words to bloody "Rocket Man".'*
> STEVE HARMISON

'He knew it was his last big effort for the season. All he had to do was bowl for one more day and he was gone. Fred is so strong physically and mentally and that huge heart he has gets him through every time.

'At the minute the bloke is the best cricketer in the world. I'd be very surprised if we can produce another cricketer any-where near as good or if we have produced a cricketer any-where near as good as Andrew Flintoff. I know that's a big statement because we've had some world-class cricketers, but the guy bowls at 90 m.p.h., bats like God in the top six and stands at second slip with buckets for hands. Now, can any-body tell me about a better cricketer in the world at the moment? Or ever?

'And when we needed a lift he was our inspiration, and it seemed to happen in every single game, when we just needed that initiative to swing back in our favour and he came up trumps. He's got so much belief in himself, not that he would ever say it, that he's better than anybody else. And it's hard to get him out of that; when he's in that mood, you've just got to let him go. Let him do whatever he wants to do and fill in the gaps around him. He's awesome. The thing is, I don't think you're a great cricketer until you've done it against the best, and he's done that now. Australia, to my mind, are still the best team in the world, and Andrew Flintoff has given them a good hiding.'

Ashley Giles says: 'It was an incredible effort and we could all sense it, you know, from a position where we were wonder-ing how many they would go past us, we were back in, bat-ting. Suddenly we were in a position where we'd taken a lead in the first innings. It was remarkable. And when he does something like that ultimately you're just proud of him. The feeling is almost one of disbelief, because this was the best team in the world and he simply overpowered them.

'They know he's a good bowler and they know he can bowl 90 m.p.h.-plus and they know he doesn't bowl many bad balls. When he comes on, they seem to be thinking, This is going to be hard work. There are no freebies. I think he's had a real hold over them throughout the series. Michael Clarke said to me that Fred is the best bowler he has ever faced.

'It was really serious stuff out there. You play for these

moments, you can't swap them for anything in the world, you can't put a price on them. Fred said, "There's no point in us leaving anything behind now, no point in us saving any energy for another day, this is what it's all about," and he was correct. This is the Ashes, that was one of the defining moments and you could see it in the eyes of the Australians: they knew this bloke wasn't going away. He was going to keep coming and keep coming and they couldn't do a thing about it.'

Paul Collingwood, witnessing the force of nature at close range for the first time in the series, was astounded. 'I went out for a meal the night before with my wife. It was raining that night, really heavy rain, and we were saying, "It'll be good if we can have another twenty-four hours of this." But I remember Fred just kept wanting the ball. And once he was on a roll he was like a runaway train. He was unstoppable. I noticed how much he was enjoying it. Because he knew I was so nervous, he was going, "You'll be all right, Collie. This is your match, this is your situation," things like that. I've had that off him before, but not to the extent that he was doing it now. He was encouraging everybody; he was really enjoying that spell, just loving it. "Give us the ball." He was having a laugh and a joke, and the way he enjoyed the cricket opened my eyes a bit. He didn't seem nervous at all, he was just having a wonderful time. That's what got him through that spell in my eyes. He loved taking the wickets – the way he was celebrating, standing in

> 'At the minute the bloke is the best cricketer in the world … I know that's a big statement because we've had some world-class cricketers, but the guy bowls at 90 m.p.h., bats like God in the top six and stands at second slip with buckets for hands.'
> STEVE HARMISON
> ON FLINTOFF

the middle of the wicket nodding his head, it was excellent. He absolutely loved the whole occasion of it, and I think that's what's taken him from a very, very good player to a world beater: going out there and enjoying himself. And that transmits itself to everyone else in the team. Just taking that very simple catch off his bowling to get Martyn out, I felt bloody fantastic. Mind you, Pietersen did come up to me and say: "Why don't I ever get one like that?"'

According to Marcus Trescothick: 'You won't get many bowlers in world cricket able to bowl a spell like that. Possibly McGrath's at Lord's was comparable, but I think Freddie's was every bit as good because he bowled so well for so long. He bowled for the whole session, pretty much, and then straight after again. He was putting it right on the spot and they couldn't go anywhere because he was keeping the pressure on them the whole time. He just kept them locked down, which meant the pressure was on both ends, and it was a completely different game of cricket. We could see wickets falling and see their strength diminishing while ours was growing. Suddenly we'd gone from thinking we might have to score 200 against Warne on a wearing pitch on the last day to avoid defeat to thinking, Ah, we could get a lead here. Then we do, and we're all thinking, You beauty.

'He has grown so much as a player but I think he's grown even more as a person. I've seen things from Freddie this year which I never dreamed I would see. His attitude has changed massively. He's just fantastic now. He's been brilliant this summer, absolutely brilliant, on and off the pitch, and he's deserved everything he's achieved.'

There was some relief when Lee hit Hoggard towards Giles rather than Pietersen on the midwicket boundary. The left-arm spinner justified the confidence by taking a good, running catch to end the Aussie innings.

All along, it had been assumed England would start batting towards the end of the day with a deficit to clear and Warne, as always, trundling in to scare English supporters out of their wits. Flintoff had seen to it that there was no deficit, but the great leg-spinner's threat was as real as ever. With a day and a half still to go, any sort of mishap could have serious consequences, and the danger became all too real when Warne came on to bowl the fourth over. Four balls later, Katich took the bat/pad catch that removed Strauss after the delivery exploded out of the bowlers' footmarks.

Warne had just beaten his previous highest total of wickets in an Ashes series, but anyone could see that he wanted more. England's lead was only 8 runs. The packed Brit Oval prepared itself for another nail-biter. A placard at the local Tube station requested: 'Wanted – One Ticket For English Masochist'. But then the weather played a hand.

Maybe Ponting would have brought on Warne anyway, but even at 2 p.m. the light was already an issue. He should have put Katich on at the other end, because a McGrath bouncer left the umpires with no option but to offer the light to Vaughan. The cry of 'Off, off, off' is normally reserved for individuals who have behaved badly on the sporting field, but The Oval crowd was just issuing a plea to the umpires to reduce their agony by cutting the time available for Warne to do his damage. Both sets of fans joined in the fun. When England supporters raised their brollies to try to con the officials that rain was falling, Australians countered by stripping to the waist as though basking in glorious sunshine. On one of the balconies overlooking the ground a resourceful Aussie fan was waving a cardboard cut-out of the sun while his mate moved behind it with a standard lamp. At one point even the Australian players came to the party, sauntering on to the field in a variety of sunglasses before the umpires took them off again at 3.42 p.m.

Play was finally officially called off at 6.15 p.m. with 59.4 overs having been lost. The greatest Test series of all time was going down to the wire: the final day of the final Test. The question was: would anyone be left standing to tell the tale?

DAY FIVE: ENGLAND 335 ALL OUT;
AUSTRALIA 4 FOR 0; DRAW

There's tension and there's tension ... and then there's the last day of the 2005 Ashes series. One day, one prize, two targets: for England, bat and bat and bat and regain the Ashes they relinquished sixteen years previously; for Australia, bowl them out, bat like demons, retain the Ashes, show the Poms who's still in charge. Take a breath and hold it, it's going to be a bumpy ride.

But for the first forty-five minutes or so, there were no alarms whatsoever. Trescothick and Vaughan played with calm assurance, and it was just like the old days in an English Test match, meandering gently to a draw. Then, at 67 for 1, the captain, who had been in sparkling form, pushed at Glenn McGrath and saw Adam Gilchrist fly to his right to pouch a sensational one-handed catch. The very next ball, the great fast bowler snared Ian Bell with a superb delivery which the young batsman could only nudge towards the slips. Warne collected nonchalantly. England were a mere 73 ahead and still had an age to bat out, most of it, inevitably, against Warne. But before that, the new batsman had to face McGrath on a hat-trick.

The new batsman was Kevin Pietersen and he nearly snapped himself in two trying to avoid a delivery that bit into the pitch then homed in on him like a missile. A huge deflection was seen and heard by everyone in the ground, and 23,000 breaths were held simultaneously. But Billy Bowden could not be swayed by the frenzied appeal: the ball had hit shoulder, not bat or glove. Not out.

In the next over, with England supporters still barely daring to watch, Pietersen pushed at a ball from his friend Warne, but a slight deflection off Gilchrist's glove altered its trajectory to Hayden just enough to put off the slip fielder. Then Warne was convinced he had trapped Trescothick LBW, but umpire Koertzen did not agree. If the gods weren't smiling on the leg-spinner, a minute or two later they seemed to be positively laughing at him. It was a moment that will probably haunt Warne for the rest of his career; a moment that allowed Pietersen to play the innings of his life. There were 8 overs to go before lunch and Pietersen, on 15, drove hard at Lee; the ball flew to first slip at neck height. It went straight into Warne's upturned hands ... then popped straight out again.

Pietersen recalls: 'I still don't understand how I nicked that. Warne told me later that the ball came to him a lot slower than he expected, whereas I thought it flew pretty quickly. At Trent Bridge I nicked exactly the same ball and I had time to turn and see Gilchrist catch it. Not this time. But I'm not the one to talk about dropped catches. Anyway, fortune favours the brave.'

Warne says: 'I saw it all the way and put my hands there ready to say thank-you very much, and it sort of dipped on me and hit me on the drumstick. I must have been done for lack of pace. Maybe the sporting gods had decided it was going to be his day.'

'I remember Vaughan saying to me a couple of days before the Test started: "I'm sort of glad KP's missed out for a couple of innings, because I can see him getting 150."'
MARCUS TRESCOTHICK

From that moment, Pietersen's attitude seemed to change utterly. If he was going to die, he wasn't going to die wondering. Trescothick says: 'I remember Vaughan saying to me a couple of days before the Test started: "I'm sort of glad KP's missed out for a couple of innings, because I can see him getting 150. I don't mind that he's had a couple of failures because it will make him even more hungry."'

'When the wickets started falling that morning I think the

Australians thought they could win the match by tea. They were buzzing, ultra-confident, and with each wicket their self-belief rose. They also thought Pietersen was there for the taking. That miss was the turning point. He'd just been prodding about trying to survive and he was going nowhere. Then, after a few balls more of this torture against Warne, he came down the wicket to me and said: "I'm fed up with blocking it, I'm just going to whack it instead." Then he went bang, bang, six, six. I can see them now, the looks on the faces of the Australians. They must have been thinking, What the hell …? Here he was, the new kid on the block, skunk on his head and diamond earrings, and they are the world champions and Warne is a genius, and he's just pushed them around. It was a really big moment.

'Batting was really hard work. Warne had been bowling so well and every ball was so tense, each one a massive event. You couldn't relax for a second. And then this happened. I've been trying to do something like that for years but I probably never will. He's done it in his fifth Test. Amazing.'

Pietersen had only just started, but Warne wasn't finished. He soon took another record when he trapped Trescothick LBW for 33. It was the spinner's 168th wicket against England, beating Dennis Lillee's previous best. Four overs later, to his delight and England's deep dismay, Flintoff went. England's all-rounder had carved the previous ball through the off side for four, but this time was deceived by the flight and gave Warne a simple return catch. Fred looked utterly dejected as he walked off. Pietersen then saved new batsman Paul Collingwood from having to face another over from Warne before lunch by calling on physio Kirk

> '*I'm fed up with blocking it, I'm just going to whack it instead.*'
> KEVIN PIETERSEN

Russell after he was hit by Lee. 'I was being a bit of a drama queen,' he admits, 'but I needed to get us off the field.'

At lunch, England were 127 for 5, still only 133 ahead. Still not nearly enough.

Unsurprisingly, the atmosphere in the dressing room was electric. Giles noticed that even his close friend Vaughan, normally adept at disguising his emotions, was in clear discomfort. But the measure of the captain's coolness under fire was that he was able to go to Pietersen during the break and reassure him.

The skipper says: 'I'd felt throughout the summer that he could do something special because he's got that ability to take the game away from the opposition. I didn't expect him to be using it on that day because of the huge amount of pressure. But at lunchtime I just said to him: "Play your natural game. You have to go out and be as positive and aggressive as you like. If you do that, you'll win us the Ashes." After lunch, when he took on Lee, you started to sense the change in the Australians that said, "We might not do this after all."'

Ponting preferred Lee to McGrath at the Pavilion End when play resumed. That was probably because the younger man had built up a fair head of steam and had already hit Pietersen three times. Most observers felt McGrath's probing would have been more likely to winkle out Pietersen, who was clearly going to tee off rather than dig in. The faster Lee bowled, the farther Pietersen hit him. Both teams were playing a high-risk strategy, but England's was the one that was coming off. Pietersen hooked two sixes, then played the most remarkable shot of this extraordinary innings.

Collingwood was at the other end: 'Brett Lee was still bowling at the speed of light but Pietersen's eyes were just gone. He was hitting sixes with half a bat and smashing fours, and the atmosphere was unbelievable. I just kept saying to him, "Keep going, keep going for it." There was no point in saying, "Come on, mate, rein yourself in," because he was so much in the zone you could tell he wasn't even listening to me. Or, if he was, he couldn't hear me.

'Then Lee bowled a length ball at him and he realised late

that it wasn't short enough to pull. So he just blatted it back past me like a baseball shot. Incredible. I'm literally just trying to get a bat on it and not give my wicket away and he's hitting length balls as hard as you like back past the bowler. I thought then, He's playing a different game to me. I was just standing there, in disbelief, thinking, How has he done that?'

Collingwood's contribution should not be underestimated, though. He calls it 'the best 10 I will ever make' because his stubborn occupation of the crease, for 51 balls and 72 minutes, largely against Warne, allowed Pietersen to plunder at the other end, and move on to 78. But when Collingwood departed at 186 for 6, to a tumbling catch by Ponting at silly point to give Warne his fourth wicket, the game was still in the balance. No one, least of all the England players, could yet relax.

'There was no point in saying, "Come on, mate, rein yourself in," because he was so much in the zone you could tell he wasn't even listening to me.'
PAUL COLLINGWOOD
BATS WITH PIETERSEN

Pietersen then scored all but one of the runs in his brief partnership with Geraint Jones that took England's lead over 200. Tea was approaching when Tait knocked Jones's off stump out of the ground, but there were still more than 50 overs left. And four an over, as cricketing teams all over the world are well aware, is nothing to this Australian side.

Cometh the hour, cometh George Clooney.

Ashley Giles explains: 'As the series has worn on my hair has got greyer and greyer, and, inevitably, I was getting a fair amount of stick for it. So I said, "It's the George Clooney look. It's back in fashion now." Big mistake. Now they all call me Clooney. Every ball I survived out there Pietersen would call out: "Come on, George. Keep going, George."

'Before I went out to bat, it was just terrible, to be honest.

Once we'd lost Vaughan and Belly – bang, bang – I couldn't watch any more. I felt physically sick and it was all too painful. I went out the back and played cards with Hoggard. And I never, ever, play cards.

'Then, when Tres got out, I had to start thinking about getting ready, and when Freddie was out just before lunch that was even worse because I thought, We're really in the mire here. There's so much time left in the game, we're really up against it.

'Pietersen's assault on Lee helped a bit, but I still couldn't go and sit on the balcony. I sat in the coach's office on my own and just watched through the open door but it was still awful.

'Then Nigel Stockill, our sports science manager, came in and sat with me. He asked me if I wanted a drink and I said, "Yeah, I'll have some water." When he came back I said, "Come and chat to me for a while ... about anything." He spoke about his wife and her new job, anything to take my mind off the cricket.

'I was just thinking: We don't deserve this. We've worked so hard and our chance is going. Then Vaughany came into the room and he said, "You all right?" I replied, "Not really," and he said, "You can go and do something about it now. It'll be like Trent Bridge." I said, "I don't really want to, to be honest."

'I was a gibbering wreck when I went out. And the looks on the faces around me were all anxious. But once I got out there with Pietersen he was absolutely brilliant. He is normally quite excitable, sort of non-stop activity. But he was so

> *'I was a gibbering wreck when I went out ... But once I got out there with Pietersen he was absolutely brilliant ... he was so relaxed ... He was amazing. I'll love him for ever.'*
> ASHLEY GILES
> BATS WITH PIETERSEN

relaxed and we were basically on the pitch saying, "Let's get through this ball, let's get through this over." He was amazing. I'll love him for ever.

'At the start we were still a long way off, about fifty-seven overs left. So initially it was just a case of getting over the first couple of balls, and once I felt a bit happier it was, like, "Let's do these overs in bunches: eighteen balls, three overs; then thirty balls, five overs." As time went on, the runs came and more time ticked by, it was really special to be out there – one of those things I'll never forget. "I was there with Kevin Pietersen." You know, it's real grandchildren stuff: "Gather round and I'll tell you about that innings I played with Pietersen, with the white stripe and the earrings."

'And I felt it was great for me to be able to do something for Flintoff, to pay him back for everything he had put into the series. You could see how down he was when he got out, wondering whether his hard work had been for nothing. But that's what we play for: we play for each other. Hoggard calls us the Band of Brothers.

'At what point did I think we were OK? It's weird, because when you're in that situation, you're batting and you know you've got to go out and bowl to a side that is going to chase a target come what may, and all sorts of stupid things are going through your mind. You're working it out: thirty overs left, that's nine an over, surely they can't get there. But they *might*. Then you're down to twenty overs, then fifteen, and half of them from Andrew Flintoff, and it's not realistic and you know it's over. But even when Pietersen was finally out it was tricky to control myself, because I was so chuffed to be batting that I wanted to stay out there longer. At the same time, I could feel myself starting to smile, taking in the crowd. I wanted to get up there with my team-mates and give them a hug.'

Vaughan considers Australia's task became impossible 'When we got to about 240. I felt at 200 Australia were going to have to bat well to get them. I knew we were in with a chance. Once we got to 240/250, I knew they'd start to feel that the game had gone. Pietersen took us past that point at around 4.10 when he hit Lee for six over square-leg then mowed Warne back over his head for another next over.'

So the struggle had finally ended by the time McGrath produced a beauty to remove Pietersen for 158 at 4.59. His dismissal was a fitting backdrop to the final live commentating words from Richie Benaud on British television. The Voice of Cricket's departure had added to the significance of this Test. The future great Australian captain and leg-spinner had been twelfth man at The Oval in 1953 when Hutton's team had regained the Ashes after almost nineteen years. Now they were coming home again after over sixteen years. Pietersen had entered Ashes legend by playing a one-day match-winning type of innings in a Test match-saving situation. Like the man himself, the innings was bold, provocative and entertaining. He faced 187 balls, hitting over a century in boundaries (seven sixes and fifteen fours), and by the end he was on his third Woodworm Torch bat, a fair indication of the power of his stroke-play.

Vaughan says: 'In this team, whatever the situation, there is always someone who comes along and puts up his hand. Pietersen has a bit of genius to play like that. It was an extraordinary effort. The guy is so positive.'

If the bold, brash, some would say arrogant, but always colourful Pietersen had needed to persuade anyone of his commitment and value, this incredible innings did the job. Vaughan continued: 'He is a show pony, no doubt about it. I think people are going to have to be careful of him in that when he does badly they're going to blame his hair and blame his earrings. But that's unfair because that's the way he is whether he's doing well or doing badly, and I don't think it affects his game. He's very dedicated when it comes to practice and when it comes to cricket.

'I do believe people have misjudged him slightly. They see the white flash and think he must take himself very seriously indeed. The point is that to wear something like that on your head you have to have a sense of humour. If you took yourself too seriously you wouldn't dare.'

According to Trescothick: 'He is the other end of the spectrum to me. I prefer a quiet life. But good luck to him because he is an amazing player.'

Harmison reflects: 'You've got to have something about you. You've got to have balls, that big-up character about you. You don't walk around with something like that on your head and go into your shell. That's his character: he's larger than life, he likes the attention and being in the public eye. But at the end of the day, if you can't back it up you're just setting yourself up for a fall and the one thing Kev hasn't done so far is fall.

'He's been magnificent. Throughout the whole of the one-dayers, the South African one-dayers, he really impressed me. Because I must admit, seeing Kevin come into the side I was thinking, Is he going to be able to do this? He's been a bully in county cricket for a long time and how is he going to attune to the demands and the disciplines of international cricket? How is he going to cope against South Africa, his home nation, when there's bound to be flak flying round? But I was so impressed by what I saw out there and how he handled himself that I thought, We've got to play him. He worked hard and he was the life and soul in our dressing room. And he stood up to all the stuff they were giving him on the field and let it all bounce off him. No matter what, I thought, we have got to pick him.

'He was awesome on Monday.'

Duncan Fletcher even likes his hair. 'It doesn't bug me. Jimmy Anderson used to have something similar and I liked that, too,' insists the coach. 'People say he is not the archetypal kind of Duncan Fletcher player, but they have the wrong impression. I've always said cricket teams need characters, otherwise it could be a very boring game. You've got to have the odd nutter. All I say is, if you've got a good attitude, you're positive and you work at your game, you can do what you like. As long as he gets results, works at his game when there's practice on, doesn't let his team-mates down or bring distractions, well, what more can you ask?'

Pietersen himself remarked: 'Yeah, you get recognised and you get a look now. You can't go anywhere. It's the stupid thing with my hair, and I'm a six-foot-four guy anyway, but you get noticed by so many people. I was walking through Soho last week [the week before The Oval Test] and these people were taking a photo. I thought they wanted me to take a photo of them, but they said, "You play cricket and you're on TV." And they could hardly speak a word of English. They were Italian. I honestly couldn't believe it.

'I had a tattoo of the three lions done on my arm just after the South African one-dayers, and I had my Test number done in Roman numerals – DCXXVI – after the third Test.

'I'm doing this because I want to do it, not so people will say, "You're incredible!" or for anybody else. I do it because I enjoy it. I think it's fun. I'm twenty-five years old and it's a really enjoyable thing that I do. I love every single day waking up to play cricket, and not many people are fortunate enough to love the thing they do. I travel and meet interesting people and make friendships all over the world.

'So I'm just enjoying life, but the big thing is not to let it interrupt and disturb my cricket, and I will never let that happen. I'll never do things when I could be training. I train as hard as anybody. In fact, I think I'm one of the fittest blokes around and I give it my best. I train as hard as possible. I work at my game as hard as I can and I never let anything get in the way of that. Because I've got a blond stripe on my head, it's not going to make me bat any differently. It's not going to make me fall over my front pad.

'I don't take myself too seriously, and I think that could be a good thing.'

Even if Vaughan had declared then, Australia would have needed to bat at around ten an over. But England's skipper had no thoughts of giving the tourists so much as a sniff. Australia were going to have to bowl England out. Giles, after hitting the winning runs at Trent Bridge, struck two boundaries to reach his fifty, and the crowd thought it was all over when the umpires moved to the boundary. But this drinks break was just the first of several false finishes.

Australia, like the true champions they are, kept going to the last, as Hoggard found out when he arrived at the crease with Lee bowling 'faster than I had ever faced before'. Warne had claimed the final 2 wickets by 5.45 to take his tally to 6 in the innings, 12 in the match, new records of 40 for a five-Test Ashes series and 172 in England–Australia clashes. Giles and Harmison (Warne's final victim) were both cheered off, as was Hoggard, undefeated on 4 after three-quarters of an hour at the crease. And the Aussies were cheered off, especially McGrath and Warne, who headed to the dressing room with their arms around each other.

Warne's final burst should have provided a bonus for England, with all the heroes on the field at the moment of triumph. As ever with this astonishing series, though, things did not go according to plan, as perhaps the greatest series ever ended not with a bang but a light-meter.

Australia came out needing 338 runs off 17.2 overs. Harmison bowled four deliveries, his second bouncer nearly taking Langer's head off. Hayden and Langer were offered the light and went off at 5.59 p.m. to resounding cheers. The crowd thought it was all over. To all intents and purposes it was, but cricket is nothing if not bound by rules and regulations, and they decreed that play could finish only at the appointed minute, which was still half an hour away. A cunning plan was hatched: Bowden and Koertzen would walk out, look up at the sky and declare that in their esteemed opinion the light was not going to improve. They would then remove the bails at their respective ends so that ancient custom could be satisfied and the match officially declared over.

It was all something of a farce as the umpires acted out

their roles, but nobody cared, and the cheering that was to continue long into the next day began. Michael Vaughan found his Australian counterpart Ricky Ponting and told him, 'Thanks for a great series.' Then he, his players and the whole nation were at last able to breathe out.

While 'Jerusalem' rang around the ground (this time with real feeling), in the dressing room assistant coach Matthew Maynard led England in their traditional team song, penned by him, to a tune of their own devising:

'Our army's been assembled, from Durham down to Kent,
A joining of all counties, to Lord's we have been sent.
Little do they know how hard the English fight,
As they trudge from their dressing room, beaten out of sight.
We are England, lions you and me,
Together we stand as the pride of our country.
We play to conquer, we play to impress,
We play for the glory of the lions on our chest.'

Pietersen, the series' leading run scorer with 473, was Man of the Match. 'Don't worry – I won't drop it' was his response when handed his bottle of champagne on the presentation stage. (He did manage to pour most of it into his eye, though.) He recalls: 'When Warne came over and acknowledged me as I walked off it brought a lump to my throat. He told me to remember this moment and savour it.

'I've been amazed at the abuse I copped,' he adds. 'It's stupid to suggest that my hair and jewellery affect my cricket in any way. I didn't have anything to prove to anybody. I am a positive player and always back myself to get runs. I wasn't nervous at all.'

Duncan Fletcher nominated Warne as Australia's Man of the Series, while John Buchanan would have been lynched if Flintoff had not been his choice in return. England's colossus was also the inaugural recipient of the Compton/Miller medal for the Man of the Series from both sides. It had been

KP's day, but it was Super Fred's series. He scored more than 400 runs at over 40 and took 24 wickets at 27.49. But mere statistics will never convey the impact Andrew Flintoff had on this Ashes contest nor the effect he had on the sporting nation and beyond. After twenty-four years, English cricket fans had a hero and summer to rival Ian Botham and 1981.

Warne remains Australia's great hero, and the man with 623 Test wickets confessed afterwards: 'It's been my best series ever, but it wasn't good enough. I took 40 wickets, but maybe it should have been 43. You can't give Pietersen too many chances and we gave him three. The England fans deserve their day in the sun. They can gloat for a bit. I like most of them, even if there are always one or two idiots. But today when they were singing "There's only one Shane Warne" and "We only wish you were English" it was a warm tribute.'

As to his immediate future plans, Warne left the speculation that he might retire hanging in the South London air. He said: 'You can't just say, "I want to keep playing." You've got to weigh up the whole package and the most important thing to you. At the moment my kids are the most important thing to me. I haven't seen them for lengthy periods of time in the last ten months and I really am missing them. Hopefully in eighteen months, if I'm still around, I'd love the opportunity to try to help regain the Ashes in Australia. If not, cricket will move on.

'England deserved to win. They outplayed us in the last four Tests. Though I was happy with my bowling: I had plans for all their batsmen and most of them seemed to work.'

One by one the England players came on to the stage to receive the rapturous applause of their supporters. In batting order: Marcus Trescothick, Andrew Strauss, Ian Bell, Kevin Pietersen, Andrew Flintoff, Paul Collingwood, Geraint Jones, Ashley Giles, Matthew Hoggard and Steve Harmison. Simon Jones was also called up to take the applause for his crucial part in England's extraordinary victory. Then Michael

Vaughan followed his team to the biggest, loudest and longest ovation of them all.

In that moment his friend and county team-mate Hoggard had to smile: 'I was just thinking how far he had come since I first met up with him at Yorkshire when we were kids, and he used to have these great long curtains of greasy hair. We didn't really get on all that well then; just a clash of personalities. He was moving on, I wasn't, and the thought of him being captain of England was laughable. But he has grown and matured and become a great captain and a great leader.

'He's our Mr Chilled, our Mr Ice Cool. When you go out to play, bat or bowl or field, you never feel under the slightest pressure from him. It doesn't help when you are a bowler and you bowl a bad ball and the captain takes his cap off and throws it to the ground. The one time he has had a go at us in my memory was at the start of the tour to South Africa, when we lost a warm-up game convincingly. He just said to us: "We didn't come here to win these matches, so put it behind you and do whatever you have to do to get it right for the Tests." He didn't need to say any more. Brilliant and totally deserving of the utmost respect.'

Ashley Giles agrees: 'All of us, from time to time in the series, suffered from nerves and edginess. But whenever one of us has started to doubt himself he has always been ready to bring us round and pick us up, even though he had everything else to deal with, including his own game. We are good mates, but I did wonder whether he had it in him. Now I know, everyone knows, he did all along.'

The captain himself says simply: 'Full credit to Australia. They made us fight all the way and we had to dig deep on a number of occasions. But our team has been fantastic. The way they have responded to the challenges put in front of them has been incredible.'

Fifth Test, Oval, London

Result Match drawn   **Toss** England

8, 9, 10, 11, 12 September 2005

Umpires B.F.Bowden (NZ) and R.E.Koertzen (SA)   **Match Referee** R.S.Madugalle (SL)
Man of the Match K.P.Pietersen   **Player of the Series** A.Flintoff and S.K.Warne

England First Innings		R	M	B	4s	6s
M.E.Trescothick	c Hayden b Warne	43	77	65	8	0
A.J.Strauss	c Katich b Warne	129	351	210	17	0
*M.P.Vaughan	c Clarke b Warne	11	26	25	2	0
I.R.Bell	lbw b Warne	0	9	7	0	0
K.P.Pietersen	b Warne	14	30	25	2	0
A.Flintoff	c Warne b McGrath	72	162	115	12	1
P.D.Collingwood	lbw b Tait	7	26	26	1	0
+G.O.Jones	b Lee	25	60	41	5	0
A.F.Giles	lbw b Warne	32	120	70	1	0
M.J.Hoggard	c Martyn b McGrath	2	47	36	0	0
S.J.Harmison	not out	20	25	20	4	0
Extras	b 4, lb 6, w 1, nb 7	18				
Total	all out, 105.3 overs, 471 mins	373				

FoW   1–82 Trescothick (18th ov), 2–102 Vaughan (24th ov), 3–104 Bell (26th ov), 4–131 Pietersen (34th ov),
5–274 Flintoff (71st ov), 6–289 Collingwood (77th ov), 7–297 Strauss (80th ov), 8–325 Jones (90th ov),
9–345 Hoggard (101st ov), 10–373 Giles (106th ov)

Bowling	O	M	R	W
McGrath	27	5	72	2
Lee	23	3	94	1
Tait	15	1	61	1
Warne	37.3	5	122	6
Katich	3	0	14	0

Australia First Innings

		R	M	B	4s	6s
J.L.Langer	b Harmison	105	233	146	11	2
M.L.Hayden	lbw b Flintoff	138	416	303	18	0
*R.T.Ponting	c Strauss b Flintoff	35	81	56	3	0
D.R.Martyn	c Collingwood b Flintoff	10	36	29	1	0
M.J.Clarke	lbw b Hoggard	25	119	59	2	0
S.M.Katich	lbw b Flintoff	1	12	11	0	0
+A.C.Gilchrist	lbw b Hoggard	23	32	20	4	0
S.K.Warne	c Vaughan b Flintoff	0	18	10	0	0
B.Lee	c Giles b Hoggard	6	22	10	0	0
G.D.McGrath	c Strauss b Hoggard	0	6	6	0	0
S.W.Tait	not out	1	7	2	0	0
Extras	b 4, lb 8, w 2, nb 9	23				
Total	all out, 107.1 overs, 494 mins	367				

FoW 1–185 Langer (53rd ov), 2–264 Ponting (73rd ov), 3–281 Martyn (81st ov), 4–323 Hayden (93rd ov), 5–329 Katich (95th ov), 6–356 Gilchrist (102nd ov), 7–359 Clarke (104th ov), 8–363 Warne (105th ov), 9–363 McGrath (106th ov), 10–367 Lee (108th ov)

Bowling	O	M	R	W
Harmison	22	2	87	1
Hoggard	24.1	2	97	4
Flintoff	34	10	78	5
Giles	23	1	76	0
Collingwood	4	0	17	0

England Second Innings		R	M	B	4s	6s
M.E.Trescothick	lbw b Warne	33	150	84	1	0
A.J.Strauss	c Katich b Warne	1	16	7	0	0
*M.P.Vaughan	c Gilchrist b McGrath	45	80	65	6	0
I.R.Bell	c Warne b McGrath	0	2	1	0	0
K.P.Pietersen	b McGrath	158	285	187	15	7
A.Flintoff	c & b Warne	8	20	13	1	0
P.D.Collingwood	c Ponting b Warne	10	72	51	1	0
+G.O.Jones	b Tait	1	24	12	0	0
A.F.Giles	b Warne	59	159	97	7	0
M.J.Hoggard	not out	4	45	35	0	0
S.J.Harmison	c Hayden b Warne	0	2	2	0	0
Extras	b 4, w 7, nb 5	16				
Total	all out, 91.3 overs, 432 mins	335				

FoW   1–2 Strauss (4th ov), 2–67 Vaughan (23rd ov), 3–67 Bell (23rd ov), 4–109 Trescothick (34th ov), 5–126 Flintoff (38th ov), 6–186 Collingwood (52nd ov), 7–199 Jones (57th ov), 8–308 Pietersen (83rd ov), 9–335 Giles (92nd ov), 10–335 Harmison (92nd ov)

Bowling	O	M	R	W
McGrath	26	3	85	3
Lee	20	4	88	0
Warne	38.3	3	124	6
Clarke	2	0	6	0
Tait	5	0	28	1

Australia Second Innings

		R	M	B	4s	6s
J.L.Langer	not out	0	3	4	0	0
M.L.Hayden	not out	0	3	0	0	0
*R.T.Ponting						
D.R.Martyn						
M.J.Clarke						
S.M.Katich						
+A.C.Gilchrist						
S.K.Warne						
B.Lee						
G.D.McGrath						
S.W.Tait						
Extras	lb 4	4				
Total	0 wickets, 0.4 overs, 3 mins	4				

Bowling	O	M	R	W
Harmison	0.4	0	0	0

Close of Play   Day 1 England 319–7 (Jones 21*, Giles 5*), Day 2 England 373, Australia 112–0 (Langer 75*, Hayden 32*), Day 3 Australia 277–2 (Hayden 110*, Martyn 9*), Day 4 Australia 367, England 34–1 (Trescothick 14*, Vaughan 19*)

EPILOGUE

The celebrations of the England players began early on the evening of Monday 12 September with the statutory showers of champagne. For some of them a long, wet night lay ahead. For one or two, sleep never came into the equation.

By 4.30 a.m. in the team hotel overlooking Tower Bridge, most of England's heroes had crawled off to bed. Marcus Trescothick was sitting in the lobby with a toasted cheese and ham sandwich. When approached, he said, 'I'm so happy. I'm so excited. I can't wait for the open-top bus ride.'

'Yes, Marcus. But why are you here, now?'

'I've ordered all the papers and I'm waiting for them to arrive.'

'At four-thirty?'

He shrugged. 'As long as it takes.'

Back in the bar, only Flintoff and his mate Harmison remained. They had vowed to themselves and to each other that they would go through the night, and they had no intention of breaking that promise.

Miraculously, a few hours later, thanks to several cups of very strong coffee, both men made it to the bus. When they saw what greeted them as it turned the corner from Mansion House into Victoria Street on its way to Trafalgar Square at around 11 a.m., every player, to a man, was shocked. For a moment, even Flintoff appeared unable to take it all in. From start to finish, in glorious sunshine all the way, the route was lined with tens of thousands of cheering, waving, ecstatic supporters. For some of them, maybe the majority, in spring 2005 cricket had been something other people were interested in.

Now the whole country seemed to be passionate about the summer game. And when the bus reached its destination the whole country seemed to be there to greet it. As the players alighted, some more steadily than others, and made their way to their seats on the steps in front of the National Gallery, they were genuinely taken aback. And the sense of happy bewilderment that all this was for them would stay with them for the rest of the day. It will probably stay with them for as long as they live.

One by one they were introduced to the cheering throng before Michael Vaughan announced: 'We all have dreams when we are growing up. This one has finally come to reality. In fact, this is beyond a dream.'

Duncan Fletcher said: 'There has been a lot of planning but at the end of the day you have got to have players who can do the business. You can be very proud of your cricketers. I still think they can improve and we can bring home some more trophies.' Then the coach who had just heard his battle for British citizenship was finally over *nearly* smiled.

Andrew Strauss thanked the crowd; Ian Bell called the day 'unbelievable'. Marcus Trescothick explained how their determination to be positive had seen them to the finish line. Geraint Jones told the fans how glad he had been to hold on to the catch at Edgbaston that gave England hope. Ashley Giles and Matthew Hoggard spoke of their delight at making a contribution with the bat. Steve Harmison and Paul Collingwood seemed blown away. Simon Jones was more forthright: 'We've 'ad 'em. We 'ave 'ad 'em,' he shouted to the delighted crowd. To which they joyfully responded with a song indicating they believed he was inebriated and he knew he was.

Then up stumbled Pietersen and Flintoff, wearing thick shades. David Gower suggested they had had a fabulous night, to which Pietersen replied: 'Speaking for myself, I have. But I'd better let Fred speak for himself, if he can.'

He could, but only just: 'To be honest with you, David, I'm struggling,' said England's hero-in-chief. 'I haven't been to bed yet and behind these sunglasses there's a thousand stories. It's been a marathon, an emotional rollercoaster. But when we needed a performance somebody always came up with it. Fantastic.' When someone asked him what he had eaten since leaving The Oval the previous day, he replied 'a cigar'.

Then the songs began. First, led by opera singer Sean Ruane and the Barmy Army's Jimmy Savile, 'Jerusalem'; then 'Land of Hope and Glory' in a stirring rendition that reminded everyone to try to learn more than the first ten words before the next series. Flintoff started up his own karaoke session, giving us his version of 'Suspicious Minds'. He got as far as 'We're caught in a trap' before someone wrenched the microphone from his grasp. Next came 'Nessun Dorma', 'None Shall Sleep' – a very appropriate choice, that. Then 'Jerusalem' was resurrected for one last time.

With the crowd still in good voice it was on to No. 10 to meet Tony Blair. 'Not much to drink there at first,' recalls Pietersen. 'Then Fred had a word and it was coming out of the walls.' Pietersen found the experience somewhat confusing. He chatted away with Cherie Blair in his usual upfront fashion, as if he had known her all his life, but when she moved on he turned to Ashley Giles and said, "Who was she?" Pietersen also recalled that the Prime Minister said 'we deserved a day or two on the sauce, and if he says it's OK, then it's OK.'

Finally, to a reception at Lord's, where the Ashes urn was formally presented to the MCC in the time-honoured tradition dating back to 1884–85.

Flintoff recalls: 'The reaction from the crowds in London was unbelievable. You never know, if you organise something like an open-top bus ride, there is always the chance no one will turn up. To be there with Rachael and Holly made me feel very proud.

'There were a few times during this series, especially on the field taking wickets, when emotions took me over and I found a side to me that I had never discovered before. I was so wrapped up in everything we were doing and so focused on trying to win these Ashes that those feelings just got the better of me. Sometimes they have been so strong that it was like I was in a trance. As part of a team and as an individual, it has meant so much. Every now and then I can't stop myself punching the air, just in a quiet moment giving it the old: "Get in there!" I can't stop smiling, to be honest. It was all such a thrill. I feel like a kid at Christmas.'

Vaughan admitted: 'I didn't think cricket could relive those moments when England came back from Australia with the Rugby World Cup. I remember watching that parade on TV and wondering if I'd ever have the opportunity to experience something like that. So seeing all those people turn out for us was a very surreal moment for all the side. I didn't think cricket could reach those heights and make so many people happy. That's the best thing about the series: we've made a nation very proud.'

> '*I didn't think cricket could ... make so many people happy. That's the best thing about the series: we've made a nation very proud.*'
> MICHAEL VAUGHAN

The last word goes to two-year-old Abbie Harmison, who joined her sister Emily and mum Hayley on the bus, and who, when it arrived at Trafalgar Square, looked up at Steve and asked, 'Daddy, what are all these people doing here?'

He'll be able to explain it all to her one day.

The Ashes Series 2005 Statistical Record

MATCH RESULTS

1st Test, Lord's, London, 21, 22, 23, 24 July 2005
Australia 190 (S.J.Harmison 5–43) and 384 (M.J.Clarke 91, S.M.Katich 67, D.R.Martyn 65)
England 155 (K.P.Pietersen 57, G.D.McGrath 5–53) and 180 (K.P.Pietersen 64*)
Result: **Australia** won by 239 runs

2nd Test, Edgbaston, Birmingham, 4, 5, 6, 7 August 2005
England 407 (M.E.Trescothick 90, K.P.Pietersen 71, A.Flintoff 68) and 182 (A.Flintoff 73, S.K.Warne 6–46)
Australia 308 (J.L.Langer 82, R.T.Ponting 61) and 279
Result: **England** won by 2 runs

3rd Test, Old Trafford, Manchester, 11, 12, 13, 14, 15 August 2005
England 444 (M.P.Vaughan 166, M.E.Trescothick 63, I.R.Bell 59) and 280–6d
(A.J.Strauss 106, I.R.Bell 65, G.D.McGrath 5–115)
Australia 302 (S.K.Warne 90, S.P.Jones 6–53) and 371–9 (R.T.Ponting 156)
Result: **Match Drawn**

4th Test, Trent Bridge, Nottingham, 25, 26, 27, 28 August 2005
England 477 (A.Flintoff 102, G.O.Jones 85, M.E.Trescothick 65, M.P.Vaughan 58) and 129–7
Australia 218 (S.P.Jones 5–44) and 387 (J.L.Langer 61, S.M.Katich 59, M.J.Clarke 56)
Result: **England** won by 3 wickets

5th Test, The Oval, London, 8, 9, 10, 11, 12 September 2005
England 373 (A.J.Strauss 129, A.Flintoff 72, S.K.Warne 6–122) and 335 (K.P.Pietersen 158, A.F.Giles 59, S.K.Warne 6–124)
Australia 367 (M.L.Hayden 138, J.L.Langer 105, A.Flintoff 5–78) and 4–0
Result: **Match Drawn**

Series result: **England won the series 2–1**

SERIES AVERAGES

England – Batting and Fielding

Player	M	I	NO	HS	Runs	Ave	100	50	Ct/St
K.P.Pietersen	5	10	1	158	473	52.55	1	3	-
M.E.Trescothick	5	10	0	90	431	43.10	-	3	3
A.Flintoff	5	10	0	102	402	40.20	1	3	3
A.J.Strauss	5	10	0	129	393	39.30	2	-	6
S.P.Jones	4	6	4	20*	66	33.00	-	-	1
M.P.Vaughan	5	10	1	166	326	32.60	1	1	2
G.O.Jones	5	10	1	85	229	25.44	-	1	15/1
A.F.Giles	5	10	2	59	155	19.37	-	1	5
I.R.Bell	5	10	0	65	171	17.10	-	2	8
S.J.Harmison	5	8	2	20*	60	10.00	-	-	1
M.J.Hoggard	5	9	2	16	45	6.42	-	-	-

Also played: P.D.Collingwood 7, 10 (1 ct)

England – Bowling

Player	Overs	Mdns	Runs	Wkts	Ave	Best	5wI	10wM
S.P.Jones	102	17	378	18	21.00	6–53	2	-
A.Flintoff	194	32	655	24	27.29	5–78	1	-
M.J.Hoggard	122.1	15	473	16	29.56	4–97	-	-
S.J.Harmison	161.1	22	549	17	32.29	5–43	1	-
A.F.Giles	160	18	578	10	57.80	3–78	-	-

Also bowled: I.R.Bell 7–2–20–0; P.D.Collingwood 4–0–17–0; M.P.Vaughan 5–0–21–0

Australia – Batting and Fielding

Player	M	I	NO	HS	Runs	Ave	100	50	Ct/St
J.L.Langer	5	10	1	105	394	43.77	1	2	2
R.T.Ponting	5	9	0	156	359	39.88	1	1	4
M.J.Clarke	5	9	0	91	335	37.22	-	2	2
G.D.McGrath	3	5	4	20*	36	36.00	-	-	1
M.L.Hayden	5	10	1	138	318	35.33	1	-	10
S.K.Warne	5	9	0	90	249	27.66	-	1	5
S.M.Katich	5	9	0	67	248	27.55	-	2	4
B.Lee	5	9	3	47	158	26.33	-	-	2
A.C.Gilchrist	5	9	1	49*	181	22.62	-	-	18/1
D.R.Martyn	5	9	0	65	178	19.77	-	1	4
M.S.Kasprowicz	2	4	0	20	44	11.00	-	-	3
S.W.Tait	2	3	2	4	8	8.00	-	-	-
J.N.Gillespie	3	6	0	26	47	7.83	-	-	1

Australia – Bowling

Player	Overs	Mdns	Runs	Wkts	Ave	Best	5wI	10wM
S.K.Warne	252.5	37	797	40	19.92	6–46	3	2
G.D.McGrath	134	22	440	19	23.15	5–53	2	-
B.Lee	191.1	25	822	20	41.10	4–82	-	-
S.W.Tait	48	5	210	5	42.00	3–97	-	-
M.S.Kasprowicz	52	6	250	4	62.50	3–80	-	-
J.N.Gillespie	67	6	300	3	100.00	2–91	-	-

Also bowled: M.J.Clarke 2–0–6–0; S.M.Katich 12–1–50–1; R.T.Ponting 6–2–9–1

BATTING RECORDS

Leading Run Scorers (300 runs or more)

Total	Player	Team	Average
473	K.P.Pietersen	England	52.55
431	M.E.Trescothick	England	43.10
402	A.Flintoff	England	40.20
394	J.L.Langer	Australia	43.77
393	A.J.Strauss	England	39.30
359	R.T.Ponting	Australia	39.88
335	M.J.Clarke	Australia	37.22
326	M.P.Vaughan	England	32.60
318	M.L.Hayden	Australia	35.33

Hundreds

Score	Player	Team	Venue
166	M.P.Vaughan	England	Old Trafford
158	K.P.Pietersen	England	The Oval
156	R.T.Ponting	Australia	Old Trafford
138	M.L.Hayden	Australia	The Oval
129	A.J.Strauss	England	The Oval
106	A.J.Strauss	England	Old Trafford
105	J.L.Langer	Australia	The Oval
102	A.Flintoff	England	Trent Bridge

Highest Run Rate (Over 66 runs per 100 balls)

Rate	Player	Team	Runs
84.50	S.J.Harmison	England	60
74.16	A.Flintoff	England	402
71.82	A.C.Gilchrist	Australia	181
71.45	K.P.Pietersen	England	473
67.69	M.S.Kasprowicz	Australia	44
67.34	S.P.Jones	England	66

Most Runs in Boundaries (170 or more)

Runs	Player	Team	Total	%age
288	K.P.Pietersen	England	473	60.89
274	M.E.Trescothick	England	431	63.57
262	A.Flintoff	England	402	65.17
212	A.J.Strauss	England	393	53.94
204	J.L.Langer	Australia	394	51.78
192	M.J.Clarke	Australia	335	57.31
182	M.L.Hayden	Australia	318	57.23
178	M.P.Vaughan	England	326	54.60

Most Sixes (5 or more)

14	K.P.Pietersen	England
11	A.Flintoff	England
5	S.K.Warne	Australia

Partnerships

Hundred Partnerships (fig. denotes wicket)

185	1st	J.L.Langer/M.L.Hayden	Australia	The Oval
177	6th	A.Flintoff/G.O.Jones	England	Trent Bridge
155	4th	D.R.Martyn/M.J.Clarke	Australia	Lord's
143	5th	A.J.Strauss/A.Flintoff	England	The Oval
137	2nd	M.E.Trescothick/M.P.Vaughan	England	Old Trafford
127	3rd	M.P.Vaughan/I.R.Bell	England	Old Trafford
127	3rd	A.J.Strauss/I.R.Bell	England	Old Trafford
112	1st	M.E.Trescothick/A.J.Strauss	England	Edgbaston
109	8th	K.P.Pietersen/A.F.Giles	England	The Oval
105	1st	M.E.Trescothick/A.J.Strauss	England	Trent Bridge
103	5th	K.P.Pietersen/A.Flintoff	England	Edgbaston
100	5th	M.J.Clarke/S.M.Katich	Australia	Trent Bridge

Highest Partnerships for Each Wicket

England

1st	112	M.E.Trescothick/A.J.Strauss	Edgbaston
2nd	137	M.E.Trescothick/M.P.Vaughan	Old Trafford
3rd	127	M.P.Vaughan/I.R.Bell	Old Trafford (1st inns)
3rd	127	A.J.Strauss/I.R.Bell	Old Trafford (2nd inns)
4th	67	M.P.Vaughan/ K.P.Pietersen	Trent Bridge
5th	143	A.J.Strauss/A.Flintoff	The Oval
6th	177	A.Flintoff/G.O.Jones	Trent Bridge

7th	87	A.Flintoff/G.O.Jones	Old Trafford
8th	109	K.P.Pietersen/A.F.Giles	The Oval
9th	27	M.J.Hoggard/S.J.Harmison	Edgbaston
9th	27	A.F.Giles/M.J.Hoggard	The Oval
10th	51	A.Flintoff/S.P.Jones	Lord's

Australia

1st	185	J.L.Langer/M.L.Hayden	The Oval
2nd	88	J.L.Langer/R.T.Ponting	Edgbaston
3rd	46	R.T.Ponting/D.R.Martyn	Lord's
4th	155	D.R.Martyn/M.J.Clarke	Lord's
5th	100	M.J.Clarke/S.M.Katich	Trent Bridge
6th	81	R.T.Ponting/M.J.Clarke	Old Trafford
7th	49	S.M.Katich/S.K.Warne	Lord's
8th	86	S.K.Warne/J.N.Gillespie	Old Trafford
9th	52	S.M.Katich/J.N.Gillespie	Lord's
10th	59	B.Lee/M.S.Kasprowicz	Edgbaston

BOWLING RECORDS

Leading Wicket Takers (15 or more)

Wkts	Player	Team	Average
40	S.K.Warne	Australia	19.92
24	A.Flintoff	England	27.29
20	B.Lee	Australia	41.10
19	G.D.McGrath	Australia	23.15
18	S.P.Jones	England	21.00
17	S.J.Harmison	England	32.29
16	M.J.Hoggard	England	29.56

Best Innings Analysis (5 wickets or more)

Figs	Player	Team	Venue
6–46	S.K.Warne	Australia	Edgbaston
6–53	S.P.Jones	England	Old Trafford
6–122	S.K.Warne	Australia	The Oval
6–124	S.K.Warne	Australia	The Oval
5–43	S.J.Harmison	England	Lord's
5–44	S.P.Jones	England	Trent Bridge
5–53	G.D.McGrath	Australia	Lord's
5–78	A.Flintoff	England	The Oval
5–115	G.D.McGrath	Australia	Old Trafford

Best Match Analysis (10 wickets or more)

Figs	Player	Team	Venue
12–246	S.K.Warne	Australia	The Oval
10–162	S.K.Warne	Australia	Edgbaston

Best Strike Rate (balls per wicket, 15 wickets or more)

Rate	Player	Team	Wkts
34.00	S.P.Jones	England	18
37.92	S.K.Warne	Australia	40
42.32	G.D.McGrath	Australia	19
45.81	M.J.Hoggard	England	16
48.50	A.Flintoff	England	24
56.88	S.J.Harmison	England	17
57.35	B.Lee	Australia	20

Most Economical Bowlers (100 overs or more)

Rate	Player	Team
52.54	S.K.Warne	Australia
54.73	G.D.McGrath	Australia
56.27	A.Flintoff	England
56.77	S.J.Harmison	England
60.21	A.F.Giles	England
61.76	S.P.Jones	England
64.53	M.J.Hoggard	England
71.67	B.Lee	Australia

ENGLAND PLAYERS' TEST CAREER RECORDS (to 1 November 2005)

Batting and Fielding

Player	M	I	NO	HS	Runs	Ave	100	50	Ct/St
I.R.Bell	8	13	2	162*	468	42.54	1	4	10
P.D.Collingwood	3	6	0	36	106	17.66	-	-	7
A.Flintoff	52	82	3	167	2641	33.43	5	17	34
A.F.Giles	50	73	11	59	1278	20.61	-	4	30
S.J.Harmison	35	45	13	42	347	10.84	-	-	5
M.J.Hoggard	45	59	22	38	319	8.62	-	-	18
G.O.Jones	20	29	2	100	803	29.74	1	4	71/3
S.P.Jones	18	18	5	44	205	15.76	-	-	4
K.P.Pietersen	5	10	1	158	473	52.55	1	3	-
A.J.Strauss	19	36	2	147	1716	50.47	7	5	25
M.E.Trescothick	66	125	10	219	5206	45.26	12	27	76
M.P.Vaughan	62	111	8	197	4513	43.81	15	13	36

Bowling

Player	Overs	Runs	Wkts	Ave	Best	5wI	10wM
I.R.Bell	7	20	0	-	-	-	-
P.D.Collingwood	20	54	0	-	-	-	-
A.Flintoff	1548.4	4621	143	32.31	5-58	2	-
A.F.Giles	1873	5297	137	38.66	5-57	1	-
S.J.Harmison	1263.1	3932	138	28.49	7-12	6	-
M.J.Hoggard	1537.1	5126	173	29.63	7-61	5	-
S.P.Jones	470.1	1666	59	28.23	6-53	3	-
M.E.Trescothick	50	155	1	155.00	1-34	-	-
M.P.Vaughan	156	537	6	89.50	2-71	-	-